The Shattered Mirror

The Texas Pan-American Series

The Shattered Mirror

Representations of Women in Mexican Literature

María Elena de Valdés

University of Texas Press, Austin

Versions or parts of Chapters 2, 3, 5, 7, 8, and 9 were previously published as

2 "Sexuality and Insanity in Rulfo's Susana San Juan," *Revista Canadiense de Estudios Hispánicos*, 18:3 (Spring 1994), pp. 491–501.

3 "Carlos Fuentes on Mexican Feminophobia," *The Review of Contemporary Fiction*, 8:2 (Summer 1988), pp. 225–233.

5 "Luisa Josefina Hernández," in *Spanish American Women Writers*, ed. Diane Marting (Westport, Conn.: Greenwood Press, 1990, an imprint of Greenwood Publishing Group, Inc., Westport, Conn.), pp. 241–253.

5 "Crítica feminista de la identidad en 'Inmóvil sol secreto,'" *Journal of Hispanic Research* 2 (1992–1993), pp. 239–248.

7 "Feminista Testimonial Literature: Cristina Pacheco, Witness to Women," *Monographic Review/Revista Monográfica*, no. 4 (1988), pp. 150–162.

8 "In Search of Identity in Cisneros's *The House on Mango Street*," *The Canadian Review of American Studies*, 23:1 (Fall 1992), pp. 55–72.

8 "The Critical Reception of Sandra Cisneros's *The House on Mango Street*," in *Gender, Self, and Society*, ed. Renate von Bardeleben, *Proceedings of the IV International Conference on the Hispanic Cultures of the United States, July 1990* (Frankfurt am Main: Peter Lang GMBH, 1993), pp. 286–300.

9 "Verbal and Visual Representation of Women: *Como agua para chocolate/Like Water for Chocolate*," *World Literature Today* (Winter 1995), pp. 78–82.

Library of Congress Cataloging-in-Publication Data

Valdés, María Elena de.
The shattered mirror : representations of women in Mexican literature / María Elena de Valdés.
    p.   cm. — (The Texas Pan-American series)
Includes bibliographical references and index.
ISBN 0-292-71591-9 (cloth : alk. paper). — ISBN 0-292-71590-0 (pbk. : alk. paper)
1. Mexican literature—Women authors—History and criticism.   2. Mexican literature—History and criticism.   3. American literature—Mexican American authors—History and criticism.   4. American literature—Women authors—History and criticism.   5. American literature—20th century—History and criticism.   6. Women in literature.   I. Title.   II. Series.
PQ7133.V35   1998
860.9'352042'0972—dc21   97-16813

For Mario
and my friends and loved ones
(they know who they are)

Contents

Is this my inheritance, grandmother,
great-grandmother, great-great grandmother,
is this the gift you left for me
in addition to your features in the mirror,
your inconclusive gestures?
I can't stand your ineffective gestures,
your indolence,
your frustrations.
Go to hell . . .

—Elena Poniatowska, *La "Flor de Lis"* (1988)

Preface

This book is a hermeneutic study of the literary representations of female identity in Mexico. Looking into questions of such identity in a nation so rich in differences, both regional and linguistic, would appear to be spurious if it were not for the unprecedented emergence of women writers in Mexico and the challenge they bring to the status quo. My inquiry begins in the second half of the seventeenth century with Juana Inés de la Cruz and then leaps ahead to concentrate on the last quarter of the twentieth century. This study is not a historical analysis of the documentation pertaining to the status of women; rather, I offer an interpretive analysis of selected texts as sources of identity. These texts can be considered primary clues for the larger undertaking.

I decided to write this book in English because I believe there is a manifest desire for knowledge and understanding of Mexican women among non-Spanish readers. All the writers included here are Mexican household names, yet all, save Fuentes and Paz, are not well known or are completely unknown outside of Mexico. Although in recent years communication and exchange with Mexico has broadened in an unprecedented way, mainly in the spheres of economics and politics, even basic information about its women, their identity, their representation, and their cultural creations, is still clouded behind stereotypes. Indeed, I believe that this encounter between an English language readership and Mexican women is long overdue and I hope that this book will help to explain the remaking of the contemporary Mexican woman. There are now, more than ever before, possibilities of active collaboration in North America and beyond, and if my work can help, I will consider my efforts worthwhile. Keeping in mind the introductory and exploratory aim of this book, I have tried to examine texts which have published English translations. The only exceptions are Cristina Pacheco and María Luisa Puga.

I have organized this book into ten chapters. In the first chapter I outline my critical and ideological position; in the second and third chapters I take a brief look at some of the best examples of the subversion of sexism by two of Mexico's leading writers, Juan Rulfo and Carlos Fuentes. The fourth chapter considers the complex relationship between Mexico's most celebrated poets: Sor Juana and Octavio Paz. The fifth to the ninth chapters study key aspects of female identity as presented by contemporary women writers. The tenth chapter is my hermeneutic conclusion. A collective configuration of the contributions each writer gives to female identity is the main objective of my work. I do not engage in reductive definitions of the vast social phenomena that constitute the identity of a nation's women. My aim, rather, is to promote collective collaborative inquiry as well as self-inquiry into what it means to identify ourselves as Mexican women, and to do so through a body of texts that belong to all of us.

This book was written over a six-year span. It began from the welcome convergence in my life of time to develop my thinking on feminist criticism as it pertained to Mexico and my association with a number of colleagues and institutions who have supported my work. I want to thank my friends Simone and Paul Ricoeur and Marie Yvonne and Etienne Guyon, whose warm hospitality in France for so many years has helped me to dedicate myself to reading and writing. I also acknowledge the generous grant given me by the Social Sciences and Humanities Research Council of Canada in 1990–91. I gratefully acknowledge the invitation of Elena Urrutia, Director of the Interdisciplinary Program of Women's Studies at El Colegio de Mexico, to participate in the program's seminars and colloquia, and thank Gloria Prado for her hospitality.

I want to thank generous colleagues for reading early drafts of this book. Thanks to Linda Hutcheon and Mario Valdés, who helped me work my way through the thickets of literary theory; José Emilio Pacheco, who read my work on Elena Poniatowska; Claudia Schaefer-Rodríguez, whose good sense helped me with the chapter on Rulfo; and Electa Arenal, who offered valuable assistance with Sor Juana. I am grateful to Janet Pérez, who read the chapter on Fuentes and as always offered much-appreciated advice, and to Nancy Gray Díaz, who read an early draft of the introduction and chapters 1 and 4. Catherine Stimpson read the introduction and first chapter, offering helpful advice on how to manage the first world and third world bifurcation in feminist criticism. Finally I want to thank Lois Parkinson Zamora for her excellent counsel on the comparative aspects of my project. I also want to acknowledge the inestimable support of journal editors who published early versions of some of my chapters. Their support and editorial advice were of immense value as I shaped these materials into the present book. To all I express my most sincere gratitude; you have helped me say what I had to say, better.

The plan of the book took shape in 1990, when most of chapters 4 to 8 were written and I recognized the need to add chapters 2 and 3, on Rulfo and Fuentes. Chapter 1 had been in progress from the outset, mostly in the form of introductions to studies of individual Mexican women. It was at this time of reorganization that I recognized the logical simplicity and the importance of the tripartite organization: theory, the subversion of existing social codes, and the contribution of women writers. The conclusion was written in 1995, and although I only briefly touch on the work of Laura Esquivel, I want to salute her talent and strength as a woman. In the course of this project I have had the pleasure of meeting Sandra Cisneros, who stands out as one of the great promises for a recognition of Chicana literature in Mexico. Cristina Pacheco and Elena Poniatowska are generous friends whose work I have read for many years and who I consider to be major contributors to the making of a new Mexican woman and to the shattering of the mirror that we have been for so long forced to look into as our only identity.

The Shattered Mirror

Introduction

In this book I am concerned with Mexican women, their situation at the end of the twentieth century, their struggle for human rights, and their ideological status as expressed in literature and thereby introduced into the linguistic matrix of the community's social culture. My work can be described as feminist social criticism; in this book I develop a feminist critical approach that is a problem-oriented examination of literary texts as an expression of ideological considerations of women.

Most feminist commentators in Mexico today question the validity of the very social structure that depends on male supremacy. The realization of an egalitarian heterosexuality is a primary objective for a number of critics like Elena Poniatowska; she recognizes that it cannot be attained without a qualitative transformation of gender attitudes toward each other. This necessary transformation is not the battle of the sexes for supremacy—this battle has been going on for a long time, with men using force and women, cunning. It is the rejection by both of a system of domination. Mexican women may reject the form heterosexuality takes in the legal and social practices of marriage, but there is a generalized idea of a different heterosexuality wherein men and women move toward a fuller realization of their physical, affective, intellectual, and creative capacities. In this advocacy for social transformation, women demand equitable social participation. The attack on sexual stereotypes is at the center of Mexican feminism's ideological critique. *The liberation of Mexican women is impossible without the liberation of Mexican men.* Both men and women, for example, have taken up arms as partners in the Zapatista challenge to civil authority in Chiapas (see Marcos; "Ley Revolucionaria Sobre las Mujeres").

I propose the following outline of social feminist criticism; it is a critical perspective that is fundamentally rooted in the social, economic, and political realities of the world of social action, with special emphasis on issues of gender. The following ten points, organized from general principles to specific applications, are proposed as the basic principles of feminist sociocriticism:

1. *Language* is a code of communication, but it is more; it is the basis of human existence as social reality. The human condition is grounded in belonging to a particular linguistic community.[1] Language is the common ground between persons in the same community of speakers in which understanding and agreement on any given subject can take place. Of course, this common ground can be examined as a code, as a system whose rules of operation can be deduced. But language does not originate with either rules of grammar or syntax; its reality is that of speech in a community of speakers. The basis of communication is therefore the commonality of action in a community. We may hold as an ideal the kind of conversation in which two people get to understand each other, in which each partner is open to the other and honestly accepts the point of view of the other as worthy of serious consideration. In the real world, however, it rarely happens like that. If one of the speakers happens to be a woman, whether the other speaker is a man or a woman, there are powerful social and ideological impediments to communication.[2] In Mexico, rigid social roles control the action and speech of women. It takes an enormous effort on the part of the woman to convince her partner in dialogue that there is more to her than a social role she is playing. The fact that in spite of these obstacles communication has been successful for women in the past and that it is today part of the feminist revolution does not remove the burden of overcoming the stereotypical reduction to fixed roles that has been thrust on the woman who tries to speak openly in Mexico. The premise is that language is much more than a code; it is a way of living, and as such it evolves for better or worse. Can it ever move beyond stereotypes?

Language usage in every community is marked by what sociolinguists have called "registers": there are different ways of speaking to different persons within the community. A woman who communicates is skillful in finding the commonality between her and her partner in dialogue, and once this ground is fixed, can proceed to give and to receive from her other. It is not true that women can speak better to other women than to men; it is only that the initial stage of finding the common ground is easier, more rapid than when she must overcome the entangled web of sexist closure which has made her an object and not a person to most men.

2. *Narrativity* is the prime source of our concept of the world and therefore also the basis for our belief systems and ideological determinations. Narrativity

is emplotted story telling, whether it be a woman telling me what she felt when she gave birth, or my mother telling me what my childhood was to her, or Proust telling me about Marcel, or Virginia Woolf telling me about George Eliot, or Kafka telling about K's vacillations. All stories that are told participate in narrativity but, most importantly, all the stories we tell are our way of constituting the world as we know it. The relation between the stories I have been told and the stories I tell is, of course, a direct one even though, like every storyteller, I may want to add or subtract what best suits my self-interest. There are, however, important differences between the narratives I receive and the ones I produce; all narrativity, because it is a process of selection and emphasis from a given point of view, is incomplete. Therefore, as listener and as reader I must complete, according to my own ability, the incomplete, emplotted sequence of events.

The discourse of power is the pornography that needs analysis in order to unmask its emptiness. The narrative of violation, like Reage's *Story of O*, with its masochistic protagonist's acquiescence in her own degradation and eventual destruction, can become the basis for the disclosure of the institutional means of violation which one can recognize with some reflection as the simulacrum of the patriarchal institutions of society, primarily educational and religious, which perpetuate the idea of female subjugation. The responsibility for narrativity goes forward and it is interpersonal; thus, we as critics become the persons responsible for Reage's writing, and the imperative is to act.

3. *Oral narrativity* is the basis of the cultural identity of most indigenous Mexican women, but we must recognize that oral texts, unless transmitted to written texts, are severely limited in scope. Oral narrativity depends on the social context of presentation, while written narrativity not only transcends its time and place of composition, it also transcends its historicity since it can be read and realized by persons remote in every way from the author. Thus we must recognize that oral texts are intrinsically tied to specific conditions of production.

Oral narrativity in a nonliterate society is markedly different from oral narrativity in a mixed society of literate and nonliterate speakers. In the former, tradition is maintained at the center of collective identity; in the latter, orality is the collective expression of marginalized sectors of the population. Such is the case in Mexico.[3]

In recent years the research of folklorists and anthropologists has made important contributions to our understanding of the continuity of this oral narrativity into present-day Mexico, but the most remarkable new direction that has emerged is in women's testimonial literature. This genre began with the research of anthropologists on the nonliterate sectors of the Mexican population.

In this context we must recognize the early work of the Mexican anthropologist Ricardo Pozas in his transcription of the autobiography of a Tzotzil, *Juan Pérez Jolote*, in 1948. This pioneering work gave a literate voice to an oral one, but nevertheless maintained the structure of oral narrativity. In the 1950s the late Oscar Lewis, an anthropologist from the University of Illinois, tape-recorded interviews with a Mexican family from the lower class and then recast the interviews into a plotted, structured literate form: *The Children of Sánchez*. But it was through the participation of women in Mexican journalism that testimonial fiction became a woman's genre. In 1969, Elena Poniatowska wrote the ground-breaking *Hasta no verte Jesús mío* (Until we meet again, Jesus), which emplots the life story of Jesusa Palancares as narrated orally to Poniatowska. The fact that Poniatowska was not allowed to use a tape recorder meant that she had to concentrate on her subject in each interview and attempt to discern her changes of mood, tone, gesture, and force as she narrated. The success of this work of Mexican testimonial women's literature was largely due to the writer's skill and her resourcefulness when confronted with the restrictions imposed by her subject. This genre has now grown and expanded throughout Latin America, from the sugarcane fields of Cuba to the mines of Bolivia, the mothers of Argentina and the Quiche villages of Guatemala. Its strength lies in that it is testimonial and not well-intentioned condescension, and, at the same time, it has given these women a public voice. Another major voice in the development of documentary Mexican fiction is also a journalist, the remarkable Cristina Pacheco, who has published a short story every week for more than fifteen years; her stories are based on factual incidents involving women from all classes of Mexican society, but primarily from the poorest and most disenfranchised. I will devote a chapter respectively to each of these two women and the importance of their work for the Mexican woman's search for identity in the contemporary world.

4. *The function of narrativity* is nothing less than the shaping of our temporal experience. Written narrativity, because it is released from the circumstances of the author's physical and temporal situation (i.e., no one is present to respond to objections or the call for clarification), can become an instrument of unlimited creativity—or it can become an instrument of distortion in service of a discourse of power.[4]

The fact that works of literature written by Mexican women account for a paltry proportion by any standards of comparison means that oral storytelling still constitutes the major contribution of Mexican women to narrativity. The entire creative area of what German feminist Silvia Bovenschen calls the "preaesthetic," that is, home decoration, table settings, fashion, the preparation of foods, and personal cosmetic makeup has been opened up for consideration, but we must recognize that the ephemeral nature of these activities, as is the case with oral narrativity, circumscribes the possibility of sharing this creative work with others.[5] The exhibitions of Judy Chicago have helped raise the consciousness of feminists regarding the creative nature of the pre-aesthetic. It should be pointed out that one of the foremost painters of contemporary Mexico, Frida Kahlo, always privileged the pre-aesthetic in her person and in her art. Her paintings are not overtly "autobiographical," but they are solidly situated in the popular culture of Mexican women.

The written text as an art form by women in Mexican literary history will remain a relative rarity unless we reconsider what literature is in its essence and what criteria we use for inclusion. The fact that letter writing, one of the few expressive modes permitted to literate women, has been an art form in Europe since the eighteenth century suggests that as women in the third world emerge from the ghetto of the kitchen and the bedroom, their extra-canonical writing will eventually become recognized as a legitimate art form.

Women's voices today are being heard as authentic and important to an unprecedented degree, although they are still far less in number than their male counterparts. And among those male writers, there are many who have written with insight into and commitment to women's rights. Carlos Monsiváis comes readily to mind. It is not necessary or desirable to deny, resent, or minimize their contributions, but it is crucial that women realize that she who helps herself will be helped most. The passive angel of patriarchy has been countered by an informed, rigorous, and forceful woman who does not ask for what is hers, but demands it in everything she does and everything she says and everything she writes.

5. *Written texts* must become printed texts and read texts if they are to fulfill their function as communication. It is commonplace in third world countries, and especially in Mexico, to hear the statement that only writers read other writers, that the general literate public does not read books, and that women read less than men because of the lower level of their educational preparation. Like much common knowledge, there is a basis in fact to these observations. But few have cared to inquire why it is that most literate Mexican women do not read books in such disciplines as literature, the social sciences, and philosophy. The obvious response, which is tied to the relative level of education, is that all but a mere 2% of literate Mexican women have not been exposed to higher education.

The female reading public in Mexico can be divided into three distinct groups: semiliterate women with a primary education (about one-half of the female population) who read comics and photo-novels; another, much smaller group, of about 10 percent who read women's magazines; and a slim minority of 2 percent who buy and read books. In brief, women, having been deprived of the educational exposure to the world of ideas, are the prime targets for commercial manipulation in women's magazines (see Appendix 1).[6] The reading matter of the first group—comics and photo-novels—is more diversified since the field is not dominated by U.S. interests. Comics range from translations of U.S. comics to native Mexican characters and from ghost stories to didactic pleas for social justice (see de Valdés 1977). The field of magazine publication is dominated by a conglomerate with U.S. interests. Hearst Corporation, with publications such as *Cosmopolitan, Buen Hogar* (*Good Housekeeping*), and *Vanidades,* dominates a great percentage of the market. Only the local advertising is Mexican. The contents of these magazines are translations of the U.S. magazines, printed in Mexico, with writers with Spanish surnames. The impact of these magazines is the crass pandering of consumerism and exploitation (see García Calderón, esp. 26–34).

In this bleak picture of repression, the only rays of hope are the tabloid newspapers *unomasuno, La Jornada,* the weekly *Proceso,* and the monthly *fem.* They are the only journalistic sources of intellectual material for and by women. *La Jornada* has published the work of Cristina Pacheco every Sunday for more than fifteen years and features articles of writers like Elena Poniatowska, Guadalupe Loaeza, and Ethel Krause. *Proceso* is an independent weekly mostly devoted to political debate but also one of the most open sources of criticism in the arts. *fem.* is a feminist review, founded in 1976 by a group of women writers and journalists concerned with changing the social condition of women; it follows a thematic or monographic line. Each issue deals with a specific topic and contains current news about women and reviews of films, theater, and books. It also publishes poetry and short stories.[7] An academic biannual journal, *debate feminista,* has been a welcome recent addition; since 1990 it has served as a feminist clearinghouse of intellectual debate.

The newspaper press is undoubtedly the medium of written communication for most women in Mexico, and it is here that the battle for inventing a new Mexican woman is being fought. The outcome is far from clear, but the turmoil of a society in crisis has reduced the traditional power of the church and the school system, and changes in self-image by young Mexican women are in evidence. Feminists who write do so for this new woman. There is, however, always strong resistance against new ideas; the 1993 decision of the Mexican government to grant legal status to the Catholic Church has precipitated renewed hostility by the Catholic press against all advocacy of birth control by both private and government clinics. Feminist critics have not merely closed ranks and imposed closure on the issue of birth control; on the contrary, they have made the issue a debate and have succeeded in opening the multiple doors of Mexican social life that have been closed for so long by the discourse of power.

6. *The target reader* for whom the feminist critic in Mexico writes is not modeled after any specific group of individuals to whom the writer belongs. This target reader is a configuration of aspirations for freedom and self-expression. Wolfgang Iser developed the idea that there are strategies of reading that a written text aims for as its realization.[8] This "implied reader" therefore is not modeled on any reader, real or hypothetical, but rather describes the design and structural strategy developed to induce interpretations among readers in general.

As feminist sociocritics, we must inquire as to the nature of the implied reader of feminists' writing in Mexico. There are at least three strategies that Mexican feminist writers bring together whether they are writing fiction or nonfiction. The first is the proposal of freedom itself as the point of departure for the text's disclosure. The freedom of the individual is not some overt trait or situation; it is not self-evident; it can only be proposed for others and believed in by oneself. As a woman I can only begin speaking about another woman's freedom because I believe in my freedom; that is, I am what I can do and I can do what I am. Freedom is realized not in itself, as a concept, but by what I do, what I produce, what I say.

The second strategy for writing comes directly from the first: this is the strategy of affirming freedom for "you." If the first person was my starting point as self-affirmation, the second person—my dialogical partner—is the second point. I will thus speak to you with the same affirmation which allowed me to speak: that you are as free as I am. It is in this movement from the first person singular to the second person that the strategy will get its power. This is the entanglement of you and me, and finding a way where each of us can maintain her freedom without taking away the freedom of the other.

The most difficult strategy to develop is the third one, which is the paradox of freedom for the third person, the person whom I do not know, with whom I may never have any contact save through the text—and who may be the enemy. How can I write a text that liberates me and you and offers freedom to the other? This is the paradoxical nature of feminist writing. My way out of this problem is to avoid endings that end. Closure of an argument, an interpretation, a descriptive piece of reporting, or a short story that leaves no room for another point of view is the denial of freedom. My third strategy, therefore, which encompasses the first two, is to open the debate but never close it completely, to state a position but allow fully for a counterposition, to argue strongly for my point of view but respect other points of view, to show no reluctance to attack ideological distortion but accept the possibility that my own prejudgments are in need of reassessment. What is the practical consequence of these strategies for a feminist implied reader? Fierce disagreement, which always holds out the possibility of a new understanding. I rule out compromise and generalized agreement as utopic, but I plan for breakthrough moments in thinking which can trigger new ideas.

7. *The literary canon of western literatures*, and specifically of Mexican literature, presents an ideologically distorted image of women, but what has not been stated with sufficient clarity is that this negative depiction of women offers us a way to directly confront the established system of values.

Feminist militants in the United States have a history of activism that is admired by feminists in Mexico, although they may not always agree. In a country like Mexico, where political censorship is part of everyday reality, the government welcomes calls for censorship of works that may violate the status quo. The argument with English-speaking North American feminist advocates of state censorship of pornography is not about the rejection of sexist images, but about tactics for confronting them. In Mexico the most pervasive pornography is the pornography of power, which may on the surface appear nonsexual, but when examined closely will yield the metaphor of the submissive abused woman as an apt representation of the Mexican people. To close one's mind to this dominant ideology in Mexico is not merely to play the fool; it is to acquiesce. Literature did not by itself make Mexico a sexist society; it reinforces what the discourse of power has institutionalized through pulpit and classroom.

Feminist sociocriticism in the third world can work by first subverting the implicit sexism in the literary canon, by undermining its authority and breaking up its cultural hold over narrativity. A lie is no less a lie because we live it. A woman is a person in spite of a cultural configuration that portrays her as a commodity. Such a critique uses formal analysis for the purpose of the disclosure of ideological distortion. Second, such a critique needs to break open the restrictions on what is and what is not worthy of being read as literature, so that the literature of women's interests can come out of the closet of the so-called women's pages in the press. Third, sociocriticism aims at changing the way persons think about women, and for this purpose the immediate need is to break down the ideological division that separates Mexican women into categories of social class. For these purposes, the better written the text, whether sexist or not, the better the opportunity it offers feminist sociocritics to address the social structure itself. Badly written texts do not last very long and are not of significant consequence. Well-written texts are to be the prime target of a sociocritique that will recognize the subtleties of the means of the prevailing, oppressive configuration of cultural narrativity.

8. *Feminist criticism* in the third world cannot be limited to the academy and foreign readers; it is a social critique which confronts the literary text as the formative source of values. The Romantic concept of literature as a manifestation of personal vision is not relevant to third world reality. The value of a well-written literary text is that it can become part of a community's worldview as narrativity; this is true whether we are talking about Proust, Kafka, or Rulfo. The difference between literary criticism in the first world and the third world is that in the latter case, we are concerned with changing social values and challenging the originating power of the literary text by deconstructing its authority. In the third world, women are striving for basic freedom rather than demanding equal rights in the workplace. The odds against our making radical changes in our lifetime are enormous, but the future lies with those who win the ideological battles, and these are fought out in everyday life, in the daily newspaper, on radio and television, and in every public verbal opportunity. Feminist sociocriticism is thus political action rather than disinterested scholarship, but the political action must be based on learning and intellectual reflection or it will be ineffective.

Finally, the old adage "divide and conquer" has never been more in evidence than among Mexican women, where differences in social class have been major obstacles to any kind of dialogue between the four main strata of women: university educated and affluent; university educated and employed; secondary school–educated, employed and unemployed; and the uneducated, including those who are non-Spanish speaking. The vast majority of Mexican women are in the fourth stratum, and the most active are in the second and third strata. Sociocritical feminists cannot, I think, hope to reach the women of the first stratum because of the vast gulf of privilege that separates them from other Mexican women. In effect, these women belong to the opulent, powerful elite. The women of the fourth stratum are to a large extent inaccessible; realistically, only their children might be reached, and only for the short time they are in school. The most fruitful area of feminist activities today is primarily in the second stratum, with expectations of making inroads into the third stratum, and even into the fourth in some distant future. We need not be demographic experts to recognize that the vast differences in the social structure of the United States, Canada, and Mexico make it impossible for one version of feminism to be serviceable throughout North America.

9. *The social paradigm in Mexico* is different from first world cultures in its basic structure. A prominent U.S. feminist critic, Susan Rubin Suleiman, describes the patriarchal ideology in terms of a confrontation between an all-powerful father and a traumatized son, a confrontation staged across and over the body of the mother. In Mexico the situation is staged somewhat differently.

We have an all-powerful European male raping a dark-skinned native woman, and the son is forever torn between hating the rapist and loving the father. In the moments of hatred toward the rapist he venerates his mother, and in the moments he loves the father, he hates the female who was violated. The mother is sacred and the violated woman is whore. The *machismo* of Mexico is a social ideology of conquered warriors condemned to a history of abuse, treachery, and infamy from Cortés to the present.

Although Suleiman (132) does not offer us a counterparadigm of how the woman becomes a person and not merely the link between the father and the son, in Mexico there is such a paradigm: she is the earth mother Tonantzin before the Spanish-speaking mestizo made her into the Virgin, mother of God. In other words, she was the female who gave birth and created all the Nahua people. There was no Yehova to create the prototype Adam and from that creation the first man and woman, Adam and Eve. The image of Tonantzin, before the Spaniards, was that of a pregnant woman whose dress changed with her attributes and functions. The conflation of Tonantzin with the Virgin Mary in her guise as the Virgin of Guadalupe imposes the patriarchal theology of Spain and makes her into the virgin mother of God, the venerated holy mother who stands in contrast to the whore who has been violated. The image of the pre-Spanish Tonantzin is that of woman as creator, creator of life on her terms, not as carrier used to produce heirs for patrilineal descent. This woman is creator of her environment; she changes the place in which she dwells into a place of her own. She dresses and adorns herself with the same spirit. She creates many guises not because she must set the sexual bait of her body for entrapment of the male. Instead, the sexuality of this creative woman is an expression of her body, not a commodity to be sold in the marketplace. This paradigm of the creative woman brings life into all she touches. She does not have the limitations of one venue, of one art form. But Tonantzin is much more than the earth goddess symbol; she is, above all, in her duality with Quetzalcoatl, the continuing principle of creativity; she embodies the creative wisdom of humanity.

10. *The individual Mexican woman* is free insofar as she has opposed herself to the will of the majority and can accomplish something, even if this work is insignificant in the general terms of society. On a superficial level, a woman's freedom in Mexico today is primarily measured in terms of her ability to pursue her own ends, ends that may coincide with social aims, but are not entirely coopted by society. In this sense, freedom coincides with the process of becoming an individual in one's own estimation. A freedom of this type until recently was virtually impossible for all but the most gifted, original, and fortunate of women, for the simple reason that their bodies—the basis of their very iden-

tity—did not belong to them, but to God or nation or family, or any combination of these.

Because of the economic and social structure of Mexican society, the desire for freedom by a woman, in the terms we have discussed, is on a collision course with the designated social responsibilities of woman as wife and mother. My principal argument is that in societies such as those of Mexico and other third world countries, wherein even a modest degree of personal freedom can be gained only through extreme personal sacrifice, women must understand that a woman's freedom in individualistic terms is utopic and of little value even as fantasy. The only freedom of consequence cannot be hers alone; it will have to be the freedom of the whole. Individual freedom is meaningless if the society in which one lives is denied human rights, and this is so not only on a practical basis of action, that is, with regard to the multiple restrictions such a society imposes and which must be circumvented, but also on a more profound level because the values expressed as a way of life in such a society are alienating and eventually destructive of the basic self-esteem that makes life valuable. This must be the supposition behind third world feminist criticism of society in and through literature.

One   The Politics of Representation of Women in Mexican Literature

Feminist criticism is a wide-ranging, sometimes contradictory, body of commentary that has developed extremely rapidly in the last twenty-five years.[1] This richness of conceptual inquiry is both an achievement and a challenge. There are signs that the time of exploration and orientation in the United States and Europe may be coming to an end; the yield of new books features many more monographs focused on specific topics as opposed to the collections of essays or abridged republication of conference papers that were so numerous twenty years ago.[2] The situation in Mexico is unique in that Mexican society and its economy belong to both the first and third worlds, and Mexico has a heritage of institutionalized sexism. This unique combination has forced feminism into a radical reexamination of the premises held in the United States and Europe.

Among new feminist studies in Mexico today one can discern a philosophical bifurcation between political activists and social critics.[3] The former seek to establish a feminist model of inquiry from the negative polemics of the last twenty-five years by retaining the features of feminist criticism that they regard as responsible for the power and success of women's studies in the United States. In contrast, the pluralists draw openly from the social sciences and in general agree on basic postmodern ideas that the world of human action can never be fully explained, that it cannot be predicted, and that no amount of paradigm manipulation will make it more accessible. If there is no privileged basic history and no final authority for the pluralist critic, she has had to begin with her own definition of the cultural problems in the specific communities whose literary expression is being examined. In responding to these issues the pluralist critic probes behind the apparently solid facade of social structures to bring out the dominant aspects of gender relations.

I do not agree with pure aesthetic positions imported from Anglo-American "new criticism" that would have us sever the literary text from its sociocultural context. Because I accept that more than one interpretation of the same text may be valid, I reject the claim that any interpretation can be a definitive or complete one. My task as a feminist social critic is to build a dialectic between the historicity of the text in its social linguistic matrix of values and my own historicity. I find myself in close agreement with feminist sociocritics in the United States like Jean Franco and Debra Castillo, who recognize the paramount importance of a dialectic of cultural historicities.[4]

With the exceptions already noted, Anglo-American feminists who have ventured into Latin America without an adequate grounding in the complex cultural mosaic of this part of the world have been taken aback by the sometimes aggressive rejection they have experienced by the very women they assumed would be their counterparts. The reasons for this barrier are varied but can be summed up briefly. Some Anglo-American feminists have assumed a position of cultural authority on the basis of their economic superiority, falsely equating these two spheres. Some have also falsely assumed that women's issues in the United States are the same as women's issues in the third world, merely expressed in other languages and cultural ways.[5] Feminist social criticism operates within the context of demographic and economic realities of cultural expression. The social feminist criticism I use addresses women's issues within the reality of Mexico's social history; this is the context within which the texts I shall consider obtain their primary significance.

Furthermore, in Mexico's intense cross fire of class distinctions, first world feminist critics must recognize that women do not constitute one social class; any commentary that ignores class issues and addresses women in general will fail to reach all but a slim minority of upper middle class women in Latin America. Spivak makes this point succinctly: "Feminist theory in the West [i.e. Western Europe, the United States, Canada, and Australia] is largely ethnocentric; often primitivist when broadly concerned with the 'third world' . . . this ethnocentrism is nowhere more evident than in the cutting edge of Western feminist speculative theory" (219). Mexican feminist social scientists and cultural critics can be excused for sometimes showing their impatience with Anglo-American feminist theoreticians, who do not yet understand that the multiple distinctions with regard to first world feminisms have limited validity in third world contexts. In the third world, the struggle for social justice and basic human rights is so fundamental that a feminist is a social critic who forces the debate into a single basic claim: a social system based on the exploitation of gender is a system where all, men and women, are victims.

On the part of Latin American feminists in revolutionary settings like southern Mexico's Chiapas state, Bolivia, Cuba, El Salvador, Guatemala, and Nicaragua, there is a strong tendency to look on the writing of Anglo-American feminists as another imperialist weapon aimed at dividing the revolutionary cause of social justice. These women take the rhetoric of women's liberation as social treason; any woman who would look to her own advantage and not identify with the social plight of society as a whole is deeply suspect. It might be argued that there has been a deep misunderstanding on the part of Latin American revolutionary women; but there has been an equally fallacious assumption on the part of Anglo-American feminists that the particular cultural issues of the United States are world issues. Domitila Barrios de Chungara and Betty Friedan represent two solitudes of discourse. The dialectic between class issues of social justice and gender issues of the status of women is the most viable basis for feminist social criticism in Mexico today.

Most Mexican women are as oppressed economically and socially as most women in the rest of the third world, but in addition they suffer a particular kind of sociopsychological loss of identity as persons because of Mexico's proximity to the dominant first world, consumer-driven culture of the United States. Mexico is a country where the first and third worlds meet in a head-on collision. Mexicans belong to a world whose main economic function has been to provide prime resources such as petroleum, silver, bananas, coffee, sugarcane, and so on, for the industrialized countries of the world, especially the United States. In this condition of economic dependence, a majority of the female half of the population has been designated as an uneducated, isolated, nonremunerated work force who reproduce the species; the illiteracy rate among women continues to be double that among men.

The exchange that countries like Mexico receive from the industrialized world is not a return value for labor and resources; rather, such countries are granted large quantities of consumer goods as part of a superficial imitation of the dominant culture. This other culture is portrayed through films, publicity, fashions, magazines, and television, imposing other ways of living and feeling about the world, with the result that the majority of Mexican women—from Chiapas and Yucatan to Baja California, and not just the affluent upper middle class—cannot recognize themselves in these images of women. These women, who carry out the most menial tasks of everyday life at the lowest remuneration, do not look like the women who have been established as role models (see Bustos Romero, 1988). The images of beauty, sex appeal, and elegance that the Mexican media accepts so gladly from the industrialized world are ethnically and socially alien. There is, therefore, a process of substitution of cosmetic products—a new shampoo or a new lipstick—for the basic needs of life. Commercial media, especially television, scorns the autochthonous and sells everything that looks like the latest images from the industrialized world. The outcome is a complex economic and social dependence. Mexico as a nation under GATT and NAFTA is more dependent than ever on the United States and, at the same time, Mexican people have to cope with an imported substitute reality.

The impact of mass media advertising and first world role models portrayed on television is at the forefront of the feminist ideological critique of media in Latin America.[6] Women who cannot recognize themselves in the models that dominate most aspects of even their most intimate lives suffer a loss of self-esteem which is a characteristic of the abused woman syndrome. Closely allied to the images of Mexican women used to sell consumer goods are the images of the television teledramas. It should be noted that 92% of the population in Mexico's cities have television and the broadcasting company, Televisa, has a monopoly on the production and distribution of these programs. Olga Bustos Romero writes that teledramas are open to severe criticism primarily for the distorted, denigrating, and fanciful images they present of Mexican women (1992, 116).

The domination of most Mexican women has a particular history which does not originate in the United States, but rather in Spain and, to a certain extent, in Rome. Spanish culture, with its entrenched Roman Catholicism and its seven centuries of Arabic-Muslim influence in Andalusia, implanted a foundation of sexual stereotypes which modern capitalism has used and developed. The basic sexual stereotypes of Latin American women are fundamentally reflections of social power. The ideology of male superiority has both a historical basis and an economic reality.[7] The status of native women changed from unequal partner, in preconquest cultures, to sexual object for the Spaniard. Such objectification is the fate of most conquered females, but in this case the Spanish administration also wanted to colonize. Therefore a dual role developed: mother and whore.[8]

I want to take up the discourse of gender ideology in Mexico from various sides; first, an examination of *machismo*; second, the reality of alienation in a *macho* society; and, finally, the ways in which this alienation is affected by foreign images and models.

Although the word *macho* has become the universal name for this social disease, *machismo* is only one means of expression of gender inequality, and it is by no means limited to Latin America. In the idiomatic usage of contemporary Mexico, *machismo* is a social relationship that promotes male superiority over the female in all aspects of life. The man comes first, has the best, receives an education, has freedom of movement, can become a productive member of society, and has his work recognized as valuable. For all these possibilities, the opposite is the lot of most women in such a social system. The male thus feels that he is a privileged being in his family and in society from birth to death.[9]

The radical differentiation of the population according to gender consolidates the social function of the two sexes. Women's primary purpose in life is to serve the male, in whatever capacity he needs her: as lover, mother, housekeeper, nurse, or teacher. In Mexico, women have not just been cast in the role of sex object, the role so prevalent in first world cultures; rather, they have been taught that their purpose in life is to serve and obey their father and then their husband. No one in Mexican letters has been more lucid in understanding and putting into practice a social feminist critique than Rosario Castellanos. She gave Mexican feminism the direction and sense of purpose it required to survive in the 1970s. One of the most cited of her essays, "Self-sacrifice Is a Mad Virtue" (written in 1971), challenged Mexican feminists; she outlined an arena of contestation where women of all classes and social backgrounds could be addressed: authority over one's person and body. She wrote:

[In Mexico a woman is] a creature who is dependent upon male authority: be it her father's, her brother's, her husband's or her priest's. She is subject to alien decisions that dictate her personal appearance, her marital status, the career she is going to study, or the field of work she is going to enter. Trained from infancy to be understanding of and to tolerate abuse from those stronger than she is, she, in turn, in order to reestablish her inner balance, treats those over whom she has power with an iron hand. The Mexican woman does not consider herself—nor do others consider her—to be a woman who has reached fulfilment if she has not produced children, if the halo of maternity does not shine above her. (261)

Before Rosario Castellanos died tragically in 1974 at the age of 49, she was working out what might have developed into a feminist sociocriticism. Although she had not yet overcome her specifically Mexican class distinctions, she was nonetheless the forerunner of a postmodern feminist social criticism that recognizes in language a way of life that if allowed to remain alien to us will continue to serve as a prison. In 1972 she published "Language as an Instrument of Domination," an essay in which she stresses that one's knowledge of the world and the value structures we accept as social order are developed, maintained, and contested through language. The man-made codes which are the inscription of Mexican reality exclude women from history. Mexican history is a man's history, manufactured by men to legitimize centuries of domination, falsification, and prejudice, and calling it "Mexico." We begin where she stopped in 1974.

The more one probes into the social status of most Mexican women, the more it becomes evident that neither men nor women have a clear idea of the domination/submission relationship which rules their lives. On the contrary, they have interiorized it into a way of thinking, a way of looking at the world, as attitudes toward satisfaction and aspirations. This interiorization has been aided enormously by the church and its misogynist clergy, who teach God's approval of this division of the world. Because of the church's traditional influence over most Mexican women, women themselves have been the prime agents of transmission and diffusion of this limited status. Elu de Leñero (1969, 82) cites a survey showing that 55% of men and 67% of women were against birth control for religious reasons.[10] Noelle Monteil's 1985 study further supports the statistical information cited above:

In response to the question "can religious and cultural conditioning be so oppressive that women themselves become an important part of the obstacles to the process of change?" it is obvious that a large part of Mexican women are part of the obstacle to change because of their religious conditioning that has made them consider it a moral obligation to maintain the established order because that order is the will of God: political order, the social division of classes, the family, etc. The maintenance of this order also signifies the transmission of a doctrine and of traditions that fix a determined status for women with a specific role to play. (172; my translation)

The status of most women in Mexico is not simply domination imposed on women by men; it is much deeper and more complex.

Women, however, are not the only ones who are oppressed under the prevailing system. The male is also the victim of *machismo* because the social system itself is structured so that a few will exploit the many. Under *machismo* the male, like the female, has been dispossessed of his identity as a social being. At an impersonal level, the *machismo* attitude, however, provides compensation for the male, for no matter how dominated he is in the work place, he has someone over whom he is master: his wom(a/e)n. The male response to the social alienation he suffers is to prove to himself that he dominates his woman, often by resorting to physical violence. This abuse of women, both physical and psychological, so thoroughly permeates Mexican culture that it is seen as a natural part of the relationship between men and women. The fundamental blindness is that the male does not realize that in alienating his woman, he has alienated himself even more.

Domestic violence against women is so widespread in Mexican society that it is seen as the silent duty of a wife to suffer beatings and generalized abuse in exchange for food and shelter (see Astelarra). If we take into consideration the incidence of rape as an indicator of violence against women in Mexican society, we are faced with some of the world's most disturbing statistics. Mexican criminologist Rafael Ruiz Harrel reports that approximately four thousand incidents of rape were registered in each of the years between 1970 and 1975. It is estimated that these reported crimes constitute a mere 5% of the actual total committed. The result is the calculation that eighty thousand cases of rape take place each year in Mexico, of which ten thousand take place in Mexico City alone. These figures are of course approximate, but by criminological standards, they are not exaggerated, since they suggest an incidence of 125 cases of rape for every 100,000 inhabitants. The incidence of murder is much lower—11.7 murders for every 100,000 persons. Ruiz Harrel writes:

Psychological explanations for rape in general and the higher incidence of the crime in certain groups are woefully lacking because all of the case studies which have been made are exclusively based on interviews with prison inmates. This group is not representative of the rapist, but only of the convicted rapist. It seems far more convincing to look at rape as social conditioning which has become prevalent in what Wolfgang and Ferracuti call a 'subculture of violence.' It has been demonstrated that certain social groups favor one response over others when faced with difficulties or frustrations. (21) [11]

As noted, there exists in Mexico a cultural substratum of *machismo* that transcends all social classes. The assumption is that manliness necessarily implies physical aggression and violence in order to take what one wants without considering the consequences or taking the rights of others into account. The corollary assumption is that the weak are meant to be victims; it is not surprising, therefore, that taking part in rape can come to be interpreted as a positive—and even praiseworthy—manifestation of male assertiveness. It should be added that this undercurrent of male aggression is maintained by both men and women.

The ideology of male supremacy is supported by the historical record, which demonstrates that all the activities valued socially coincide with the work that men do. Thus it is that art, philosophy, religion, and scholarship have been the exclusive domain of men. Prior to the twentieth century, are there any Mexican women artists or writers of consequence besides Juana Inés de la Cruz? This question has been answered negatively by historians of art and literature. The argument put forth is that there was a trickle of women writers from the sixteenth through the nineteenth centuries, but that with the notable exception of Juana Inés de la Cruz, none of these women produced a single literary work of art of lasting value. And this was so, we are reminded by the more open-minded historian, because they lacked exposure to the great works of the past and the stimulus of contemporary writers. As women they were denied access. It was only the remarkable Juana Inés de la Cruz, with her influential patrons in the higher clergy and in the person of the vicereine, who was able to develop her genius. In the four hundred years prior to the present century, no paintings, works of sculpture, or even decorative designs are attributed to women. Leaving aside for the moment that in Mexico until very recently most historians of art and literature have been men, the fact still remains that the critical marginalization of Mexican women intellectuals is unparalleled even in Latin America. While any response must be tentative because this question has yet to be examined by feminist historians, it is my contention that the artistic work of Mexican women has been ignored because the norms of what constitutes a work of art are largely Eurocentric and phallocentric, and that this is also the case among Latin American specialists. The 1990 publication of *Women, Culture, and Politics in Latin America,* by Emilie Bergmann et al., demonstrates the continued marginalization of Mexican women. This book, the result of the work of a study group formed at the University of California at Berkeley and Stanford University, is admirable in terms of the specific aims of each essay, but the book is Latin American in name only. With the exception of one chapter on Juana Inés de la Cruz, Mexican women are mentioned only in passing, if at all. More than half of the book is closely focused on Argentina and to a lesser extent, Chile. This lack of scope and balance stems from a conscious decision of the participants to concentrate on the struggle of women to participate in public culture in the southern cone nations. My objection to the book's misleading title goes deeper: by excluding all consideration of Mexican women since the seventeenth century, it effectively dismisses them as part of Latin America.

A handful of literate Mexican women from the sixteenth to the nineteenth centuries who wrote poetry have been recognized; in 1893 José María Vigil published an anthology of ninety-five women poets of Mexico. The majority of these poets were in the religious orders—the only place for a woman to attain some semblance of a literary education. The subject matter of their poems was ideal or divine love, the sense of order in the perfect home, correct comportment for young ladies, nature, and the nation. Most of these poems were written to commemorate a special event. These poems of occasion, compared to the production of men, both in Mexico and in Spain, are correct and trite imitations of higher poetry. What has yet to be done is to examine this poetry in terms of the ideological repression of women as creative writers. Through their celebration of special events, these women were transferring their artistic sense of form from the confines of the home to the public domain. The recent re-edition of Vigil's book has given us the opportunity to explore these closet poets.

With regard to plastic arts, it is true that women were completely excluded from acquiring any training, but what has not been recognized is that the popular arts of needlework and weaving have been the exclusive means of artistic expression of Mexico's native women. It is only in the last twenty years that the exquisite, original, and elaborate work of textiles has been considered an art form.[12]

Women in the third world suffer from the same gender bias as their counterparts in the first world, but their response, in large part owing to the fact that their sociopolitical situation is so different, differs markedly. Much feminist political thinking in the United States, Canada, and Europe continues to define itself according to the ideological structures of male versus female. Stated in political terms, the goal of feminism is seen as the liberation of women. This version of feminism limits itself to individualistic relations: women must be paid as much as men, women must be treated the same as men, women must have access to the same facilities as men, and so on.

Feminism in Mexico cannot but address issues of women's rights in the context of the generalized social injustice that prevails. The first world demand for social and economic justice can be easily distorted into utopic essentialism or into a bitter vindictiveness over a history of discrimination; its first world models are often androgynous women—for example, the tabloid image of Margaret Thatcher—who are behaving more *macho* than men, with popular cultural images of women (Wonder Woman et al.) attacking men with physical violence. But, in all of this imported pop culture wave of anger and revenge, the basic social structure that embodies gender discrimination is utterly untouched. Mexico as a third world partner with the United States is especially given to this distorted view of feminism. Popular comics depict women superheroes as sexy and lethal (see Lima, 1989). Elizabeth Badinter argues effectively that *macho* behavior is an ideological construct. It does not take long to reflect politically that the inverting of old values does not destroy them; on the contrary, the status quo is perpetuated. In Mexican usage the counterpart of *machismo, hembrismo*, reinforces the former, and an authentically egalitarian society will forever remain inaccessible. *Machismo* as an ideology of behavior has been examined by social scientists in numerous studies; what I want to stress here is that the female complement (of submissiveness, dependence, and exclusive devotion to family and home) to the sexual bravado, authoritarianism, and even violent domination of the male conceals the hidden agenda of *hembrismo*. There are Mexican women who, as mothers, become exploitative and ruthlessly dominant from their power base in the family. *Hembrismo* should, therefore, not be considered as a response or a corrective to *machismo*, for it reinforces the most violent features of *machismo*'s exploitation of women. *Hembrismo* is merely a female variation of oppression.[13]

The Making of a Mexican Feminist Sociocriticism

The conventions, assumptions, and methods of literary criticism do not simply come together; they are developed within a community of critical commentary. This book is addressed to, and thereby participates in, at least three separate critical communities that have come together in my work over the last decade: Latin American literary criticism and specifically criticism of Mexican literature, feminist literary criticism and issues of female characterization and social identity, and, finally, cultural hermeneutics, which examines literature as part of social narrativity. All three communities have a multiplicity of concerns which are reflected in ongoing debates. I make no claim to encompass all or even part of any of the three critical communities, but I do take from all three to form what I believe is a consistent body of thought and I trust an effective critical approach. The three communities have a number of areas of overlap, but also show marked differences from one another. My appropriation is quite deliberate and is the result of carefully constructing a critical approach that will respond to the cultural reality of Mexican literature as I understand it.

The foundation and therefore basic frame for my criticism is the idea that literature is written and read in a situated condition—the sociocultural context of text and reader—and therefore is best examined in a critical context drawn from the social and historical conditions of production and reception; this, in turn, means that the literary critic will draw upon the research of the social sciences. The schema I use within this framework is the particular concern with the representation of women in literature and social discourse. Finally, the focus of my work is on the images of Mexican women which make up the current ideological currency of Mexico and their ties to literature.

In my view, a feminist study of Mexican literature that would concentrate exclusively on work by women would fail if the objective is examining social values on gender issues as expressed in literature. To be effective, feminists must deal with the most powerful forces of a literature, irrespective of the authorship, and, in so doing, bring out the social, political, and economic factors that affect women. The unmasking of the discourse that makes a sexist society pass as one that respects human rights remains the single most important objective for feminist critics around the world, and it has particular urgency in

Mexico now, when both state and church oppose social justice. Beneath the obvious surface violence of the Zapatista uprising of January 1, 1994, there flows a deep undercurrent of continuous violations of the human rights of Mexico's native people in all sectors of the country. It is in such a social context that we must examine sexism. In Mexico the status of women throughout the social diversity of class and privilege is consistently one of inferiority to her male counterpart. Besides the formidable opposition of church and state, the supremacy of class consciousness over social conscience makes the task of feminist social criticism extremely difficult.

In this book I comment on works by Carlos Fuentes and Juan Rulfo because they have given a new direction to the expression of gender relations in Mexican literature from mid-century to the present. At midpoint in this book I turn to the work of Juana Inés de la Cruz (1648–1695), not only in its own literary accomplishment but also as a heretofore unacknowledged formative direction in the development of Mexico's most celebrated poet, Octavio Paz.

The other women writers I have chosen reflect different aspects of women's writing in Mexico. Rosario Castellanos (1925–1974) is recognized not only as a poet and a novelist of some significance, but also as a formidable voice for the women's movement in Mexico. I present her here in her direct advocacy of the feminist cause in her last writings, especially her farce *Lo eterno femenino (The Eternal Feminine)*. Luisa Josefina Hernández (1928–) complements Rosario Castellanos as representative of the generation of university-educated Mexican women who were born in the 1920s and came to maturity as writers in the 1960s. Hernández, unlike Castellanos, is adamant in her dismissal of the women's movement. As a prolific writer, Hernández has been a major voice in the theater but has been largely ignored as a writer of prose fiction. María Luisa Puga (1944–) is from the following generation. Her skill as a writer of both short stories and novels is well recognized today. She has given Mexican literature some of its most intelligent pages on gender relations.

In Chapters 6, 7, and 8 of this book I comment on three very different and remarkable writers: Elena Poniatowska (1933–), Cristina Pacheco (1941–), and Sandra Cisneros (1954–). Elena Poniatowska is a journalist and writer of prose fiction and hybrid works of immense importance in the making of Mexican culture today. She is perhaps the most innovative writer of her generation, having introduced the literary collage as well as the testimonial novel to Mexico. In this book I consider two of her novels. Cristina Pacheco is a journalist and also a short story writer who invented Mexican hard-edge writing. Although she is one of the most popular writers in Mexico, her work is either ignored or rejected for a presumed lack of artistic merit. Finally, I must explain why I have felt compelled to include a non-Mexican writer in a book on female identity in

Mexico. I include the work of the Chicana writer Sandra Cisneros not only because of its lyrical quality, but also because she represents marginalization in a way that no one writing in Spanish in Mexico today could. The marginalization of the Chicana within an alien dominant culture in the United States and an overwhelming sexist Chicano culture provides us with insight into the situation of the silent marginalization of the millions of Mexican native women. Nowhere is this comparison more poignant than in Chiapas and Southern California. The Chicana has struggled against the double oppression of Chicano sexism and Anglo-American alienation through song, dance, art, and a powerful literary creativity. As "women of color" they have demanded to be heard on their own terms and they have been heard. In Chiapas, the women insurgents have demanded and won political as well as social and sexual rights over their own bodies. They have also lived in the double marginalization of an extreme sexist society that was itself alienated linguistically and culturally from the mainstream of Mexican life. Both Chicanas and Tzotzils live in closed patriarchal communities with limited contact with the larger national group or groups, but both have found the means to break out.

In my concluding chapter, I take up the work of Laura Esquivel (1950–). She is from the post–World War II generation and represents writers who have come of age in the midst of the women's movement. She and her contemporaries have made the move from the rejection of the institutionalized sexism of Mexico to the celebration of Mexico's women artists and art forms. She is part of the postfeminist recovery of the past of women's art. In her novel and film *Like Water for Chocolate*, she uses parody to recover the past of women's magazines of the late nineteenth century.

This book concentrates on the literary representations of women in Mexican writing and aims to bring to light the main procedures through which authors, both men and women, have sought to invest their view of life in Mexico with a particular significance for the public. Collectively these depictions of social practices have represented reality for Mexicans. From the television serials and newspapers' short stories to books, this narrativity has characterized the social images of women held by the Mexican people. My analysis of specific texts ends up pointing to some of the ways in which figurative representation of forms of life such as wife, mother, daughter, lover, and so on, and the remembrance of particular life events, both physiological and social, such as maternity, sexual intercourse, success or failure in work, play a symbolic role in making the story an "as if" truth claim for women. In this respect my selection of texts should be regarded as analysis for social criticism and not as a comprehensive history of women's writing (see Appendix 2).[14]

The plan of this book in terms of content is therefore based on fundamental issues of the discourse of social identity. I would now like to outline the methodological basis for the form of feminist sociocriticism I have developed. It is, like most things Mexican, a hybrid phenomenon—a combination of Anglo-American feminist criticism, philosophical social criticism, Latin American social sciences, and, finally and importantly, postmodern hermeneutic criticism.

Hermeneutics and Sociocriticism

Critics respond to a number of ideological, cultural, intellectual, and academic directions, most of which claim unmitigated allegiance, and many of which are mutually exclusive. Others allow for coexistence with some modes, but not with all. Some of these warring modes of operation cluster around the historicity of the text, while others swarm around the historicity of the critic herself. The demands on the feminist sociocritic in Mexico are explicit and unyielding. My response to this challenge has been developed through practical criticism over the last ten years. A synopsis of this development follows.

There are, to my mind at least, three distinct ways of organizing the work to be done: the critic can choose to concentrate on the formal and historical aspects of the text, exclusive of their significance in the world in which she lives; conversely, she can attempt to read the text as a part of her cultural situation and place the emphasis on its present significance, irrespective of what may have been the original place and circumstance of composition; or, finally, she can accept both poles, both historicities, and concentrate on how they interact. The third position, my own, evolved through the course of my personal and intellectual development. I have been trained as a literary critic to value rigor of exposition and attention to the textual discourse and structure, but I am also a feminist who is culturally and existentially identified with one of the most regressive systems of sexual domination and repression: the sexist culture of my native Mexico.

Thus there are two poles in my criticism: one belongs to the text and the circumstances of composition, the other is mine. I shall be explicit about these two historicities because my criticism will involve a constant movement from one to the other. Why have I chosen such a demanding way of working, instead of just getting on with the commentary? The reasons are many and varied, but two should suffice for starters. I am concerned with the close analysis of the text because I anticipate that my readers may have read differently, and I want to establish a common ground between us so that we can debate the meaning and significance of my reading of the text. And I insist on ultimately responding to the text as part of my cultural situation because it is as cultural narrativity that literature achieves sociocultural reality. Because I am concerned with the status of women and the ways in which literature supports, adds to, or rejects the status quo, my criticism is part of my participation in a broader feminist sociocultural critique in Latin America. In the following paragraphs I will outline the theoretical premises of my criticism.

Literature is a socially determined and privileged body of texts which are widely read because they contain ideas, images, or notions that move the receptors to reflect on life as they know it. Literature is, therefore, knowingly or unknowingly, an expression of the values and prejudices of the community wherein it was composed and the community in which it is received. Writers organize and give specific identity to situations and ideas shared at large in the social group to which they belong. The personal intentions and prejudices of the writer merge with the conventions of the artistic form (be it oral epic, novel, or poetry), and both become fused with the shifting ideological currents of the larger cultural context. This ideological outlay of life, however, can only be reconstructed on the basis of its effects on readers, an undetermined number of readers, present and future, in that changing community of readers to which the text passes. It is for this reason that I consider Kate Millett's designation of a literary text's prejudices as the private property of an author to be unacceptable as a critical principle.[15] If the writer's language were merely a private means of expression, it would be unreadable. It is precisely because the writer's language is not private but rather communal that the text as communication can exist in the first place. This statement does not mean that I want to exonerate the writer of responsibility or take away praise, but only to insist that whatever personal intentions were behind the author's writing, they have been transformed through language into an effect, and it is the effect that concerns us. Part of the reader's response is, of course, determined by how much or how little is known about the writer and the community to which he or she belongs. Therefore, the study of a text's effects on its readers, a significant area of study, involves the consideration of the time, place, and ideology in which the text was composed in relation to the situation of the reader. The kind of essentialist criticism that takes up a novel like D. H. Lawrence's *Women in Love* or *The Rainbow* in order to lash out at the author's arrogance is irrelevant and misses the point, which is that Lawrence as an individual is not what interests us; what does concern us is what Lawrence did with language; his texts, with whatever shortcomings they may have, do provide us with the material to discuss the ideology of gender relations. The other side of essentialist blindness is to take the work of any woman who has rejected the restricted position society may have imposed on women and to make of her work a new anti-canon regardless of whether it has any literary value or whether we as readers can respond to the text as an imaginative configuration that will serve as a threshold to a re-description of the world we live in. Literature is a primary formative means of supporting dominant ideology *or* challenging it. The criticism I practice examines those texts that have the power to challenge the reader from a sociofeminist position. The cultural construct we call reality has been developed over centuries by the discourse of power and the distortions of ideologies. Literature constitutes a most valuable depository of discourse for examining the relationships of social interaction.

But these ideas on the nature of literature would be incomplete and inaccurate if we did not take the reader into consideration as the maker of the reading experience. Readers respond only to those aspects of the text that have struck a resonance of confirmation, confrontation, or, in some cases, revelation in the reader's experience and knowledge. Most formal critical methods are in fact an attempt to mitigate partial readings by setting up organizational patterns for the study of the whole of the text. Without disparaging formal methods, on which I am also dependent, for I recognize that they make possible a meaningful debate of interpretations, I would claim that they do not eliminate partial readings and the result of these partial interpretations. Consequently, any interpretation of a text that claims to be definitive is another reductionist application of doctrine. No one can take such claims to omniscience seriously except in those cases where the critical reader is swept up in the name of a cause or belief. This is indeed the strength and the curse of feminist criticism. Feminists believe in the advocacy of women's rights, but the invocation of the cause should not lead us to accept reductionist, dogmatic criticism. Although some feminists may reject my position as one dominated by a self-serving notion of pluralism, I hold that dogmatic or essentialist criticism is in the long run destructive of feminist goals, for it isolates and imposes closure on debate. The ending of the debate plays into the hands of sexists, who have always opposed it. The cause is not served when criticism becomes doctrine.

The aim of my work is to engage in the debate in a way that will give us the opportunity of claiming control of the reality we make. In the case of Mexico, feminist literary criticism must be a part of social criticism. There are as many responses to a novel like *Pedro Páramo* as there are readers, but there are at the same time socially conditioned ways of reading, socially induced patterns that are recognized as such by critical readers. Noncritical readers respond to the exploitation of women with an affective distance. In other words, they do not recognize the social consequences because they respond to the specific scene or description as singular and not general. They do not see the "fallen woman" as the fictional representation of an "as if" situation, but rather as an object that the social system has always had.

The feminist sociocritic in Mexico has two practical tasks to perform in addressing the multiplicity of readings of literary texts. The first is to expose the sexism of narrativity—the stories that make up our reality; by so doing the critic will have begun the unmasking of the ideological distortion that turns the representation of a woman into a sex object or a commodity. The other task for the feminist sociocritic is to introduce readers to new ways of writing by women. The personal space, or, to use Virginia Woolf's metaphor, "a room of one's own," that women have created through their writing has been traditionally exiled to marginal publications; the loss incurred because of their lack of participation in the making of that shared cultural construct we call social reality has been enormous.

Interpretations that do not take the reader's reception of texts into consideration can only offer a singular viewpoint which may be supported by close analysis. On the other hand, interpretations that begin with the acknowledgment of the plurality of readings and inevitable differences of interpretations recognize that each reader must read in his or her own way; criticism then becomes a discussion of differences rather than an advocacy of uniformity.

The problem for feminist sociocriticism in Mexico is to present the critic's viewpoint in terms of the larger context of a collective position and not as individualistic revindication. The urge to pursue a personal interpretation of a sexist text or of a feminist text is very strong, but our objective is not one of personal justification, but rather the much more important goal of social criticism.

The text itself must also be considered. There are at least three distinct textual realities: the text before reading; the reading of the text; and the text as presented in discussion about the reading. These distinctions as well as the ties that link these textual realities together are important; the focus of study here is social critique within the community, not the purported meaning of the text itself.

The first textual situation, the text before it is read, establishes the virtual nature of texts: they are made to be read and they have the essential characteristic of potentiality before they are read. All references to the text for the person who has not read it are external references; these can include reviews, commentary in literary histories, and literary criticism, as well as conversation. Because the text has not yet been actualized, the external references may predispose the reader, but they remain external to the experience itself.

The second situation is the reading of the text. As we are all aware, this is neither a uniform operation nor a simple matter of decoding the message. The full operation of reading a literary text is a complex interaction between what Iser calls the textual strategy and indicators and the reader's linguistic, affective, and experiential repertoire of making meaning. The interaction between text and reader as a part of experience can be new and different with each reading. What is the same is the mutual dependence between the textual indicators and the reader's world-making capacity.[16] Reading a literary text involves much more than linguistic competence; it involves above all the imaginative figuration of the reader. By figuration I mean the ability to discern figures and project them into an imaginative extension and expansion of reality.

The third situation is writing about the text after reading it. The critic has no access to the author's idea of the text or to a fixed text that does not change in the reading. The text is always the text as realized in a reader's interaction with it. Therefore when I write about the text, I am in effect writing about a reading or series of readings of the text, and not the text itself. The critic writes about the ways in which she has read, and she directs these remarks to an undetermined number of other readers who have also responded to the text or who are interested in others' responses. What the critic has to say about the text is entirely what can be reconstructed from the effects of the text. She writes with a specific community of readers in mind with whom she hopes to debate the effects of reading, but this audience can also change.

This organization of the critical enterprise forms a paradigm for poststructural feminist criticism in general and, in Mexico, opens the possibility of a social critique that rejects dogmatism. The writing that we produce as criticism cannot be in any way taken as individualistic reduction of the text to one viewpoint, since the text itself remains open to all readers and is not the direct subject of our commentary. Rather, it is our reading experience of that text that is explained. Second, emphasizing the ways in which one reads the text provides an analytical means for discussion of particular readings. And, third, by directing our remarks about reading to the effects of reading, we engage in the collective realization of how the narrativity of the many texts that comprise our lives expresses the ideological makeup of the world we live in. We comment on our reading in order to discuss the nature of our reading as part of the response to the collective social situation as it is embodied in language. Thus through literature we are participating in the narrativity of what we call the real world or, simply, reality. This cultural construct is made collectively; it is not given or fixed; it is changing. In what direction it will change depends on those who participate.

The Politics of Pornography in Mexico

The issue is not whether we oppose or disapprove of degrading portraits of masochistic women. Nor is the issue whether or not we want children to be exposed to such distortions. The issue is that Mexican women live in a society where their purported inferiority is institutionalized through religion, education, and tradition. The image of the heroic abnegation of Mexican women is propagated in the name of religion and family. Both church and state vehemently denounce and oppose pornographic degradation and violence to women, but they also oppose an open forum on the topic, fearing that the popularity of pornography would reveal that beneath the Mexican image of the family stands a psychology of abuse of the weak by the strong. In the interest of preserving the family, the church safeguards women by keeping them under wraps. The blindness of this way of thinking is an integral aspect of our colonial heritage. The rhetoric of the sanctity of the family hides the objectification of women and enlists women themselves into supporting the status quo. In Mexico, as in most of Latin America, censorship on matters of sex and morals is but another aspect of political control (see Eltit and Honsiváis).

A life, as depicted in literature, could hardly be conceivable without a number of small indicators that mark it as male or female activity. But there is a difference; until recently almost every object the writer gave to the reader that was marked female, either in perspective or in its functionality, was so marked because of an underlying assumption that a generalized view was not a female view. A worldview is assumed to be male unless it is specifically marked as female. This state of affairs should not surprise anyone, since in Mexico almost all writing in literature and history before 1975 was by men. Therefore, we must remember that both the general and the specific viewpoints were written by men. Quite obviously, the assumed general perspective was male. The point is that even in the case where the general viewpoint was not concerned with gender issues, it was a destructive agency for the part of the readership who were female, for it unmistakably led to one conclusion: the male point of view is the norm and the female is a derivation of it, with obvious limitations, like a sort of Eve derived from Adam. Against this destructive agency, which with unquestioned ease dismissed one half of the population from the written narrativity that makes up our lives, there is one primary weapon: to deconstruct the apparent validity of the male viewpoint promoted as a generalized perspective of life. Institutionalized exclusion of women in Mexico is still a reality. The 1992 history textbook used in all Mexican schools mentions only nine women in passing; everything was said, done, and written by men.

It is against this institutionalization of the male perspective as reality that women writers of the second half of this century have had to struggle. We can only be certain that there is no going back, that times are different, and that once the lie has been revealed, there is no recovery of the way things were. At the same time, the amazing growth of women's writing in Mexico since 1975 cannot not hide the dominance of a male perspective in many areas of Mexican public life, especially in popular culture.

The major historical development that has emerged since 1975, coincident with the women's movement, is the fundamental change in the definition of cultural production. The breakdown of the iron grip of monopoly over cultural production by a specific sector of the social elite has in particular favored women writers who had been almost completely shut out before. Of course, Mexicans still recognize the traditional cultural forms of painting, sculpture, theater, literature, and musical composition, but the technical innovations accessible to the general public in computer desktop publishing and video and audio recording have not only opened up access, but have also changed genres and forms. A good example of this innovative creative dimension is the work of the young playwright and director Jesusa Rodríguez, whose performance pieces are often presented at the "Teatro de la Capilla" (Theater of the Chapel) and the adjoining "El Hábito" (The Habit); several of her pieces deal with lesbian parodies of traditional gender roles.[17] Although women moved into journalism in a significant way during the 1980s, today women have gained an unprecedented role in the full range of cultural production. The exclusion of women from artistic expression has ended.

The Politics of Prescriptive Criticism

In 1989 prescriptive feminists in the United States reprinted Cheri Register's 1975 list of five essential characteristics, one or more of which, they asserted, literature must perform in order to earn feminist approval: (1) the work must serve as a means of communication among women as women read and write about their common interests; (2) the work must explicitly promote the creation of an androgynous culture; (3) the author must create role models for young readers to emulate; (4) the work must promote sisterhood of all women; and (5) it must raise the consciousness of women's status in patriarchal society. The list is naive by Mexican standards because it does not address the disease but only offers remedies for some of the symptoms. In our view misogyny derives from social alienation. The social structure that perpetuates the domination of women is the ideological construction of an institutionalized abuse of power. When women are denied their place as social persons, it is the same political process by which certain social classes have been denied access to full social participation. But perhaps the most naive aspect of this qualifying list is that it refers to the works of literature that ought to be written, thus prescribing what ought to be rather than addressing what there is.

Although the editor of *Feminist Literary Criticism*, Josephine Donovan, referred in the 1975 edition to Cheri Register's article as a "bibliographical essay" that "provides an excellent interpretive introduction to the body of existing feminist criticism," the article is in fact not a report but rather an uncompromising advocacy of what feminist writing should be in the future if it is to earn feminist approval. In her discussion, Cheri Register states that prescriptive criticism "is best defined in terms of the ways in which literature can serve the cause of liberation" (18). Her prescription of liberation, however, is a reified matriarchy for the affluent middle class Anglo-American woman, and thus offers no recognition of the social reality of her own country, let alone that of the third world, in which the majority of the women of the world live. In short, it is little more than a self-serving individualistic response to misogyny that does not address the social structure that produces it.

I have no wish to overstate the case against prescriptive feminism or to imply that it is more than a small part of the highly diversified feminist scene in the United States. The work of Sandra Gilbert, Susan Gubar, Margaret Higonnet, Nancy K. Miller, Elaine Showalter, and Susan Rubin Suleiman, to name only a few, continues to offer Mexican feminists intellectual stimulus of the most effective kind: a challenge to develop our own thinking and respond with our own criticism. There is another fundamental common cause between feminists north and south of the Rio Bravo. The increase in violence against women that has been a side effect of the rapid growth of the women's movement, although expressed in different ways in Mexico and the United States, is rampant in both countries. In Mexico the main arena today is with a male-dominated judiciary and a sexist, often corrupt, police force. In the United States the arena has been primarily political through the virulent opposition of the neo-conservative alliance with fundamentalist religious groups. Susan Faludi's *Backlash: The Undeclared War Against American Women* has documented the extent and the depth of the war against women, and in her epilogue she comes closer than any other U.S. feminist to recognizing why the Mexican feminist priority is one of changing the social structure rather than addressing the symptoms of sexism. In Mexico the political system must respond to the will of the people. Until that is accomplished there is no hope for women's rights because there are no rights. In the United States, where the political system is by and large responsive to the public will, the problem has been one of fighting for a change of attitude with regard to such basic demands as self-determination and economic equality. The situation in the United States is by all standards of comparison more hopeful in spite of the backlash. Faludi writes: "Men need women as much as women need men. The bonds between the sexes can chafe, and they can be, and have been, used to constrain women. But they also can promote mutually beneficial growth and change" (457). The struggle for a change in attitudes is, we hope, just ahead for Mexican feminists as we await democracy.

In our world we must respond to life as it is in the ordinary affairs of living. Thus it is that in place of the preparation of a well-intentioned but naive list of qualifications, we propose the following set of goals for feminist sociocriticism; these are the practical aims for Latin American critics rather than a program to promote ideal literary works: [18]

1. *Feminophobia.* We begin with the analysis of the symbolic degradation of women in social reality. I shall refer to this practice as feminophobia; it is the symbolic representation of *machismo.* The best of our literature offers a wealth of material; see my study of Carlos Fuentes, Chapter 3.

2. *Attention to pre-aesthetic arts.* We recognize that centuries of denial of access to education and even to literacy have led women to channel their creative talents toward the decorative or pre-aesthetic arts. A strong literary criticism has begun the long effort of recovery from exile. [19]

3. *Ideological dimensions.* Literary texts as value-laden cultural constructs have an ideological dimension, whatever the genre or topic presented. It is the task of the feminist critic to expose the sometimes subtle, sometimes overt, political discourse that depersonalizes and objectifies women. The loss of women's identity as social persons is one of the main concerns of this book.

4. *Writing as transgression.* Because writing has been traditionally a male domain, for a woman like Juana Inés de la Cruz to write was a form of transgression, a breaking of the social code. The fact that as a young woman she wanted to dress like a man in order to be allowed access to the university emphasizes the degree of her transgression. The act of writing by women in Mexico is a relatively contemporary phenomenon: between Juana Inés de la Cruz and Rosario Castellanos there is a deafening silence. Hence it is a primary task of feminist sociocriticism to investigate the development of feminine modes of writing and the revision of existing genres. [20] In the chapters devoted to Elena Poniatowska, Cristina Pacheco, and Sandra Cisneros, I address the topic of women's writing as a means of transgressing prevailing social codes in order to gain freedom.

5. *Social development and the status of women.* One of the fundamental issues feminists in Mexico have discussed in depth from 1975 to the present is the re-

lationship of the status of women to the economic and social development of the general population in this part of the world. The consensus, with which I concur, is that the exploitation of women and their alienated situation cannot be separated from the social structure. Thus it is that feminist sociocriticism in Mexico addresses the symbolic distortion and loss of identity of women in relation to the social structure. The significant contribution that the monthly *fem.* (founded in 1976) and the biannual *debate feminista* (founded in 1990) have made to the women's movement and to feminist criticism cannot be overstated. They are the cornerstone of feminist discourse in Mexico.

The political elements of literature are to be found not so much in the thematic or descriptive elements as they are in the value judgments and truth claims that the reader accepts uncritically. In this sense, all literature has a significant ideological effect. By ideology, I mean a system which promotes certain values and disparages others. Since language itself, as the expression of a community of speakers, embodies a specific social organization, there can be no neutral statements. Value judgments are implicit even in such ordinary statements such as "*no te rajes*," usually translated as "don't give in." This phrase carries powerful sexist values; the verb *rajar* literally means "to crack," and the admonition "don't crack" also means "don't be a woman." Implications of weakness, dependence, and cowardice, as opposed to strength, independence, and courage—which express sexist attitudes toward women and men, respectively—are embedded in the ordinary spoken Spanish of Mexico. Consequently, every work of literature carries strong and weak ideological messages encoded in the discursive level of the text.

Feminist social literary criticism is not the exercise of authority or of special privilege; above all, it is a dialogue about the effects of reading works of literature. I am engaged in dialogue not only with the text or other critics, but also with all readers who have read the text and are willing to pursue a discussion of that reading experience. I am not addressing the author because I am not concerned with the private person, but with the person's public writing. And, when I speak about the intentionality of the text as distinct from the intentions of the author, I refer to a strategy that includes aspects of the writer's biography which may stand behind the development of literary structure and the anticipation of a climate of reception. This intentionality of the text can be discerned only through the effects on the reader. Therefore, my concept of criticism is the ongoing discussion about effects and to a certain extent about formal causes but, most emphatically, about the effects not on the individual alone but on the ever-changing community of readers. My topic is the literary discourse of and about women in the social structure of Mexico. This is an inquiry of subversion and transgression and, of course, of survival.

Two

Rulfo's Susana San Juan

Woman as Subject and Object of Desire

In reviewing Mexican novelists, critics might dispute the relative merits of some or most authors, but there is a wide consensus that Juan Rulfo and Carlos Fuentes are two of the most important novelists not only of Mexico but of all Latin America in this century. I take up their work in this book not only because of its aesthetic features but, primarily, as powerful examples of the way literary texts can subvert the social codes of alienation and domination of the other. Chapters 2 and 3, both of which treat the subversion of Mexican social codes, convey important historical literary background material on the status of women in Mexican letters at the time I began this project.

Juan Rulfo's[1] masterpiece, *Pedro Páramo*, published in 1955, has become a classic novel of contemporary Latin American literature and, consequently, has been studied from a large variety of critical perspectives.[2] Here, I draw upon the novel's textual richness in order to examine the language of female identity. The principal female character is the enigmatic Susana San Juan.[3]

One of the most difficult of all critical tasks is to discern and describe those generic features of our experience which we take for granted. One such feature is presence: a state of affairs we resort to describing by contrast with absence. In this book I have approached presence primarily through the self-conscious act of reading a literary text. The structure of this experience is put together from the abundance of vivid details which crowd our lived experience as we respond to the text in reading. The factual impact of experience comes to us in a stream of occurrences and is held together through images. We focus on only a small fraction of the manifold experience that the text offers us. Most of the time we focus the way we do out of habit or because of professional training; we are, of course, capable of changing our focus and of pursuing an epistemological analysis of it. But in the reading of a literary text, the initial selection of particulars has been made for us by the writer and it is our task to build up consistent images by supplementing the writing and following the textual injunctions if we are to claim that we understand it. The U.S. historian Louis O. Mink sums it up succinctly: "Memory, imagination, and conceptualization all serve this function [to hold in mind], whatever else they do: they are ways of grasping together in a single mental act things which *are not experienced together*, or are even capable of being so experienced, because they are separated by time, space or logical kind. And the ability to do this is a necessary (although not sufficient) condition of understanding" (49; emphasis mine). Mink's clear and concise analysis of imaginative thinking gives us a basic outline of what happens when we read works of fiction like *Pedro Páramo*. One reads and constantly puts into play an enormous diversity not only of textual details but also of points of view. Thus it is that, against the general outlines of the historical background of rural Mexico, we encounter a diversity of voices from the past. This period extends from 1886 in the second decade of Porfirio Díaz's thirty-four-year regime to the last phase of the Mexican revolution, the Cristero upheaval of 1928.[4]

Juan Preciado, the first-person narrator and guide into the ghost town that is Comala in the 1950s, hears voices from the town's past, including that of his mother Dolores, recalling the town of her youth in the 1890s, the voices of her friends Eduviges Dyda and Damiana Cisneros, and, quite unexpectedly, the voice of an adolescent Pedro Páramo from the 1880s. This is the voice of the boy who would one day be Juan Preciado's father and father to many others in the town, including Abundio Martínez, who killed him in the 1930s. Whether Juan Preciado hears Pedro's voice is not clear, but what is obvious is that he is plunged into terror by the voices he does hear. As the textual world of Comala develops in the second half of the novel, we learn that Juan has died and lies in his grave with Dorotea, commenting on what they both hear, and it is at this point that we encounter Susana San Juan, the would-be last wife of Pedro Páramo, a woman who died in 1928. Her voice stands out as intimate and lyrical among the voices of numerous men and women who lived in Comala from the 1880s up to the time of the town's last survivors, the incestuous brother and sister who see themselves as an Adam and Eve after the apocalypse. It is the presence of Susana San Juan, both as object and subject, that will concern me in this chapter.

At the center of this text is language as subjective presence in the midst of the discourse of power and domination. Pedro Páramo, the *cacique* (strongman)[5] of Comala, owns the land that surrounds the town and, consequently, rules. He owns the *Media Luna* lands, not through inheritance, work, or even speculation, but only by means of violence and treachery that know no moral constraints. His power is entirely based on the disregard and abuse of all others who are caught in his sphere of influence. In this text Pedro Páramo is the center of gravity of the discourse of power against which all voices are heard.

The discourse of power is the calculated language of distortion that converts a rape into "virile love." The basis for the discourse of power is that the prescriptive aim controls the cognitive phrase in the most direct manner possible. Thus it does not matter what there is, or what has been done before, or what the community has accorded; the only concern of this discourse is *what must be done* in order to accomplish the prescribed aim. To do something, to accomplish an end, is what we recognize as practical, but when the discourse of accomplishing an aim becomes the discourse of power, the multiple constraints on *how* the aim can be met disappear. Thus the discourse of power invoked in the name of the mythical *we* and used under the cover of the practical becomes a conscious calculation of phrases and of their complications, measuring the response on the part of both subordinates and adversaries. The discourse of power remains abstract and therefore ineffective unless it is expressed together with a description of the means whereby the end is to be accomplished. The discourse of power is the pornography of the linguistic construct of the world of action, which it distorts in seeking self-gratification. When this discourse is coupled with an effective taking stock of resources and capacity, as well as the probable response of victims, it emerges as a plan to violate the rights of others. I have argued above that sexual desire is only incidentally related to pornography, that only the surface referent is the male eroticism of the female as other; the deep referent is always the will to power and domination, and rape is the violent exercise of power by the insecure and weak on the necessary victim who can be considered weak only in terms of brute physical strength. It is instructive to note that in Mexican Spanish, the most insulting attribute that one male can hurl at another is that he is *rajado*, that is, that he has a crack, a vagina in place of a penis. In this sexist society, women are all assumed to be willing victims. In *Pedro Páramo* all the women are real or potential victims; Susana San Juan is the only woman who through madness escapes and thwarts the exercise of power over her.

In this chapter I shall follow a direct plan of discourse analysis; first, I examine the discourse of power in general as it is depicted in the novel; second, I turn to the consideration of the female as object of desire within the language of the *cacique*, thus linking up the discourse of power with a hermeneutics of desire. Third, and last, I want to comment on the language of progressive introversion by the female object of desire, Susana San Juan, who personifies the tragedy of women in the world of all the *cacique*-ruled Comalas of Mexico— women whose only form of escape from victimization is madness or death.

The common stratagem of the language of power is to create a situation in which the abuse of other's rights becomes accepted as the privilege of the strongman. Power needs targets, and the language of power generates a steady supply of targets for domination. Jews, gypsies, and homosexuals were the targets for Nazi aggression because of long-prevailing prejudices in the German population. In Mexican society, women are the targets for aggression on account of an entrenched sexism which fixes their social roles as subservient objects of desire, venerated mothers, or abnegated scapegoats.

The language of power in *Pedro Páramo* deals with four areas of action: the acquisition of property, the granting of surrogate license to authorize subordinates to rape and murder, personal sexual gratification, and terror. These four areas of action are, of course, common to the tyranny of strongmen whether they be *caciques*, generals, or politicians; in effect they are all the manifestation of the realization of the discourse of power. In Mexico this is the only social reality many, if not most, of the population have known.

When Pedro Páramo inherits his father's lands, and with them a long list of debts, he begins to exercise his role as would-be *cacique* by taking over his major creditor's lands—those of Dolores Preciado—through marriage and the conjoint holding of land and property. Under Mexican law of the time, a marriage with conjoint holdings led to effective control by the husband. On taking over after his father's death, Pedro immediately takes on the *cacique's* discourse:

"Tomorrow you're going to propose to Lola."

"She wouldn't even look at me. I'm too old."

"Propose for me. Tell her I'm very much in love with her. And while you're at it, tell Father Rentería to arrange for the wedding. How much money have you got?"

"None, Don Pedro."

"Promise it, then. Tell him it'll be paid. I don't think there'll be any trouble. Do that tomorrow." (34)

Fulgor does not at first get the full sense of Pedro's statement: that it does not matter how much is owed, but to whom it is owed. The strategy is to assess the capabilities of the adversaries, for that is what anyone is who has a claim on Pedro Páramo's property or, as we shall see, who has property the *cacique* might want. Once the assessment is given by Fulgor, Pedro's response is immediate: go ask for her hand in marriage, not for you but for me. The cynical remark (in the Spanish text, omitted in the English translation) that after all she does have some charm only serves to heighten the calculated nature of the language of power. The admiration Fulgor shows for his young boss is part of a *macho* code that admires strength and audacity and scorns weakness personified by the priest and, of course, by women.

This use of the language of power is dramatized in the passages that deal with Toribio Aldrete, the owner of a neighboring ranch who has his land surveyed with a view toward drawing up a land map. The law as emanating from the will of the community is irrelevant to the discourse of power. In place of the rule of law there is only the will and whim of the strongman. Fulgor asks Pedro what he is to do about the law. Pedro responds: "What law, Fulgor? From now on we're going to make the laws ourselves" (38).

The significance of this statement is that it unmasks the *macho* code as the rule of irrational bravado to the detriment of the community. The strongman need not be literally strong himself, as long as he can demonstrate a strong will and can draw upon the *macho* code that equates the proving of manhood with risk-taking and indifference to all communal values. At a time when there are not sufficient armed conflicts in society, those caught up in the irrationalism of perpetual adolescence must invent new ways of proving their manhood. In Spain today young men sit blindfolded in the middle of a highway after a blind turn, in Lebanon they play Russian roulette, and in Mexico they rush down winding roads in the dead of night in cars without lights. This *machismo* in Mexico is, however, not merely a symptom of adolescence; it is an institutionalized part of the social makeup and of gender relations.

In the discourse of power, the desire for power becomes the opposite of the will to truth, but the desire for power itself is not the source of such action; it is only the manifestation of a deeper human trait which is desire itself. In order to examine this deeper aspect of the discourse of power, we must probe through a hermeneutics of desire into this wellspring of human longing which can become destructive of collective social values.[6] The language of desire is fed by the image of the target of desire. The construction of this image takes fragments of the absent reality and manipulates them into an all-encompassing configuration of an ideal state of satisfaction, well-being, fulfilment, and happiness. When the target of desire is a woman, her image becomes a figure, an object that maintains only the external aspects of a woman, but is propelled by the inner psychological needs of the male who has created the object of desire. Susana San Juan is the object of desire of Pedro Páramo. Her image has been given the following characteristics: (1) In spite of the fact that she has been absent for thirty years, she is the figure of a young girl and is constituted through the remembrance of the sexual daydreams of a masturbating adolescent. (2) Because there was no sexual experience to remember, the figure has been made into an imaginary sexual partner. (3) The economy of remembrance has transformed the image of the young girl into an ideal of female beauty. (4) The sexual drive in the male leads to the routine substitution of any young girl for the body of the object of desire. (5) The sudden presence of the mature woman in place of the young object of desire does not rupture the imaginary longing because she is incapable of responding to the dominating male; that is, she cannot acknowledge that she belongs to him. (6) The deferment of sexual union and domination prolonged over three years augments the passion for possession. (7) The mourning for her death is the culmination of the frustration of thwarted desire. (8) Revenge becomes the manifestation of frustration at the death of the woman who was never possessed. The community serves as scapegoat for Susana San Juan's death. There are, therefore, eight stages in the creation of the female as object of desire and the eventual destruction of Comala.

The projection of the figure of the female as object of desire intrudes into Juan Preciado's narrative in the opening pages of the novel. The enunciating voice, unknown to Juan Preciado, is that of the adolescent Pedro in his sexual daydreams about Susana:

I was thinking of you, Susana. In the green hills. When we flew kites in the windy season. We heard the sounds of the village down below us while we were up there, up on the hill, and the wind was tugging the string away from me. "Help me, Susana." And gentle hands grasped my hands. . . .

Your lips were moist, as if they had been kissing the dew. I was remembering you. When you were there looking at me with your sea-green eyes. (9–10)

The young boy shut up in the outhouse imagines the girl with the aquamarine eyes. His emphasis is on their being together, and on the sensuality of her lips and eyes. The special nature of his remembrance of the childhood friend in adolescence is that their relationship as intimate friends now has the sexual overtones that come with puberty. This passage, as well as the two that follow, are in the first person, in the mode of an apostrophe, as the boy addresses the absent girl who has become his imaginative figure, his object of desire. "I was watching the drops fall, Susana, in the glare of the lighting, and every breath I breathed was a sigh, and every thought was a thought of you" (12). The remembrances of the young Susana are linked in the imagination with specific natural phenomena: the rush of the wind, the dew, the sunset, and, primarily, rain. The significance of rain and sun in the parched arid ghost town in which Juan has encountered these evocations is that of the contrastive force between the imaginative ideal figure and the scorched reality. The pre-hispanic myth of sun and rain as the burning water of life[7] and the separation of the two as death cannot go unheeded in what is an imaginative construct of the union of the two young people.

The sense of loss in the voice from the past comes into the narrative not only as one of the many moments of Comala's past, but also as an essential aspect of the psychological alienation of Pedro Páramo. The return of Susana San Juan to Comala marks the return of Pedro's direct address to the absent woman, subject of the figure he has created as object of desire. This discourse is the most potent of the entire novel, for he is close to the attainment of a lifetime of desire and his possession of the object: "I've waited thirty years for you to come back, Susana. . . . I hoped to have everything. . . . I felt as if Heaven had opened. I wanted to run to you. To surround you with happiness. To cry. And I did cry, Susana, when I knew you were coming back" (80–81). The discourse of desire is clearly marked: "to have everything. Not just something: everything. Everything we could possibly want . . . and all of it for you" (80). The object of desire created throughout thirty long years, invested with countless days and nights of sexual desire, fed by the need to possess the loved one, encompasses life itself. The figure of Susana has been elevated to an ideal image of female beauty: "'Do you know, Fulgor, she's the most beautiful woman in the world. I thought I'd lost her forever. And now I don't want to lose her again. Do you understand, Fulgor?'" (83) The encounter with the real woman, with all the ravages of time, does not materialize. Dorotea tells Juan Preciado, and us, "'When she was delivered to him she was already worn out and half crazy'" (my translation; omitted in the English publication). The possession is deferred.

One of the most basic aspects of an object of desire is that although it is a creation of the ego, its very nature is unknown to the ego and forever remains a mystery. The construct is entirely a one-sided projection onto the object. There is no attempt to know the person behind the construct, nor can there be such an attempt, for the ego is not interested in knowing but only in possessing the object dressed in the colors of the ego's desire. The text makes this fundamental condition explicit. Even if Susana regained her sanity, would it be enough for her to know that she was the most loved creature in all the world? Would it be enough for her to know that she would transport him from this world drunk with the ecstasy of her image that erases all other memories? But Susana San Juan was not of this world.

Pedro Páramo's deepest frustration comes when he has Susana San Juan in his house, but cannot have sexual intercourse with her because she is progressively sinking into insanity. Instead of going through the pretense of making love to her, Pedro prefers surrogate lovers whom he can imagine to be Susana. The use of the surrogate raises the obvious question of why Pedro does not merely force himself on the hallucinating Susana, who is more often than not lost in an erotic reverie both auto-erotic and heterosexual. The surrogate responds physically and can be made into an extension of the object of desire by the same ego that has created it. On the other hand, the unconscious body of Susana cannot be made to respond to the stimulus that it receives. The text offers this scene of Pedro and a surrogate Susana:

He thought of Susana San Juan, then of the girl he had slept with a short while ago. That startled, trembling, little body. Her heart in her mouth from fear. "A handful of flesh," he called her. And when he embraced her he tried to change her body into that of Susana San Juan. "A woman who isn't of this world." (107)

Pedro Páramo's drive to possess Susana becomes desperate as he is condemned to look on helplessly at life slowly draining from the semiconscious body of the woman he has made into the sole object of his affective being. He opens the door and goes over to her, letting a ray of light illuminate her face. Her eyes are shut tight, as if she were in pain. Her mouth is moist and half open. With a sudden movement she pulls off the sheet and reveals her naked body.

The death of Susana is the death of a woman; but to Pedro Páramo she was more than a woman: she was his creation of more than thirty years. This creation has been the only other to whom Pedro Páramo has directed his affection. Yet this other is fabricated and utterly false. The Susana San Juan of Pedro's desire is only superficially related to the woman who is dying in his house. Without a true other, the self that is Pedro Páramo sees all men and women as objects of his power. The death of the insane Susana is only the final stage in the process of alienation that goes back to Pedro Páramo's adolescence. The absence of a real other throughout the thirty years that have elapsed cannot be set right with the presence of Susana. The denial of an affective union that would transcend sexual intercourse began when Susana left Comala, and its culmination, which Pedro now faces, is her death; it is marked by the onset of a silent rage for revenge against everyone and anyone.[8]

Susana is buried in the town cemetery but hardly anyone in Comala realizes that she has died. The village is all lights and fiesta, and the Media Luna is sunk in shadows and silence. Pedro Páramo swears he will take revenge on Comala, and he does. He burns everything and allows the barren lands to be depleted through wind and rain erosion.

In this novel Comala is a village like any other in rural nineteenth-century Mexico, with its traditions and modes of governance. But like the rest, because of the continued exploitation of the many by the few, the irrational code of *machismo*, and the obvious failure of both church and state to offer any hope of social justice, it was fertile ground for strongmen to take over and force it into an orgy of self-destruction. The Mexican revolution is the macrocosm of the history of Comala. What makes the story of Comala utterly different from all other villages is that its history is evoked through voices from the past in the present, and at the center sits not a larger-than-life *cacique*, but a rather ordinary, ambitious, and ruthless man whose entire community paid the price of his affective alienation. The discourse of power has behind it the figure of evil, but behind the mask of ruthless power is a lovesick adolescent boy yearning for his girl.

The names of Susana San Juan and Pedro Páramo are extraordinarily lyrical names. Both would make a five-syllable verse; both have alliteration and internal rhyme. The stresses are different, the first and third syllables of the dactylic stress in Pedro Páramo coupled with the explosive P make it a rather abrupt, hard succession of sounds. The stress in the name Susana San Juan is on the second and fifth syllables, which together with the three sibilants make it a far more fluid series of sounds. The names are more than the signs of identity; they become lyric motifs because of the extraordinary frequency with which both names are used in the text, and in the second half of the novel, they are used in relation to each other. There is, however, one remarkable and consistent contrast in the textual presentation of the two names. Whereas Pedro is constantly enunciating the name of Susana San Juan, she never speaks his name in the text. This contrast is part of the major separation in the discourse of the two main characters. I have characterized Pedro Páramo's language as the discourse of power and of desire, but what about Susana's own language?

Susana's discourse is the language of introversion. Hers is a process of a gradual internalization of sensation and sensuality, slowly receding into the darkness of an introverted mind engulfed in fear. Susana's discourse begins with the expression of a hermaphroditic sexuality, and slowly becomes the enunciation of the memory of moments of sexual exuberance. She does not offer us any remembrance of Pedro Páramo, her would-be lover, who has made her his object of desire ever since their childhood together in Comala. Among her memories from childhood, one in particular is filled with terror. She remembers the day her father lowered her into a dark cave to look for gold coins and the fear she felt as she handed up to him, piece by piece, the scattered bones of a human skeleton. The sexual joys of her past are remembered with exuberance in her reverie, but her present in the house of Pedro Páramo is filled with an overwhelming dread of darkness and with the partial awareness of her ensuing descent into madness.

In contrast to Pedro Páramo's earliest evocations, hers are the words of a mature woman recalling her youth. She remembers with sensual pleasure the winds of February and the playful antics of birds, but although this is the same period recalled by Pedro, when the two of them would fly kites in the hills above Comala, she does not mention him. Her mother's death at this time is remembered in the apathetic tone of an impersonal observer. The affective emphasis is entirely placed on the sensual experience of the fragrance of fruit trees, the cool sensation of mountain winds, the remarkable clarity of blue skies, and the play of birds.

I think about that season of the year when the limes ripened. . . . The wind came down from the mountains on those February mornings. But the clouds stayed up above, waiting until it was time for them to enter the valley. They left the sky a blank blue. The sunlight shone down on the games the wind played as it made circles on the earth, stirring up the dust and shaking the boughs of the orange trees. And the sparrows laughed. . . . They chased the butterflies. . . Then my mother died. . . . The down had begun to grow on my legs, between the veins, and my hands were warm and trembling when they touched my breasts. The sparrows were playing. The wheat swayed on the hillsides. I was sorry that she couldn't see the wind playing in the jasmine, that she'd closed her eyes to the sunlight. (74; published translation corrected)

The voice of Susana San Juan evokes an introverted and distant remembrance. There are no references to others until the flat simple statement announcing her mother's death. Clouds, wind, sky, birds, and butterflies are the agents imbued with action. This is a remembrance of blissful happiness in which she is quite alone. The death of her mother ends this pre-sexual, almost embryonic reverie full of playfulness and laughter and announces the beginning of puberty.

Susana's remembrances shift abruptly from her sensual perceptions to the voluptuous sexual feelings brought on by her entering the sea nude. This highly erotic description of sensations culminates in what we can only term hermaphroditic orgasm. The male who is present leaves because he feels excluded. He will wait to make love in the bedroom; she does not need him. The capacity for introversion and self-fulfilment is marked and will carry over even when later she recalls the physical force of the male in sexual intercourse.

"I like to bathe in the sea naked," I told him. That's why he followed me that first day. He was naked too, and he glowed when he came out of the water . . . He followed me that first day, but he felt lonely, even though I was there with him.

"You're just like one of those birds," he said. "I like you better at night when we're together in the darkness, under the same sheet, with our heads on the same pillow . . . ."

And he left.

I went back to the sea. I always went back. And the sea washed my ankles, my knees and thighs. It clasped its gentle arms around my waist. It encircled my breasts, and kissed my throat, and hugged my shoulders. Then I let myself sink in fully. I give myself up to its strength and gentleness. . . . (93–94; translation corrected)

The sensations of sexual intercourse with a male partner are remembered by Susana twice; at first only Juan Preciado, our guide and primary narrative voice, hears her and reports, but subsequently, her voice is heard directly when she speaks about what she would no longer be able to feel because of her husband Florencio's death.

"She says . . . she used to sleep all nestled up in him, hiding herself within him. She says she used to feel lost in a dark nothingness when she felt her flesh being broken open like a furrow being opened by a burning spike. Then it wasn't burning, it was warm and sweet, striking hard blows against her soft flesh. She felt she was sinking, was being swallowed up, and she moaned." (98)

Although the words of sexual climax as reported by Juan Preciado are a repetition of what Susana was saying, the emphasis on her sensations to the exclusion of all else cannot be overlooked. The report is entirely taken up by what she felt; there is no mention of what Florencio said or felt. His sexual penetration of her is metaphorically described as the sensation of being opened by an ardent spike. The description of physical sensation is dominant in this remembrance of her sexuality. The mind has blocked out all but the images of sexual activity.

When we hear the voice of Susana San Juan directly it is in response to the news that Florencio is dead. She does not cry for Florencio, the man, her husband, her partner, but for the loss of his body. Her loss of a realized passion becomes an object of desire with his absence:

"And what I want is his body. Naked . . . hot with love . . . boiling with desire. Pressed against my trembling breasts and arms. My transparent body suspended from his, sustained by his strength. And what will I do with my lips now, without his mouth to kiss them? What will I do with my poor lips?" (99)

As Susana's mind recedes into deeper introversion, the most powerful sense of reality she retains is that of physical sensations which are evoked, when not directly relived. When the priest is whispering the terrifying preparation for death in her ear, she blocks out his words and recalls sexual pleasure:

"And the terrible agony never lessens: it is kindled forever by God's wrath."

"He held me in his arms. He loved me." (113)

Later, the same night of her death, after an agitated violent sleep, the priest awakens her, Pedro lifts her head, and the priest gives her the communion wafer:

Susana San Juan, between sleeping and waking, extended her tongue and swallowed the Host. Then she said: "We've had a happy time together, Florencio." And she buried herself again in the tomb of bedclothes. (109; translation corrected)

The extreme introversion of the last three years of Susana's life begins at the time of her return to Comala with her father. They had come from La Andrómeda, Bartolomé's mine, which is located deep in the sierra. In Greek mythology, Andromeda was the princess who was offered by her father, King Cepheus, to the sea monster that plagued his kingdom, Ethiopia. The hero Perseus rescued her from the rock where she was chained; he turned the sea monster to stone by exposing it to Medusa's head, which he carried in a bag. Freud interpreted the severed head in terms of castration. If Susana plays the role of Andromeda, as sacrificial victim, she is in need of a hero to rescue her from her father's victimization. There is no severed head, however. The monster of fear dominates her; Pedro cannot save her, he is too late, for she was offered to the monster as a child. The initial trauma came when she was lowered into the dark hole in search for gold. This event, which traumatized Susana, partially explains her hatred for Comala and her turn inward toward her body, her sensations, and, finally, the inner recesses of her mind.

When she was a child her father lowered her into a cave; she was hanging from a rope. It hurt her waist and made her hands bleed, but she didn't want to let go because it was the only thing that joined her with the world outside the cavern. Her father lowered her, swaying and rocking in the darkness. Susana trembled at her father's shout:

"Bring me up what's down there, Susana!"

She picked up the skull, and when she saw it in the light she dropped it. . . . The skull crumbled into fragments. The jawbone came loose as if it were made of sugar. She gathered piece after piece until she reached the little bones of the toes.

"Look for something more, Susana. Money. Round wheels of gold. Look for them, Susana."

Then she lost consciousness until many days later, when she felt the ice and the icy stares of her father. (89; translation corrected)

The introversion, the fear of darkness, the indifference she has for all others are all part of Susana San Juan's other world. The language of Susana San Juan is the inversion of the discourse of Pedro Páramo. They are opposites because each form of discourse is going in the opposite direction from the other. The language of Susana is moving inward as she recedes further and further into the closed world of her mind. She goes from external sensations of the body to her inner voices until she becomes immersed in the phantom world of her closed mind. On the other hand, the discourse of desire enunciated by Pedro is aimed at the object of desire which is the figure of the girl/woman he has created. The drive is toward the other, not as person, but as a creation of desire to possess and consume. He wants to consume her; she is consuming herself. The two will never meet; they are two projectiles, one rushing out, the other rushing inward. The divergent course of their relationship has been plotted by contingency and circumstance in a society that values an exaggerated image of the *macho* man who always takes whatever his desire may be unless another *macho* contests it.

The political structure of Mexico derives from a series of social upheavals, beginning with the conquest and culminating in the 1910 revolution, which have left as their legacy this *macho* value paradigm, which strongly favors a succession of local and supra-local strongmen. The values of cooperation, pooling resources, and communal action, which were so strong in preconquest Mexico's village life, are still present, but they have been subordinated to the discourse of power of the *cacique*.[9] The woman's place in this metapolitical spectrum has been alternatively that of victim and rebuilder of the community. In the latter activity, however, women act in conjunction with other women. They are all, as women, subject to the same misogyny and know that their only hope for building is through common action. The latest example of this extraordinary social force of Mexican women was their cooperative efforts to resurrect the community from the rubble of the earthquake of 1985 (see Poniatowska, *Nada, nadie* [Nothing, nobody]).

A universal male perversion of power is exemplified in this novel. Egoism establishes itself by the absorption of force derived from each destructive act of the strongman's tyranny. The perversion is that the more ruthless the tyrant is, the more he will be elevated into a deity by the collective imagination. In other words, the power of the tyrant grows strong feeding on the collective fears of the social group.

The novel ironically presents a community whose identity extends continuously through its dead members as well as through the living. There is a historical cycle of power and abuse. The dead are still part of Comala in the same way as the living, each having a role in the cycle. Life is renewed out of death, and humanity appears to be condemned to relive the same destruction again and again.

What is final in this novel is the death of the object of desire, for with her death die the particular fantasies of the individual Pedro Páramo. There will never be another chance for this would-be Perseus to rescue his Andromeda or this Orpheus to save his Eurydice. This aspect of Susana was created in the desire of Pedro; as object of desire, she dies, and he dies all but bodily. Others will create new objects of desire and will also fail, each in turn doing his part to punish the collective for the deficiencies of the individual. Such is the history of Mexico and the role of women as long as there are *caciques*, strongmen, and tyrants.

Susana San Juan rejects not only the social authority of the church but also, what is more significant, the ideology of death which elevates the church and its priests to the role of necessary intermediaries between the individual and salvation, for the church is the sole agency of dispensation of sacramental grace. When Susana is dying and the priest Rentería attempts to induce her to make a general confession, she blocks out his words with her exultation of her sensuality, and when he gives her holy communion, she opens her mouth and takes it, but then speaks to her deceased husband, Florencio, about sexual intercourse.

The Mexican social order has given women the role of custodians of spiritual values. Consequently, from birth, they have been tutored in the unquestioned truth that their primary function in life is motherhood, whether it be by physical birth and nurturing of children or within the religious orders; thus it is that Mexican women have been brought up to believe that their obligation in the economic order of this society has been to attend to the needs of the family group. Therefore, by education, training, and custom, Mexican women are the primary guardians of the family, and they perform this role in the name of God and under the influence of the clergy, usually in the person of the parish priest. But the events of the Mexican revolution have also demonstrated that Mexican women are quite capable of separating spiritual issues from the authority of the church. In present-day Mexico, the clergy has taken a position of unmitigated condemnation of all efforts by women to win the right to be full participants in society with the same civil rights men have. In the world of Comala, the only woman who escapes the church's domination is Susana. Although her escape is a mental one, it is still a rejection; Ana, Rentería's niece, is her submissive counterpoint. The Woman with the Moon Face in Carlos Fuentes' *The Old Gringo* bears testimony to the arduous battle Mexican women have had to fight in order to attain self-esteem in the face of the church's repression. I shall take this up in the next chapter.

The richness of Rulfo's text is nowhere more apparent than in the brilliant assimilation of preconquest myth into the discourse of Susana San Juan. This richness of basic inherited sensibilities of universal attributes of goddess figures is an inexhaustible source of imaginative creation for all readers. The reductive simplification of some critics only emphasizes with more acuteness the failure of criticism that approaches a text through a subtext. For example, José Carlos González Boixo is most reductive in his critical use of an interview with Rulfo which limits the significance of the text. Authors' intentions should be left to the biographer and have no place in criticism posing as an interpretive norm. At the other extreme is the work of Nicolás Emilio Alvarez, who would impose a fixed archetype paradigm on the novel where it fits and where it does not, like some interpretive juggernaut crushing all creativity out of the text by the imposition of a fixed paradigm on selected passages.

The mythic dimensions of Susana San Juan run deep in Mexican culture and have explicit links to goddesses in general, but the text cannot be tied to the sequentiality or attributes of any one myth, not even those from Mexico's preconquest heritage.

Susana San Juan has two textual sides to her: first, Pedro Páramo's object of desire, which obsesses him and ultimately will destroy him and Comala. This image of Susana San Juan is Pedro's and must be examined in the light of his own adolescence and the psychology of power that interprets the Mexican *macho*'s wanton destruction of society as a result of his rage of insufficiency. In this capacity she carries the attributes of the Nahuatl goddess Chantico, an earth-mother figure who embodies the burning water symbolism. In Pedro's fantasy she is associated with rain in conjunction with the warmth of the sun or the burning water of an agricultural goddess of fertility.[10]

The other face of Susana is a magnificent collage of fragments that form one of the most seductive and indeterminate configurations in literature: Susana as a life goddess, in the tradition of Isis, associated with the moon and with sexuality in an unrestricted sensuality that rejects the Christian denial of the body. There is an exuberance in her body, with its joyful delight of sexual intercourse and the physical experience of living. This goddess of sensuality speaks through a fictional self that has had an all-too-common life of abuse and deprivation with some moments of pleasure. Whether this pleasure is physically experienced or imagined is not significant; what is most important is that in these moments she evokes traces of the life goddess through her sexuality.

Susana is the daughter of a poor miner and a woman who dies of consumption. After the death of her mother the preadolescent girl is taken away from Comala by her father to live in remote mining areas; he subsequently makes her his sexual partner. She escapes from her father, in fact or in her mind, by marrying Florencio, who gives her sexual satisfaction and unleashes in her a sensual awareness and joy of her body, including an auto-erotic state of bliss in the sea and on the sand. A number of critics have suggested that Florencio may be a creation of Susana's feverish imagination, sexual frustrations, and need for an escape from her father's sexual enslavement.[11] The evocations of Florencio and of sexual intercourse are, of course, the personal psychotic responses of the semiconscious Susana. But the remarks made by Bartolomé and, especially, by Pedro [12] about her marriage to Florencio and his death clearly rule out the possibility that Florencio existed only for Susana. After Florencio dies she resumes her role as her father's sexual partner and reverts to an escapist mental state. The final stage in her life comes when she returns to the Comala of her childhood to become the wife of Pedro Páramo, a man she had known as a preadolescent boy. Pedro forces the father to give her up and then has him killed.

In Pedro's possession, Susana sinks deeper and deeper into a fantasy world, afraid of the dark and the trauma of the black cave into which her father had forced her to descend. She wavers between sleep, dream, and semi-wakefulness. She is almost entirely in the grip of the imaginative reenactment of sexual intercourse with Florencio or the remembrance of auto-eroticism. Her convulsions are the external sign of violent orgasms. She is given the communion wafer by the priest and imagines it as the sperm of her lover. The identity of Susana San Juan therefore offers us one of the most dramatic contradictions of fictive characterization: on the one hand, she is an object of desire, the most beautiful and unrelenting magnet for the love-deprived Pedro. She is to him not a woman of this world but an ideal of the female that he must possess. On the other hand, she is an ordinary Mexican woman who has been a victim of abuse, but who has the capacity through her sexual imagination to evoke traits of the great mother, the goddess of life and death.

Some critics have seen Susana's madness as a limiting characteristic in their assessments of the relative significance of her language. My reading, on the contrary, stresses the fact that it is only through madness, or extreme marginalization, that a Mexican woman in rural Jalisco can break out of the prison of repression and reject the ideological dictum that her body is sinful and her role is that of perpetual servitude. Susana forcefully expresses the joy of being a woman and knowing the pleasure of her body. Whether she actually experienced the sexual pleasure or she only imagined it, her verbal enactment is undoubtedly subversive because her society condemns pleasure of the body for the female.

The madness of Susana San Juan is a narrative technique of revelation with regard to sexuality. An account of female sexuality from a phallocentric point of view fails to measure the significance of the female body, and the sexual organ, to the woman herself, and the effect it has on her unconscious. From the beginning of a young girl's consciousness, self-love can move her to privilege the interior of her body and her vagina; this is as true in the modern individual as it is in archaic cultural experiences of the meaning of being female. The anxiety that plagues women in repressive societies is that the woman's relation with her own body, a relation which quite naturally tends to be narcissistic and erotic, is condemned. The self-love that she bears for herself can become self-hate if she is taught that her body is a tool of evil.

Julia Kristeva has given us the idea of feminine *jouissance* as the woman's celebration of her body; Kristeva also elucidates the ways in which this celebration has been condemned in modern society: "If there is a problem today with regard to women's position in the social code, it does not rest on the mysterious question of feminine jouissance (but rather is a consequence and derivation); it rests profoundly, socially, and symbolically on the question of reproduction and the jouissance which is articulated" (1974, 462; my translation).

Susana San Juan expresses the jouissance of being a woman; unfortunately she can do so only because she is mad, and this is so because Juan Rulfo has given us a fictional character who manifests the celebration of the female body within a society that can only conceive of it as an object of desire and, therefore, an object that must be denied, hidden, and, ultimately, condemned as evil.

| Three | **Carlos Fuentes and the Subversion of the Social Codes for Women** |

The feminist social literary criticism I have outlined in the first chapter and put to the task of bringing out the wanton destructiveness of male sexism in Juan Rulfo's masterpiece *Pedro Páramo* must be extended into the larger consideration of examining the subversion of *macho* ideology in Mexican society. No other novelist has probed deeper into the issues of social alienation and identity in Mexico than Carlos Fuentes. I comment first on subversion as demonstrated in his short novel, "Mother's Day," and on the basis of this analysis I then turn to *The Old Gringo* for an inquiry into female identity through the experiences of three women: a middle class woman from Washington, D.C., a Mexican middle class provincial woman turned camp follower in the Mexican revolution, and, finally, the regiment's prostitute.

Fuentes' two works are functionally feminist texts, whatever the author's intentions may have been (and these need not interest anyone but Carlos Fuentes). Rita Felski is not far off the mark when she writes:

. . . an increasing interest in the political dimensions of literary forms has emerged within feminist criticism, accompanied by a consciousness that linguistic and textual structures need to be questioned at the most fundamental level. . . . The political function of art is consequently redefined; it is not the text which reflects female experience that best serves feminist interests, but rather the work which disrupts the very structures of symbolic discourse through which patriarchal culture is constituted. (30)

I would put the point slightly differently, for I believe that the term "political" is too reductive. I prefer to talk about the social function of literature. "Mother's Day" is a subversive text in that it undermines the discourse of power in Mexican society. *The Old Gringo*, however, goes beyond confronting the social discourse of power that has been instituted as a master/slave relationship for five hundred years, for Fuentes also succeeds in creating fleeting glimpses of a woman's space, especially in the extraordinary monologue of the Woman with the Moon Face.

In political terms, as Rita Felski would put it, there is always a time for the angry protest and a time for a reasoned plea for justice that will challenge the juridical and social systems of the community, but there is also the more fundamental task of questioning social discourse itself and its overt sexism. The social discourse in which we live is the very air we breathe into our identity as women. We have in the past accepted the sexist discourse of male power because it has been repeated again and again throughout the great writing of the past from the Bible to the high literature of modernism. The ideological structures which maintain power and authority as a male domain have led us to ingest the distorted caricature of a human being called a Mexican woman and to do so against our intelligence, which rejects such female characterization.

Up until the last thirty years, Mexican literature was a male-dominated world of male priorities and interests. Male writers like Carlos Monsiváis and José Emilio Pacheco have joined to directly oppose the discursive wall of sexism, and others like Carlos Fuentes and Juan Rulfo have done so indirectly through irony and the use of the autonomous fictional character. But it is the large number of women writers who have entered into Mexican literature since 1960 who have changed the situation in a radical manner. Sor Juana began in the seventeenth century, Rosario Castellanos took up the challenge in the twentieth century, and at the end of the century, Mexico is finally showing signs of plurality.

An ironic subversion of the truth claims of the discourse of *macho* power is a beginning, the autonomous fictional self like the Woman with the Moon Face is an achievement, but it is only with the creation of a woman's space inside a shared world that we find a woman's discourse with a sense of female identity. "Mother's Day" (El día de las madres) is one of the short novels published in *Agua quemada* (1981).[1] The English publication, *Burnt Water*, includes several short stories in addition to the original narrative quartet. This text is of particular significance because it transcends the empirical reality of present-day Mexico City, goes beyond the commonplace depiction of *machismo* in Mexican society, reaches into patriarchal ideology, and discloses feminophobia (fear of female difference).[2] Although feminophobia is not limited to Mexican society, it has taken on a unique form of institutionalization in this society. In general terms, for those who are caught up in this psychotic state, there are basically two personae for women: the virgin mother and the whore.[3] In Mexico these personae have become symbols of good and evil.

In "Mother's Day," three men and their aging servants live alone in a large and ostentatious house in the Pedregal district of Mexico City. The old general of the Mexican revolution, Vicente Vergara, who is at the time of the narrative action about seventy years of age, rules the house he shares with his son and grandson. The son, Agustín Vergara, is a polished, suave lawyer whose every gesture is an imitation of scenes from sentimental cinema, especially of the roles played by Arturo de Córdova; he is about fifty years old. The grandson, Plutarco Vergara (named after the general, turned president, who founded the forerunner of the Party of the Institutionalized Revolution [PRI], Plutarco Elías Calles), is nineteen years old in 1965 and thirty-four at the time of the narration in 1980, when he remembers the extraordinary days of his "liberation."

There are no women left in the family. Clotilde, the grandmother, died years before, while still a young woman; Plutarco's mother, Evangelina, also died young; she was killed before her son was five years old. Although long since dead, both women have a presence in the house: Clotilde is venerated as a household saint; Evangelina is mourned as the innocent whore who had to be killed. Both women are commemorated in the yearly visit on Mother's Day, May 10, to the French cemetery where they are buried side by side.

The time of the narration is set in 1980 and in the remembrance of April and May of 1965; the place is Mexico City, its streets, its low barrios, and the opulent Pedregal. The story's first page is narrated in a free-indirect style that establishes the framework for the more intimate characterization of the grandfather, General Vicente Vergara. The rest of the story is narrated entirely in the first person by the now-mature grandson Plutarco, looking back some fifteen years to the days when he was nineteen. The narrator probes into the past in a deliberate attempt to understand the present. After the initial four pages of first-person narration, the text's narrative presentation is counterpointed by dialogue on every page. The dialogue is all between the three men; the women are not remembered as speaking because the narrator was only five when his mother died and was not yet born when his grandmother died. This silence can also be seen as symbolic of the muting of Mexican women. The longest dialogue sequence is between the grandfather and the grandson; a shorter but highly charged sequence between the young man and his father comes at the climax.

The institutionalized social symbol of the virgin mother in Mexico is, of course, the Virgin of Guadalupe. As a social symbol she permeates all sectors and classes of Mexican society but, as a gender symbol rather than a religious one, she contributes to the denial of individuality to Mexican women. This does not mean that there are not millions of Mexicans, women and men, who daily turn to the Guadalupana as an essential refuge against the harsh realities of life, for this is certainly the case. What we are concerned with in this study is not the Guadalupana as the focus of religious piety, but the social symbol of the virgin mother, that is, maternity without sexuality.[4] This bifurcation of procreation and birth symbolically makes all women guilty of having been blemished by sexual intercourse in order to become pregnant and give birth.

The text of this story explicitly presents the Guadalupana as a social symbol and not as the object of religious piety: "After our love for the Virgin and our hatred of the gringos, nothing binds us together more than a treacherous crime," says the old man (30). His grandson reminds him of his lifelong antagonism to religion and the church. The old man responds: "The Virgin of Guadalupe is a revolutionary Virgin; she appeared on Hidalgo's banners during the War of Independence, and on Zapata's in the Revolution, she's the best bitchin' Virgin ever" (31).

The old man is correct historically. Both Hidalgo and Zapata's troops fought under the banner of the Virgin of Guadalupe for the obvious reason that the European transplant had taken root in Mexico by merging with the Aztec goddess Tonantzin, but beyond historical accuracy, he is sociologically correct when he says: "She's the best bitchin' Virgin," which is the translator's rendering of the expression "a toda madre." In the colloquial Spanish of Mexico, this means "the best" and its application to the Virgin of Guadalupe as a revolutionary symbol means she is powerful.

Just as the old man respects the power of the Guadalupana as a social symbol, rather than a religious figure, so he has over time created of his wife a symbol of sexless purity, motherhood, and domesticity.[5] The grandson observes the old man in his bedroom as he looks on his ancient wardrobe with affection. Every time the grandfather opens his wardrobe, he is reminded of his wife Clotilde: the smell of her clothes, the memory of her bustling about the house; this nostalgia is encapsulated in the image of ironed and starched linens neatly folded on the shelves. The middle-aged narrator recalls these experiences from his youth in an attempt to gain some insight into the significance of the woman who was also his grandmother: "This ancient young woman who was my grandmother looks like a little doll. The photographer had tinted the photograph a pale rose, and only the lips and cheeks of Doña Clotilde glow in a mixture of shyness and sensuality. Did she really look like that?" (36). The grandson's question is answered indirectly: "'Like something out of a fairy tale,' the general says to me. 'Her mother died when she was a baby, and Villa shot her father'" (36). When Plutarco asks, "'You didn't take advantage of her, just because she couldn't protect herself?'" the old man's response is instantaneous: "He glared at me and abruptly cut off the light" (36). Plutarco has seen a girl with youth and sensuality in the old photograph and has asked his grandfather not about his grandmother, but about the young girl. He has inadvertently broken the taboo and has made allusion to her sexuality. Plutarco has female sexuality on his mind; he would have liked to have his mother as his sexual partner: "I would have liked a relationship with a real lady, mature, like my father's lover, not the 'proper' girls you met at parties given by other families, filthy rich like us. Where was my Clotilde to rescue, to protect, to teach, to love me? What was Evangelina like? I dreamed about her in her white Jantzen bathing suit" (40). Plutarco's sexual fantasy of making love to his mother, or a mother substitute, is in striking contrast to the rigid separation of motherhood and sexuality which the old man observes.

The hidden skeleton in the family closet—the murder of Evangelina, Plutarco's mother, by his father—is confessed by Agustín himself in the climactic dialogue. Evangelina is imbued by all three men with sensuality. The father-in-law portrays her as a whore, perhaps because she was not able to resist his advances, and portrays her husband as the victim of her attractiveness; for the son who does not remember her, she is the object of sexual desire. None of them, however, are prepared to think of her except through the stereotypes of their own obsessions: whore, sentimental heroine, or sex object. She appears for the first time in the story through the narration of Plutarco: "I was thirteen when one of my classmates at the Revolution High School showed me a photograph of a girl in a bathing suit. It was the first time I'd ever felt a twinge of excitement. Like Doña Clotilde in her photograph, I felt pleasure and shame at the same time. I blushed and my classmate, guffawing, said, 'Be my guest, it's your mommy'" (39). Plutarco's mother is the central figure in his sexual fantasies from puberty through adulthood. In the dialogue between the old man and his son Agustín, Plutarco hears this description of his mother: "'When you married a whore, you dishonored only yourself'" (43). Later, when the old man and Plutarco are in a brothel, he asks if his mother was like the prostitute Judith:

"Was this what my mother was like, Grandfather? A whore like this. Is that what you meant?" . . . "Did she put the horns on my father?"
—"He looked like a stag when she got through with him."
—"Why did she do it? She didn't have to, like this girl does." (48–49)

Finally, Evangelina receives her most enigmatic characterization by her husband as reported by Plutarco:

He said that my mother had not taken proper care of me, she'd been dazzled by the social scene. . . . It was inevitable that it would impress Evangelina, a beautiful girl from the provinces who'd had a gold tooth when he first met her, one of those girls from the coast of Sinaloa who become women while still very young, tall and fair, with eyes like silk, and long black hair, whose bodies hold both night and day, Plutarco, night and day glowing in the same body, all the promises, all of them, Plutarco. (53)

At the climax of the discussion between father and son, Agustín confesses: "Evangelina was so innocent, so without defenses, that's what galled me more than anything, that I couldn't blame her, but I couldn't forgive her either" (56). So he strangled her to death in keeping with the B-class cinema he had imitated all his life. To add effect to his confession, he puts on the phonograph record with Avelina Landín's sentimental clichés of Mexican popular culture: "something about silver threads among the gold." Then Agustín falls into an armchair in perfect simulation of Fernando Soler's melodramatic acting in the film *Soulless Woman.* Of the three portrayals of Evangelina, the most shallow and empty is that of Agustín; she has been turned into the victim of a sentimental, cliché-ridden, melodramatic cinema: the unfaithful wife whose death restores the husband's honor. The old man can see women only as mother or whore, but Agustín tries to live the clichés of the cinema and is never able to experience anything that is his own. Plutarco sees through his mannerisms: "I felt sorry for him; these were gestures he'd learned at the movies. Every move he made he'd learned at the movies. Everything he did was learned, and pompous" (52). The viewpoint of the narrator, Plutarco, is also empty but in a different way:

Now that I'm past my thirtieth year, I can remember that night when I was nineteen as if I were living it again, the night of my liberation. Liberation was what I felt as I fucked Judith, with all the mariachis, drunk as hell, in her bedroom, pumping and pumping to the strains of the ballad of Pancho Villa's horse, 'in the station at Irapuato, broad horizons beckoned,' my grandfather sitting in a chair, sad and silent, as if he were watching life being born anew, but not his, not his ever again, Judith red with shame, she'd never done it that way, with music and everything, frozen, ashamed, feigning emotions I knew she didn't feel, because her body belonged to the dead night. I was the only one who conquered, *no one shared the victory with me, that's why it had no flavor,* it wasn't like those moments the General had told me about, moments shared by all, maybe that's why my grandfather was so sad, and why so sad forever was the melancholy of the liberation I thought I'd won that night. (49; emphasis mine)

At the end of the story, Plutarco recalls standing between his father and his grandfather at the graves of his mother and his grandmother the next Mother's

Day, after the "liberation" when he found out the truth about his father's drug dealings and the murder of his mother: "My grandfather sobbed again, and uncovered his face. If I'd looked at him closely, I'm sure I would have asked myself for whom he wept so bitterly, and for whom he wept more, his wife or his daughter-in-law. But at that moment I was simply trying to guess what my future would be. We'd gone to the cemetery without mariachis this time. I would have liked a little music" (57).

Plutarco knows about loneliness: "No one shared the victory with me, that's why it had no flavor." These are the words the mature Plutarco uses to describe the emptiness of his sexual performance with the prostitute Judith. As he stands in the cemetery not knowing what is to become of his life, the void he now feels is a consequence of his being alone even in the intimacy of sexual intercourse.

The three men are of three different generations, and each has a very different view of women. To the old man, they are sexless mothers or whores, to the father they are clichés from sentimental cinema, and to the young man they are sexual objects. What all three men have in common in their attitudes toward women is that they are all incapable of knowing one. The barrier between man and woman is built up through the institutionalized stereotypes and roles that govern the behavior of both sexes.

But there are numerous occasions when these sexual objects speak, think, and express feelings that are not intended for the sole gratification of the male. Herein lies the root of feminophobia: this "other," who is not a man, who has breasts and a vagina, has to be depersonalized, must be made into a type rather than a person. The two most powerful and time-honored forms of depersonalization are the virgin mother and the whore; one is all-nurturing support and is venerated: the other is only a sexual object and is abused; neither thinks. All three male characters in this story operate through the depersonalization of the women in their lives. All three have to assign roles to women so that they can function in their feminophobic world. We have noted how the old man assigns the standard roles of the virgin-whore syndrome, and how his son Agustín has recast women into trite roles, but for the grandson, Plutarco, the search for the mother in women has led to an emptiness. His sexual desire is expressed through symbolic transference of the gardens of the Pedregal. High walls are like a chastity belt and open flowers like the genital openness of the whore: "They sowed the rock with dramatic plants, stark, with no adornment but a few aggressive flowers. Doors locked tight like chastity belts, Grandfather, and flowers open like wounded genitals, like the cunt of the whore Judith that you couldn't fuck and I could, and what for, Grandfather" (51).

He is the only one of the three to realize that the self without the other is incomplete, and consequently sexual intercourse with a woman who is not a person is the same as fornicating with an inflated plastic doll: "And what for, Grandfather."

The structure of the story is a subtle interplay of relationships: between grandson and grandfather, between grandfather and father, and, finally, between father and son, and the core of these relationships is the exercise of power. This structure is one of generational juxtapositions in the context of the power struggle that is life in Mexico. The first set, Vicente-Plutarco, engages the generational poles, a man from the end of the last century who came out on top of the revolution, contrasted with a man from the beginning of the second half of this century. The second set, Vicente-Agustín, exemplifies the generational clash between the viewpoint of the veteran revolutionary and that of a modern businessman. The third set, Agustín-Plutarco, presents rejection and nostalgia for the loss of a mythical vitality.

It is significant that the story is narrated from the point of view of Plutarco, who gives present-day values to the three sets of relationships. There is admiration on the part of the young man for the spontaneity of the grandfather and a fantasy of being able to relive the revolution with him. This is a nostalgia for the revolution and the desire for the power to kill, pillage, rape, and castrate those who stand in his way. Plutarco reports on the relationship between his grandfather and father as one where there is only disdain and arrogance on the part of the old man because Agustín never proved himself. On the part of Agustín, there is the distaste for the old man's crudeness and an abject servility to him. Finally, the relationship Plutarco presents as existing between himself and his father is one of pathetic sympathy on his part and self-serving melancholy on the part of his father.

The wealth of the family, it must be recalled, is entirely derived from the abuse of others, first, through the spoils of war and subsequently from drug trafficking. The ostensible victim of these relationships is Evangelina, but at the most intensive level of reality, the three male characters are also victims of abuse in the societal power struggle which they expiate through their feminophobia. This is a social system where the rule is exploit others or be exploited by them. The essential point is that feminophobia is only incidentally about sexual differences and is fundamentally about power: the power of authority, of force, of money, of domination of the other through any and every means available. The raw use of power that is prepared to abuse or to kill in order to win is the fine narrative thread that runs through the story. And the symbolic demonstration of power is made manifest by the veneration and abuse of women. Feminophobia was born of sexual repression by medieval introverts, but it has become institutionalized in cultures where the power struggle is always just beneath the surface. It is fitting that the only one of the three who knows that he is caught up in a system of domination is Plutarco. Agustín sobs to Plutarco:

"You and I, Plutarco, what battles are we going to win? What women are we going to tame? what soldiers are we going to castrate? you tell me. . . . He [the grandfather] laughs and says, let's see whether you can do what I did, now that it can't be done any longer, let's see whether you can find a way to inherit something more difficult than my money. Violence with impunity." (55)

He is crying because of his own desperate search for power. Since he could not match the old general through his open violence in war and sexual domination, he chose the role of the dishonored husband and murdered his wife.

The power struggle within Plutarco is all in the past; from the point of view of the narration, some fifteen years after the events being narrated, it is all over. There remains only the melancholy of the person who surveys the bleakness of his life without knowing how to overcome the fact that the other that has been absent and will remain absent from his life is the woman as person rather than a goddess on a pedestal or a metonymic vagina.

The popular culture of Mexico, with its ongoing alternating attitudes of servile passivity or superiority toward the United States, runs throughout the story as a subtle reminder that Mexico as a society sees itself as bound up with a fate similar to that imposed on women. Mexico, as a participant in the economic and political reality of the North American hemisphere, is similarly caught up in the either/or law of life: abuse or be abused. This is an ethical malaise that ultimately destroys both men and women. Few writers have been able to express the deepest fears of their culture with the power, the insight, and the effectiveness of Carlos Fuentes. The short novel "Mother's Day" is not an isolated example in his work of this cultural disclosure. It is the literary achievement of Fuentes to present female stereotyping as the social manifestation of the male characters' pathological distortion of reality.

Because the narrator remains incapable of understanding the nature of his alienation, he becomes its most visible victim. At the time of the narration he has reached a state of psychological estrangement. There is no possibility of going further than self-pity, because there has not been any contact with a female fictive self. There is an irreducible difference between the female object and woman as subject or social self. The two cannot function in the same society except in complete negation of each other. This is an ideological confrontation of either/or, for one can function only as the (ab)use of women and the other as the participation of women.

And, what can we ultimately say about modern men like the narrator of "Mother's Day" and our relation to them? If it is true, as Michel Foucault has written, that power increasingly influences our daily lives in our relations with others as well as in our relation to ourselves, do Mexican women have any choice? The struggle of Mexican women against feminophobia passes through two initial battles against subjugation, as Sade knew so well. The first and most basic one is that of asserting one's individuality in spite of the constraints imposed by patriarchal power. The second is that of finding an identity that can reconcile one's individuality with the need to surpass the crippled, mutilated social persona we have been given. In other words, opposition has to give way to growth. If we lose the first battle and our will to be is broken, we remain objectified. If we lose the second battle, we become intellectually invisible.

Let us now turn to the most feminist of Fuentes' works: the creation of an autonomous female character in *The Old Gringo*.

The Old Gringo was published in Mexico in 1985, and, as with all of Carlos Fuentes' work, the English translation was printed immediately.[6] The plot is straightforward; the year is 1913. The novel narrates the unforeseen meeting of a young general of the Mexican revolution, an old writer from the United States who seeks death, and a woman from the United States who seeks life. Harriet Winslow, thirty-two years old, is the typical puritan, imprisoned in an empty routine devoid of any serious purpose, burdened with sexual and social repressions. She dreams of her liberation. Opportunity comes her way when she is hired as governess to the Miranda children, scions of a Mexican family of vast wealth and power, owners of half of the state of Chihuahua. Harriet arrives late in Chihuahua, following the arrival of Pancho Villa's Northern Division and the flight of the Miranda family.[7] Instead of teaching children, she finds herself in the midst of the initial campaigns of the Mexican revolution in the country's northern region and is witness to the fury of the revolution, the passion of the Mexicans, and an unforgettable experience which will mark her for the rest of her life. The narration is via Harriet Winslow's remembrances, when "she sits alone and remembers" (3) many years later in Washington, D.C. The novel explores human relations and the meaning of the patriarchal paradigm for the three principal protagonists and for the others. In the short time lapse of a month, the embittered old writer, the repressed Miss Winslow, and the impassioned General Arroyo each find their identity by liberating themselves from the father's authority.

Among many powerful undercurrents which move through this novel, the role of the father acquires significance among the three principal characters. The old gringo is a father figure to both Arroyo and Harriet, but for opposite reasons. Harriet feels the absence of the father who abandoned her and her mother. Tomás Arroyo must kill the father over and over again in order to gain his own identity; the presence of the father weighs heavily on him. Harriet, quite naturally, turns to the old gringo as a fellow compatriot, a man about the same age as her father and, most of all, a man who sees her as both daughter and possible lover. Through the old man she can begin to survive paternal meaning in the arms of Tomás Arroyo. Julia Kristeva (1980) puts it this way: "*To love* is to survive paternal meaning. It demands that one travel far to discover the futile but exciting presence of a waste-object: a man or woman, fallen off the father, taking the place of his protection" (150). In the case of Tomás Arroyo, the passion runs deeper: as the bastard son of the owner of the *hacienda*, he hates his father for the rape of his mother and for the lingering image of his power and domination, which still threaten the adult Arroyo. Kristeva gives this insight: "Obsessed man never sees his father as dead. The corpse under his eyes is the waste-object. . . . Through this opening, he might look for woman. But the Other, the third-person father, is not the particular dead body. It is Death; it always was. It is the meaning of the narrative of the son, who never enunciated himself as anything else, save for and by virtue of this stretched out void of paternal Death, as ideal and inaccessible" (1980, 150).

Harriet falls in love with the Mexican revolutionary and loses her aversion to sexuality. The old gringo finds the death he wanted when Arroyo kills him for burning the hacienda property deeds. Harriet goes to the U.S. authorities to claim the body and Villa, not wanting to give the United States an excuse to invade Mexico again, orders Arroyo to take the gringo's corpse to his encampment. There he decides to solve the problem with revolutionary justice: he has both the old gringo and Arroyo shot for disobeying orders. And Harriet? Harriet will be "the one who will remember it all" (183).

In *The Old Gringo*, a woman's sexuality is neither an uncomfortable duty nor an instinctive disturbance but rather an essential part of being a woman. There are three notable women in this novel. Harriet Winslow; the Woman with the Moon Face, partner to the young villista general, Tomás Arroyo; and la Garduña, the regiment's prostitute. All three women fulfil different functions, establishing the feminine condition in this novel.

Four other women in this novel are mentioned by the other characters. Harriet is wont to remember her mother as an embittered and repressed woman, and, from time to time, she also remembers her father's black mistress, a sensual and generous woman. Tomás Arroyo remembers the beautiful Yucatán girl whom his father raped and who was avenged by her family, who killed him. He also remembers his mother with fervor, seeing her as the Yucatán girl's twin. These characters fulfil the service of the sociocultural referentiality needed for the development of a contrast between the feminine condition in the two countries. The two Mexicans are victims of the *macho* code. The two women from the United States are the opposite sides of the moon, white and dark, repressed and sensual.

By "feminine condition," I mean the distortion of the human condition which is the legacy of all women within patriarchal social structures. This condition consists of the systematic repression of all signs which could indicate an active and free participation, independent of the social subject within the community. The feminine condition results from the ideological canalization of a perpetual state of repression of any personal aspirations outside the social functions of womb, servant, and object of desire. Neither women's bodies nor their persons belong to them. Like the virgin of the gospels, woman in patriarchal societies has been born to be the handmaid of the lord she will serve from childhood to death. This feminine condition of inequality or inferiority constitutes women's sociopolitical reality with some differences of degree in countries such as those of Spanish America and those that are Islamic. The feminine condition can be depicted through the media, but only via the refiguration generated by readers in their realization of the literary text does it acquire a figurative form; that is, it is shared. The space between text and reader is what we usually call the poetic space, and when this poetic space is filled with the realization of the feminine condition, art fulfils its highest task: to communicate intersubjectively the human being's truth and catalyze a redescription of institutionalized and ready-made values.[8]

Harriet's fictive self creates tension between focus and focalization, with a well-assigned and clear distance between the focused one who remembers and the focus of the remembrance.[9] Distance is temporal and sociocultural between the present of the remembrance and the past remembered by an old gringa wrapped in the stormy and strange world of revolutionary Mexico. Besides being a structural element, this tension marks Harriet's discourse in its dialogical opposition between the woman who represents her social class and the intimate person.

On the other hand, the Woman with the Moon Face is, first of all, the embodiment of a middle class woman from provincial Mexico who reveals herself through introspective confidences, firmly rooted in the social reality of Mexico.[10] The Woman with the Moon Face does not participate in dialogue; she carries on a monologue and only in one chapter, eighteen, shares the focalization with Harriet.[11] In her case, I shall analyze a social symbol.

Finally, there is the secondary character La Garduña; she is presented as a stereotype, but she also expresses herself with authentic humanity. She wears a carnival mask, the prostitute's, but instead of hiding behind it, she reveals her deep feelings.[12]

Harriet Winslow's character is both the focus and the focalizer. In the past, she is protagonist of the plot and, in the present, she is the woman who sits, alone, and remembers. This temporal duality is realized not only in the first person of remembrances, but through a third-person narrative voice, which works more like a cinematographic focalization than as a mimetic narrator. The world of Chihuahua in 1913 is recreated, mixed with some images from Harriet's life in Washington before she goes to Mexico. This montage of images, present and remembered, creates an immediate and private totality of the Yankee protagonist, but, at the same time, Harriet is a character with very particular ideas, frustrations, and dreams, only understandable as the center of consciousness of an existence built on a series of social and intimate lies in which she lives. Time has given her the necessary distance to be able to articulate these images.

Precisely because of the time gone by, Harriet now remembers and understands that the complaint she took to Villa against General Arroyo—the complaint that cost the young revolutionary his life—was not to avenge the old gringo's death, but rather to make Arroyo pay for what he had done to her. Arroyo had destroyed her hypocritical defense as a scandalized gringa, knowing that the woman who throbbed behind the puritan would never be the free woman he showed her she might have been if only she could have overcome patriarchy's established preconceptions about feminine virtue and the sin of sexual excitement. Arroyo knew she would return to her country, her house, and her lie, and she could not forgive him for being right.

This character moves in a troubled muddle between her social place and her internal demons. Harriet retains clear in her imagination the memory of her mother's hypocritical coldness and the open sexuality of her father's black mistress. The novel's discourse uses montage to create an intimate conflict between the images of her father with his mistress and her mother's rejection of sexuality.

Gaze can be a way of domination in interpersonal and social relationships, and in the case of a man's gaze upon a woman, it is a form of domination that objectifies woman as the desired object, an object whose sole function is to give pleasure to the male. Harriet Winslow is Tomás Arroyo's object of desire, but she rejects his gaze and faces the male with her own gaze.[13]

It is the gringa, not the title's gringo, who is the center of consciousness and dominates the narrative. The focalization is concentrated on her, playing back and forth between her social persona (desired woman) and the strong character underneath the persona, with her own vision of the world:

They danced slowly, repeated in mirrors like a sphere of blades that cuts wherever it is grasped.

"Look. It's me."

"Look. It's you."

"Look. It's us" (109). . . .

She pressed closer to Tomás Arroyo, as if she were afraid of losing something, but she held her head away to see her own wild surprise in the eyes of the Mexican.

"I've been here before but I won't know it until I leave" (111). . . .

This would not be only a man's story from now on. A presence (my presence, said Harriet) will alter the story. *I only hope that I also give him a secret and a danger that events in themselves could never guarantee* (112). . . . When she moved from Arroyo's arms, she saw herself in a ballroom lined with mirrors. She saw herself entering the mirrors without looking at herself, because in reality she was entering a dream. . . . She looked at Arroyo and kissed him with wild surprise. (113–114)

The man's gaze surrounds Harriet Winslow. She knows she is desired. She understands perfectly Arroyo's blackmail when he threatens the old gringo if she does not take him as a lover. Nevertheless she does not allow him to dominate her; she does not allow the gaze to go unanswered. Fuentes' text lets the reader participate in the woman's challenge to counter the male's gaze with her own. She does not look at herself in the mirrors as an object possessed by the male; when she looks at herself in his eyes, it is to see her own reflection, just as he sees himself in her eyes. They will make love that night, but he will not possess her as a submissive female; she will meet her lover. He will attempt to have her as the object of his desire, but she will force him to face her as a woman with her own will and world, with an independent sexual desire. She will try to show him that beyond sexual desire there is a desire which is more basic, that of domination.

Harriet discovers her body and her sexuality with the young Mexican, not as an unresisting maiden but rather as a woman who wants to give as much as she wants to receive:

Truly her own fire, saved for her own grace after Arroyo had kindled it, but not his, no, his only momentarily, he the instrument for reviving a fire that had always been there but that was hers, that belonged to the fall of the house of Halston, to summers never seen on the Sound and to her mother and her father and her father's black woman, a fire that belonged to all of this, a fire which was hers and which he now wanted to attribute to himself, with *macho* petulance and unrelenting theatricality. (137–138)

Faced with this *macho* demonstration, Harriet responds with her own will, turning the tables; instead of being the passive female who bears the male's weight, she flings herself upon him to take him: "as though, before, she had been possessed by him and now he were possessed by her: that was the difference . . . before, she could have been his victim, and now he could be hers" (138). But Arroyo does not allow her to overcome him; he withholds from reaching sexual climax and she pushes him away: "'What is it with you, what makes you what you are, you damned brown prick, what makes you refuse a woman a moment as free and powerful as the one you took before?'" (139). The narrative voice concludes: "And, for this, Harriet Winslow never forgave him" (139).

The character known as the Woman with the Moon Face (La Luna) has no proper name in the novel; she is identified only by her round face and sad, almond-shaped eyes. The fact that she lacks a name and is designated only with a descriptive name has important symbolic implications. First, her identity with the moon, woman's basic symbol, serves as representative discursive background. She symbolizes generic woman and, as such, she expresses herself in the monologue which takes up chapter eighteen. Second, the description of her features links her to the Mexican people, and her not having a proper name opens more emphatically the possibilities of functioning as social symbol. That is to say, the Woman with the Moon Face is simply a provincial woman of the middle class whose daily life is representative of a social feminine routine.

The monologue of the Woman with the Moon Face recounts a Mexican woman's daily life, softly moving from everyday verisimilitude to the most intimate confidence of woman to woman. Let us recall the narrative context. The Woman with the Moon Face is trying to explain to Harriet why Mexican women behave the way they do and, specifically, why she is there as General Arroyo's camp follower. Her discourse assumes the natural rhythm of an intimate conversation even though it is only the Woman with the Moon Face who speaks. Now and then she asks Harriet's permission to confide such personal details, such as only a woman can tell another woman. The focalization is unadorned, straightforward. The Woman with the Moon Face carries on a conversation with Harriet, in the manner of a confidence between female friends. Harriet tries to understand this submissive, self-denying woman who waits outside the door until her man leaves, after making love to another woman. Harriet, deep inside, feels contempt for this woman who speaks softly, fearful of being heard by men. The Woman with the Moon Face tries to explain herself. The chapter consists only of her continuous monologue. After each explanation, there follows a question in order to make sure Harriet is listening and has understood. Throughout this movement, back and forth, from explanation to inquiry about understanding, the discourse deepens. The Woman with the Moon Face begins by speaking of social customs and daily life, passes on to religion, and then finishes by breaking the barriers of shyness to speak of her body's intimacy, sexuality, and, in general, the human condition of being a woman in Mexico.

The chapter begins with the omniscient, third-person narrator which has dominated the text up to this point: "The woman called La Luna said it was strange to hear a bell and not recognize the reason for its sound. That's how she knew the Revolution had arrived at her small provincial town in Durango" (150). The narrative voice begins then to alternate with an indirect free style, presented in parentheses; for example: "(that was extremely important, not to see your own body ever)" (150). Finally, in the middle of this long paragraph, the narrative changes from third to first person, as the woman begins expressing herself through a monologue full of introspection, frank and revealing in its female intimacy.

Before examining the first-person monologue, I would like to analyze La Luna's views and concepts of church and religion. For her there is something false, something that makes no sense in the Roman Catholic religion, and that is the teaching that God consists of three men in one, when the very nature of life requires that there must be female and male, not three males. To her, the idea of God as a magician who transforms himself into an old man with a white beard or into a young man who is sacrificed makes no sense. All human life begins in the mother's womb. The divine trinity of patriarchy is a divinity of oppression. It is the magician called spirit and, on top of it all, holy, who makes the Virgin pregnant in order to be born from her womb, die sacrificed as a victim, be resurrected, and join the other two in the unity of the consecrated wafer, which is divided up in thousands of little pieces.

The difference between the designation "superstition" and "religion" has more to do with ideological differences between cultures than differences of knowledge or thought. When a cult becomes institutionalized with professional priests, all other cults are designated as superstitions. The more different this cult is from the institutionalized one, the more clearly it is designated as superstition. It is thought that the superstitious cult has sprung by chance from infantile minds that are culturally rudimentary. One definition of superstition is respect or excessive fear of the unknown. Therefore, a religion has mysteries, but a superstition has excessive respect or fear of the unknown. The trinity doctrine, Christ's divinity, the immaculate conception, the resurrection of Christ, the transubstantiation of bread and wine into the body and blood of Christ—all are mysteries of faith. But what can be said of a female cult, based upon the veneration of virginity, "the child bride," and fear of the penis as instrument of domination, which makes matrimony "a ceremony of fear?" This is the way the Woman with the Moon Face puts it:

That life became dark, repetitive, as things are when they come to a standstill and do not blossom forth from what they were before, before the man, the father, the husband was there to see to it that you remained a child bride, that marriage was a ceremony of fear: fear that you might be punished for not being a little girl anymore; yet this man takes you, señorita, and punishes you with his sex for not being a little girl anymore, for betraying him with your sexual blood and your sexual hair. (151)

Religion, with its mysteries of faith, disguises the patriarchal ideology of the subjugation of women, which fixes woman's role as the submissive handmaid of the Lord, so that his will be done.[14] The social economics requiring women to propagate the family and serve men have converted her into a unit of mercantile exchange through which power and property are bought and sold. Thus, the education of a "decent" woman is that which eliminates any signs of individuality, condemns sexual pleasure, and emphasizes her servile status and her dedication to the family and social well-being.

The woman called La Luna can tell Harriet all this because she has been liberated, albeit temporarily, by the revolution's cataclysm and, specifically, by a young revolutionary who has made her realize she is a person, one who can enjoy her body and her sexuality. She has escaped the prison of having been born a "decent" woman in provincial Mexico.

The Woman with the Moon Face's monologue moves away from the omniscient third-person narrative after her commentary concerning the magician's religion. The first-person speaker swiftly deepens and expands her disclosure of subjugation and liberation in the cited passage of matrimony as a ceremony of fear. This monologue's structure is a dialectical one between an explanation of what her life is like, followed by a question to her listener, Harriet, as to whether she has understood, if she begins to understand, if she can follow. The sentences state in detail the dialectic of explanation and looking into the eyes and presence of her listener for a sign of understanding, even if it should be a silent response: "'Señorita, amiga, friend, may I call you that?' 'You see, señorita, amiga, may I call you my friend?' 'Tell me, señorita, my friend (may I?),' 'for when will we know, señorita, mi amiga, who was just and who was unjust. Not me. Not then. Not yet'" (153–158). The chapter of the Woman with the Moon Face ends with these questions: "'Señorita, mi amiga, may I call you friend now? Do you understand, Miss Winslow?'" (160).[15]

The monologue's smoothness takes us into the intimacy of the remembrance of lived time, of its daily routine, now seen as negation of her being:

"I was not to have any pleasure, and I refused to, with him or without him; I betrayed all my teachings and saw myself a few times in front of a mirror, but then did not do it anymore, not because I was tempted to let my fingers wander down from my flourishing nipples to my heavy dark crotch, but because I started seeing myself in that mirror as an ancient child, a silly crone muttering childish babble, a ruined doll singing obscene nursery rhymes and sticking the imaginary dicks of stuffed animals into my withered, prune-like vagina." (152)

La Luna's destructive reflection reveals her hatred of her body and of herself, instituted by her husband and the misogyny of the Mexican *machismo*. The Spanish psychologist J. Rof Carballo makes the following pertinent observations about misogyny in terms of social psychology:

When an individual affirms his masculinity strongly [as exemplified by the total social code of the Mexican *macho*] the psychologist knows that, down deep, the individual is expressing his anguish in the face of subconscious impulses of signifying completely the opposite to that which he pretends to express. But let us understand each other. It is not that cultures that make ostentation of their masculinity at each step are, in their subconscious, not masculine enough. To affirm this would be absurd. What happens is that they are more afraid of their unconscious femininity. (209–210; my translation)[16]

In the case of Mexico and, specifically, of the social symbol which Fuentes' Woman with the Moon Face is, the *macho* has to degrade the woman because of his fear of seeing himself cracked, that is, weak.[17] In the vertical social structure of Mexico, there is a vast gulf between middle class morality and the reality of a lower class woman like La Garduña, and any treatment of misogyny would be incomplete if it did not treat both. Fuentes' sensitivity to these differences is highly developed in this novel.

La Garduña is described as "an appalling whore from Durango" (18). This woman wears a makeup mask: "the paint on her fat cheeks cracked like varnish dried in the sun" (19). Like La Luna, this rural Mexican woman does not have a name. She is known only by the sarcastic nickname of La Garduña; in slang, a thief who works at night, an attribution derived from the nocturnal habits of the weasel. As an orphan she lived with an aunt until she left home to follow a young revolutionary. Upon her partner's death she found a way to survive as Arroyo's regimental prostitute. She has a two-year-old daughter.

Contrary to the normal use of the mask to hide the wearer's identity, in carnival the function is reversed. Inside the commotion of carnival, the mask serves to reveal the wearer, affirming that which in normal times is hidden. In carnival, masked men and women uncover their passions, say what they think, do what they have wished in their fantasies. Women can use makeup as a mask to hide their intimate selves or to make the secret self public. For La Garduña, the Mexican revolution is a kind of carnival which destroys established life patterns, breaks down social codes, and impels a whole people into an accelerated frenzy of death and life. La Garduña is a woman of laughter and easy guffaw, without inhibitions or caution, who says what she thinks. She ridicules social and religious codes which would condemn her for surviving the upheaval as a prostitute, but she is also the character with the greatest compassion for others. When she sees the old gringo arrive at the *hacienda* where Arroyo's regiment is encamped, she tells the others: "He has sorrow in his eyes" and the narrative voice adds: "and from that moment respected him" (19). This respect for others' grief is an acknowledgment of her recognition of them as human beings. On another occasion we see La Garduña distressed because her daughter is dying: "La Garduña, brutal, rouged face, small sharp teeth, was weeping beside her; she was shaking her, she was telling her a hysterical, melodramatic tale she couldn't understand; she understood only one thing: Help us, miss, my baby is dying" (97). The obvious and pathetic love of La Garduña for her daughter contrasts openly with Harriet's relationship with her own mother; she cannot resist the pleading and she takes out with her own mouth the phlegm which was asphyxiating the child. Ironically, the maternal role—object of constant manipulation in all representations of women—in this novel finds its only positive presentation in the characterization of the prostitute.

I would like to examine this trio of women as a group who realize a feminine space in an old woman's remembrances, in a woman's whispered confidences to another, and in the revealing makeup mask. Harriet Winslow sits alone, old, distant, and remembers the bitter truth that the young Mexican general taught her: that she could have been other if only she had had the courage to be. This is a terrible truth because existentially it makes her responsible for what her life has and has not been. The generalized guilt of a society which represses women finds its clearest reflection in the very woman's guilt for not having fulfilled her own life. It must be remembered that Harriet acquired full consciousness of a woman's possibilities, and, having rebelled against the Yankee puritan tradition, she tried to confront the Mexican *macho* in their sexual relations by attempting to enjoy the relationship as one between equals, not one between dominant male and submissive female. Arroyo fears Harriet's sexual initiative because it would make him feel feminine. Harriet's instinctive choice in taking the initiative and the *macho*'s rejection reveals to her the possibility of emancipation which her Mexican sisters do not have. Now, years later, the old woman remembers and in so doing recreates the reality of a liberated sexuality between active and reciprocating lovers who share pleasure and give as much as they receive; but in Harriet's case, the attempt was not successful because the man could not accept sexual reciprocity. She denounced him, and after his death, she returned to her country to cultivate her bitterness.

The Woman with the Moon Face, the social symbol of the Mexican woman during the revolution, has been liberated momentarily from an oppressive society, degrading and medieval, ruled by men in their capacity as fathers, husbands, or priests, who perpetually keep women in servitude in the name of family and God. The Woman with the Moon Face recovers her dignity as woman when she is liberated from the stigma of her "dirty femininity." She discovers sexual pleasure and self-esteem because of the cataclysm of the revolution. She lives day to day, but each new day is another day of freedom from the fear to which she was subjected as a Mexican wife.

La Garduña follows the revolutionaries, not as a camp follower, but as a prostitute. It is in prostitution that she has found the only usefulness that a disintegrating society has allowed her. The revolution, like the carnival, temporarily breaks with routines and norms and offers greater opportunity for self-expression. In this situation, La Garduña wears her makeup mask and expresses herself as an honest person, as a woman willing to forgive, to love, and to defend life without rancour.

The analysis of the feminine characters at the level of intratemporality—remembrance, confidence, mask—anticipates fully the conclusion about feminine space. The tale of the remembrance, combined with the paradigmatic example of narrating memories, is elucidated in public time even though it deals with private revelations. This public time is not the anonymous time of idle chatter but the time of narrated interaction from the point of view of the omniscient narrator. In this sense, this public time of the novel is the time of being-in-common for all the characters. But we must remember that public time is fixed in one's mind by the personality of the evoker, not necessarily that of the one who is narrating. Harriet Winslow is present, seen from outside with moments of personal revelation.

What is the purpose of reminiscences and of the recreation of a past in which the interaction of the characters is revealed? Above all, these remembrances are communication, not only between the living—Harriet, who remembers; her narrator, who tells the story—and the reader, but, principally, between contemporaries in this interaction, which is the past remembered. Thus, besides the public time of the novel's plot there is a narrative time, the time that continues after the characters' deaths, the time of realization implicit in their story. Harriet is part of public time as well as of narrative time. The Woman with the Moon Face and La Garduña function in Harriet's public time and in the narrative time of our reflection. The reading of a novel, even if it is a private activity, is inexorably a collective act of repetition, of refiguration, of beginnings, of making the story affective, sensible, and moral for each reader who is part of the community.

The narration redirects a character's time, the interaction time in a possible world to the time of the historicity of readers. But I would like to stress that the story's analysis can carry the community of readers into still more radical movement than that of the sole refiguration of the isolated reader's world. When we read and think, our reflection has that characteristic of refiguration. When we read, we reflect, and if we then share our reflection, we have passed from personal refiguration to collective refiguration.[18]

Woman's space is achieved with the dialectic between the text in its historicity and the readers' historicity. Only within the community of readers does there exist the possibility of recognizing the feminine condition and transforming it into a feminist liberation, which is nothing more or less than creating a woman's space of authentic revelation of the person each one of us can be if we are not distorted by the concave patriarchal mirror in which the Woman with the Moon Face looked at herself.

Carlos Fuentes' work represents the new Latin American novel, which has been accepted as universal in cultures as disparate as those of Japan and Russia, under the rubric of magical realism. However, Fuentes is also the most restless and prolific Mexican novelist of his generation. No other writer of contemporary Mexico more aptly illustrates the break with modernism and the steady radicalization of writing into a postmodern force. The two stories I have examined demonstrate Fuentes' extraordinary narrative range. The unintentional irony of the first-person narrator in "Mother's Day" presents an acid bath for the Mexican *macho* who has in the final analysis become his own victim. The narratives of Harriet, La Garduña, and, especially, La Luna in *The Old Gringo*, on the other hand, draw deeply from the most subversive well of Hispanic narrative technique: the autonomous fictional character, created by Cervantes, expanded by Pérez Galdós, and, I would say, given a soul by Carlos Fuentes. The Woman with the Moon Face is a female fictive self within a fictional structure that allows for such radical departures. The sense of her worth has been renewed in spite of the abuse she has suffered at the hands of her husband and the social forces that have destroyed all basic human dignity in her because of her childlessness. She has found emancipation from the repressive misogyny of patriarchy through the social chaos of the revolution. Only at the most superficial level is La Garduña related to that stock figure of modern fiction—the prostitute with the heart of gold. Unfortunately, this is the representation she receives in the film version of the novel. In the novel, on the other hand, La Garduña's lower class origin and manner serve as a significant counterpoint to La Luna's small town, middle class manner and her sense of escape from that social prison. La Garduña and the women she represents are, above all, survivors. They are women endowed with an indomitable spirit and a love of life.

Four	# Juana Inés de la Cruz and Octavio Paz

The Crucible of Poetry

From the death of Sor Juana at the end of the seventeenth century until the mid-twentieth century, with Rosario Castellanos, there has been an almost complete absence of recognition of women in Mexican letters. Two hundred and fifty years of silence in the colonial capital of New Spain, heir to one of the most advanced civilizations of Mesoamerica, is a fact that demands some explanation. There is no better place to begin than with Sor Juana Inés de la Cruz in the second half of the seventeenth century. Sor Juana's transgression of the social codes of seventeenth-century Mexico is nothing short of remarkable. In one of the most sexist and restrictive societies in the world, led by a misogynist archbishop, Sor Juana was able to state publicly and repeatedly her demand for the intellectual independence of women, for the right to literacy and for education. No political or moral thinker in Mexico has expressed the woman's struggle for equality with more clarity or persuasive power.

Octavio Paz enters our discussion of Sor Juana and the literary representation of Mexican women because his work on Sor Juana is a prime example of historical revision and restitution. He closes his 1988 book on Sor Juana with the assessment that "political-religious orthodoxies strive not only to convince the victim of his guilt but to convince posterity as well. Falsification of history has been one of their specialities. In the case of Sor Juana the travesty nearly succeeded" (488). Why should the most renowned poet in the Spanish-speaking world and the most influential intellectual in Mexico turn his full attention for ten years, from 1971 to 1981, on this seventeenth-century woman? His poetry and essays had been for many decades identified with European surrealism and André Breton, or with the almost mythical pre-Hispanic culture of Mexico. The answer to this question is also the answer to my previous question: how do we explain the apparent silence of women in Mexico? Paz's reasons may be quite varied, but I want to argue that his fight for the historical restitution of Sor Juana stems from his own appropriation of her poetic sensibility and also that he points us toward answering the larger question when he addresses the orthodoxy of falsifying history. This chapter aims at introducing Sor Juana to a larger audience and also at sketching out Paz's role in the historical revision of her work and her person.

Female identity is to be found in the woman herself, how she sees herself as a woman and in the images she accepts as valid. Our inquiry, if it is to be a hermeneutic examination of culture in Mexico, must begin with a closer look at sexism and hatred of women. Feminophobia is not to be confused with sexism, which is a commonplace social prejudice. Feminophobia goes much deeper into the psychological makeup of a community or an individual. Misogyny is the hatred of women, and feminophobia is the irrational objectification of women into nonpersons who threaten, mock, and reduce the male's purportedly innate virtues of courage, honesty, and productive work.

The history of misogyny is a heritage of deprivation and wanton violence which ranges from the burning of witches, widows, and heretics to the institutionalized rape of thousands of victims of every war that man has thrust on the world. Here, I focus on the institutional misogyny of the archbishop of Mexico in the seventeenth century and his persecution of Sor Juana Inés de la Cruz. Archbishop Aguiar y Seijas was only one of a long line of predators in the history of Mexican misogynists. Women who have threatened the patriarchal system of values, few in number to be sure, have been subject to censure, isolation, and, if possible, elimination. Institutional misogyny as an ideology in our society is both psychological and physiological. The rapist is a criminal who attacks women primarily because of hatred; the institutional attack on women, however, emanates from the social structure itself. One of the notable differences is that while some rapists are convicted as criminals, social institutions such as armies, police, and religious authorities are not. The status of women in seventeenth-century Mexico was, unfortunately, not unique in the world, nor was it an extreme example; rather, it was the destructive norm. Francisco Aguiar y Seijas, the Spanish-born archbishop of Mexico from 1681 to his death in 1694, was one of the most notorious misogynists in the history of the church in Mexico (Paz, 1988, 407–409).

Juana Inés Ramírez de Asuaje was born in 1648 in the village of San Miguel Nepantla, at that time a few kilometers from Mexico City, now part of the urban spread of the city.[1] She was the illegitimate daughter of a Mexican woman, Isabel Ramírez de Santillana, and a Spaniard, Pedro Manuel de Asuaje. She had two sisters and three other half-brothers and sisters born from the mother's subsequent partner, an army captain, Diego Ruiz Lozano. Juana Inés' father is believed to have been from the basque country because of his surname; nothing more is known about him except that he abandoned the family when Juana Inés was eight years old. She was a precocious child who learned to read at an early age and composed her first play before she was ten. She yearned to be sent to school and wanted to disguise herself as a boy in order to attend university. She had to be content with her maternal grandfather's small library. A radical change in her life came when her father departed and her mother took a new partner. It was arranged for Juana Inés to go live with relatives in Mexico City. After some months of requesting access to formal education, she finally got her wish and was given instruction in Latin. In fewer than twenty lessons, she was writing with the ability of an advanced student. Her fame as a prodigy reached the viceroy, who invited her in 1664 to live at court. With the approval of her family, she accepted and soon became the center of attention at the viceregal court because of her extraordinary learning, wit, striking beauty, and charismatic personality. Her intellectual fame was put to the test in 1668: she was given an oral examination, arranged by the viceroy, by a jury of forty professors from the university. Their verdict was that she had the learning of a doctor. She was twenty years old. When she was twenty-one, in 1669, she entered the convent of San Jerónimo. From 1665 she had been under the special protection of the vicereine, la Marquesa de Mancera.

From 1669 to 1690 Sor Juana Inés de la Cruz enjoyed a remarkable period of twenty-one years of scholarship and writing. She assembled a library of four thousand books, a variety of musical instruments, and a collection of scientific apparati. Her rooms in the convent became the closest imaginable in Mexico to an intellectual salon for the discussion of arts and letters, the performance of plays, and poetry readings. The funds she had originally received when she entered the convent, as well as those she earned with her writing, were administered with consummate skill. By 1690, at the age of forty-two, she was relatively independent financially. But the most significant achievement was that this woman was the center of intellectual and cultural activity in Mexico. She had managed against all odds to have the kind of life that was exclusively reserved for the male heir of an aristocratic family, who would have the indulgence of his family to pursue literature and science.

Her very success was to be the cause of her downfall. With her insistent pleas that women be taught to read and write, she came to the attention of the archbishop of Mexico, Aguiar y Seijas, whose generalized misogyny had become a feminophobic obsessive hatred that filled him with rage against "this affront to God's laws."

During the twenty-one years when Sor Juana enjoyed the protection of the viceroys, she was the confidant and friend of two vicereines, Leonor Carreto and María Luisa Manrique de Lara. She also had influential friends in Madrid, Seville, Lima, and Quito. Her literary and learned works were much admired throughout the Spanish-speaking world. Although she was a nun, her writing was characteristically not religious, and she discretely avoided all religious discussion. There were some among the clergy who were critical of her poetry because it included love poems. She was the most admired and prestigious writer in the Spanish-speaking new world and, indeed, certainly the finest stylist. It is not difficult to understand why she provoked such a high degree of envy among her contemporaries. The church permitted her this unusual license because she had not only the powerful protection of the court, but also the admiration and the friendship of the best writers of Mexico, like Carlos Sigüenza y Góngora, and of the most learned among the clergy, including Fray Payo de Rivera, Diego Calleja, and, until he betrayed her, Fernández de Santa Cruz, bishop of Puebla.

Sor Juana was also an able administrator and, most importantly, prudent in her political relations. There were two topics she never touched in writing or conversation: theology and the politics of the colonial empire. But things were to change rapidly, and she was to facilitate her own entrapment by her enemies. Her belief that she as a woman was as competent as any man on intellectual matters was stronger than her prudent avoidance of theology and government.

The political climate changed rapidly; 1692 was an exceptionally difficult year for the Spanish authorities in New Spain. A number of factors came together to provoke the first insurrection in a century. Unrest was provoked by several factors: the mercantile policies of inept ministers in Spain (these were the last years of the Hapsburg monarchy under the mentally unstable Charles II), a series of the worst floods in sixty years, a failure of the main crops, and the excesses of the local corrupt bureaucracy combined to create a tense situation. An anti-government sermon by the Franciscan Escaray set afire the unrest among the *criollos*, who were rapidly followed by the *mestizos* and the native majority. Had there been an intellectual middle class able to lead the uprising, revolution might have ensued, but since the only capable educated population were the clergy, the unrest was quelled. It was at this time that Manuel Fernández de Santa Cruz, bishop of Puebla and until that time close friend and advisor of Sor Juana, published her critique of the famous sermon of 1650 written by the distinguished Jesuit Antonio de Vieyra. The critique, *Carta atenagórica* (Letter worthy of Athena, 1690), was all her enemies needed to begin the process that would in two years time silence her. Why did Sor Juana break her own prudent rule not to write on theological topics? We do not have an answer, but it is clear that the bishop of Puebla urged her to write the critique of the Jesuit's sermon, "The Attributes of Christ." It is also evident from her own writing that she believed that there was no intellectual task she could not perform as well or better than any man, so the critique might have been put to her as a challenge. The possibility of entrapment cannot be ruled out; or, it may be that she was unwittingly involved as an ally, albeit one who was vulnerable, in the rivalry and political infighting between the misogynist Archbishop Aguiar y Seijas and her supposed friend and supporter Fernández de Santa Cruz, bishop of Puebla.[2] The shock waves caused by Sor Juana's theological critique were threefold. First, the sheer audacity of a woman, a nun, challenging a distinguished theologian with intellectual argument outraged the authorities of the church; second, her argument itself with its clear deistic overtones and its espousal of the philosophy of reason, which does not reject God but discards the benevolence of divine providence interceding in human affairs, was cause of great consternation even among her friends; and third, the letter which preceded her treatise, written by the bishop of Puebla under the pseudonym of Sor Filotea, condemned not only her treatise but also Sor Juana's dedication to art and learning.

Sor Juana fought back with logical argument in her *Answer to Sor Filotea de la Cruz* (1691). In this, her last written work, she argues for the right of women to seek knowledge and to take their rightful place in society as active participants in all levels of life. She cites classical sources and those church fathers whose writings were at all favorable to her position, but her most brilliant arguments are taken from what the next century would call natural law—she pleads for women's right to study, think, and speak; she understood full well that the attack on her, which had started because of theological differences, had now become entirely an argument about a woman's right to learning. In 1994 the Sor Juana scholar Electa Arenal, in collaboration with Amanda Powell, published a critical edition of Sor Juana's *Answer to Sor Filotea de la Cruz*.[3]

The conclusion of the attack on Sor Juana was not long in coming: she was ordered to subject herself to a life of penance and silence. Because of the departure of her viceregal support, she found herself isolated, without any protection against the ruling. She had to obey or leave the convent; she had nowhere to go. She submitted, sold all her books, scientific and musical instruments, and her silence was heard all over the Spanish-speaking world. Sor Juana died two years later, in 1695, from an epidemic she contracted while she was working in the infirmary. She was not yet forty-seven. The Hispanic world of letters still reverberates from the injustice, and Sor Juana criticism, three hundred years after her death, is stronger than ever (see Appendix 3).[4]

This historical sketch of Sor Juana lays the ground for examining Octavio

Paz's interpretive studies of her life and writings. He develops a number of significant issues; I will touch on the five of these that I think have most affected his own writing and his influential historical reexamination of her place in Mexican letters. It is a case, I propose, of direct and indirect poetic appropriation which Paz himself often states marks the writings of poetry. I will begin this probe into intertextuality by sketching out the five issues: (1) the imagery of her greatest poem, *Primero sueño* (Dream); (2) the erotic nature of some of her love poems; (3) her status as a woman in colonial Mexico; (4) her philosophical platonism and deism, and (5) her fight for women's rights.

Primero sueño, an intellectual autobiography written around 1686, when she was thirty-seven, is Sor Juana's masterpiece. It was not published until 1692, at the end of her public life, but it was read and discussed by her many friends before that date. The poem begins in the darkness of the night, and the enunciating voice contemplates the fantasy of the imagination. She first enjoys the creations of the mind, but slowly breaks away from this contemplation and looks at the things of the world around her. The diversity of the world blinds her in its richness. Astonished, she falls, but she gets up and begins again the long and arduous climb. She cannot take a leap of fantasy but must ascend toward knowledge step by step. In response to her sense of limitation at not being able to comprehend the world, she turns to Aristotle's categories and begins to master the world, one part at a time. By taking separate account of each thing, she is able to[5]

> scrutinize all things, one by one,
> which come to our attention   580
> through the artifice of what
> are the Categories, two times five,
> a metaphysical concentration
> (which configurates generic entities
> through a few ideas or images,   585
> thus reason abstracts what is essential
> from concrete matter)
> science creates universals and
> wisely repairs with artfulness
> our defect—the inability   590
> of knowing all of natural creation
> through perception of our senses
> step by step
> we must ascend in our effort
> to understand the order   595
> of things in their relations.
> Dependent as we are on reason and
> limited by the relative vigour

of our intellect we entrust
understanding to subsequent discourse. . . .   600
My understanding now sought to pursue   617
the method in ordered succession.

The poem describes the spiral ascent of the search for knowledge from inanimate matter to the animals until she reaches humanity and its symbolic manifestation in the triangle. The three angles represent the physical attributes of humanity, the divine will, and the spiritual dimension of humanity. The unique nature of the human being in all creation is described as the union of body and soul in the person.

By these steps I thus sought to proceed
but at times I desisted,   705
thinking it excessive impertinence
to inquire into all things when
I could not understand what
was most obvious and accessible.
. . . .
If one solitary object of nature
lies beyond understanding—my thought
said timidly—and discourse
in fear flees; if a species of nature   760
—which like the rest is singular,
taken in isolation—
evade understanding
and astonished discourse cower
before the rigor of scrutiny   765
because it fear
not understanding well, or never or later,
how can reason expect to confront
the immensity of the cosmos . . . ?

But there is a growing frustration in the lyric voice as she realizes that she does not understand relationships: the relationship of the soil of the earth to the plants that grow, the relationship of plants to animals that depend on them, and, finally, the relationship between lower animals and humanity. Is there a hidden unity in creation? The lyric voice senses the presence of unattainable knowledge beyond this unity. Perhaps it is better to retreat? She is forewarned of the inevitable failure of human efforts to attain absolute knowledge. The act of seeking knowledge, rather than knowledge itself, emerges as the reward for her struggle. The lyric voice recovers, garners strength from defeat, and sets out again.

thus with the light of reason
cast on the natural order   970
of things, recognizing color
and reconstituting visible features,
returning them to their functions
before my sense perception,
their operations coming into clear light   975
the World illuminated and I awakened.

The body inert until now begins to awaken and demands sustenance. The sun comes up. The reality of life imposes restrictions, but the now-conscious lyric voice emerges prepared to resume the struggle to know "the world illuminated and I awakened."

There is the cyclical alternation of night and day: the night, a time of the never-ending struggle to know; the day, the time of attending to the things of the body. This is a dialectic between night and day, the seeking of knowledge and the continuation of the world. They repeat each other in a cyclical pattern, but sustaining the soul throughout is the insatiable desire to know and the courage to be and to continue knowing full well that there can be no end, no final summit to scale. She turns the defeat of her human limitations into victory, for the climb itself, the seeking of knowledge is its own reward. The seeker of knowledge must overcome hostility, silence, and opposition everywhere, must survive the demands of the day in order to return renewed in the night to the continuation of the struggle to know.

It has only been in the last few years that Sor Juana's work has received new readings not determined by the constrictions of either Spanish or Mexican literary history. In the former, she is described as a late baroque follower of Luis de Góngora; in the latter, as the finest example of the creole culture of New Spain. In fact she was both, but much more. Her poetry was certainly linked in form and thematic topos to Góngora, and she certainly reflected the culture of colonial Mexico rather than Spain, but there also develops in all of her work a passion for free inquiry that was quite foreign to the seventeenth century in Spain or New Spain. The emphasis on rational discourse and the belief that the universe is knowable through the disciplined application of the intellect was seen as heresy in a culture where human fallibility was continually held in contrast to divine omniscience. The sin of intellectual pride was the label awaiting anyone who held Sor Juana's views. The most lasting effect of the counterreformation and the Inquisition was to severely stifle emerging scientific inquiry in the entire empire at the very time that it was flourishing in northern Europe. The center of power shifted dramatically from the Mediterranean to the North Atlantic because of economic reasons. Catholic France, in contrast to Spain, began what was to be a long tradition of deistic free thinkers, while Spain and its colonies would continue to deny that study of the natural world was not subject to revealed scripture. The magnitude of Sor Juana's rebellion must be seen in this context.

Octavio Paz wrote his first commentary on Sor Juana's *Primero sueño* (Dream) in October 1950;[6] shortly after that, he wrote his own long poem about the seeking of knowledge, "Piedra de sol" (Sunstone), published in 1957. The intellectual relation of his commentary on *Primero sueño* to his own poetry is more indirect than direct or explicit. He observes that Sor Juana's night is not the sensual night of lovers. Nor is it the reflective night of the Spanish mystics. Hers is an intellectual time of scrutiny, a night constructed by sheer willpower in the conquest of empty space; it is a rigorous discipline of the mind. This intellectual impulse has only the slightest reminder of the night of the soul of Saint John of the Cross. The mystics are drawn up in celestial reverie as depicted in paintings of El Greco. In *Primero sueño* the heavens are empty and hostile to comprehension. Silence faces the human soul, the desire to know is illicit, and the soul that dreams of knowledge is rebellious against authority. Nocturnal contemplation brings dryness, vertigo, and fear. To think one knows is but a dream, but this dream is all we have. This dreaming dreamer has self-awareness, the recognition of herself; she dares to make the universe according to her own viewpoint. In Paz's foreword to *A Sor Juana Anthology*, it is evident that the vertiginous and cyclical night of Sor Juana has revealed its center to him; Paz writes: [*Primero sueño*] "is the poem not of knowledge but of the act of knowing" (Trueblood, x).

The imagery of a fall into an abyss and the painful arduous climb which creates in the self the courage to be and to continue to search in spite of the awareness that one will never attain one's goal is familiar to us from a wide variety of literary works ranging from the Sisyphus myth to existentialist writing of the nineteenth and twentieth centuries. However, the extraordinary characteristic of the dialectic struggle to know, singled out by Octavio Paz as the center of Sor Juana's poem, is that it is also the center of his own "Piedra de sol."[7]

The lyric voice in Paz's poem has also fallen and is desperately seeking order and purpose to life. The following verses from "Sunstone" will put us into the midst of the lyric voice's desperate search: "I search without finding, I write alone,/there's no one here, and the day falls/ . . . I walk through my shadow in search of a moment." The essential difference, aside from poetic form, is that the identity of the lyric voice is at issue in Paz's poem while in Sor Juana's poem the fall is an epistemological despair, a response to diversity dramatizing the confusion and despair at not being able to understand the complexity of the world. Sor Juana's seeker does not doubt who she is; her doubts are all about what she can understand. Paz's lyric voice, in contrast, falls into sameness and struggles for identity: "There's nothing in front of me, only a moment/salvaged from a dream tonight of coupled/images dreamed."

Sor Juana found the clue of unity amidst diversity in the human capacity to reason. Intellectually, this glimpse of unity as the mysterious union of animal and God in the person foreshadows not only Enlightenment writings on humanity's independence from divine providence, a deistic philosophical tenet that would survive primarily through political writing, but also the romantic hero's radical solitude.

The rationalism in Sor Juana's writing generally, and particularly in *Primero sueño*, is both a mode of inquiry and a profound conviction. She insisted that any conception of the life of the spirit that excluded women and accorded them a lesser place or assumed their subordination could not be demonstrated through rational argument. Sor Juana was a proto-feminist pre-Cartesian thinker in a nun's habit.

Paz's enunciating voice also seeks knowledge, but his is not a rational quest. His voice is one of a desperate, anguished persona in search of his identity. Paz is writing in the second half of the twentieth century and is part of an intellectual world that is heir to the loss of faith in God and rational thought. Sor Juana's seeker believes in an ordered universe and in the human mind's capacity to know it. Paz's voice believes in nothing and finds only chaos beyond the consciousness of self. Sor Juana's lyric voice seeks knowledge as a way of being rather than as an acquisition. She begins her quest, like Descartes, looking within the self. Reason in both Sor Juana and Descartes is the faculty of control and focus.[8] To free oneself from the constraints of the passions of the body and to obey reason is to gain control over the world. The intellectual argument of *Primero sueño* can be readily found in Descartes' statement: "The true function of reason, then, in the conduct of life is to examine and consider without passion the value of all perfection of body and soul that can be acquired by our conduct" (170). Sor Juana's strong belief in reason and in the corresponding axiom of free will enabled her to internalize the moral strength she needed to believe in herself and to develop her argument that gender has no bearing on the capacity to reason.

Sor Juana's views on free will are so central to her thinking that we can only lament the fact that she most likely did not read Descartes on free will: "Now free will is in itself the noblest thing we have because it makes us in a certain manner equal to God and exempts us from being his subjects; and so its rightful use is the greatest of all the goods we possess, and further there is nothing that is more our own or that matters more to us" (228).

Sor Juana wrote that free will gives human beings the possibility of moral responsibility, moral judgment, and, finally, salvation. Without free will, all sense of divine justice would be a mockery. The Cartesian dualism of self and world, or body and soul, is assumed in Sor Juana's seventeenth-century view. Paz's poem presents the terror of a void beyond the self. But both questing voices recover from their initial obstacles and slowly take on the role of god-like world-makers. She is deistic, he is existentially anguished. Yet in both poems the self emerges with renewed strength and the realization that knowledge is self-knowledge.

Paz has received this poetic tradition and transformed it to address the twentieth-century malaise—the loss of personal identity. The lyric voice glimpses identity in a single moment and expands this fleeting glimpse: "they crumble/for one enormous moment and we glimpse."

Paz has incorporated the lyric apostrophe of love poetry; there is now not only an *I* but also a *you* that is essential for the reality of *we*. The lyric voice discovers the truth of self that the poet Paz had found long before in the love poetry of Sor Juana: "When I am I am another, my acts/are more mine when they are the acts/of others, in order to be I must be another . . . I am not/there is no I, we are always us."

Sor Juana wrote a number of love poems to her friend and protector, María Luisa, marquesa de Lara, the beautiful and talented vicereine. The poetry suggests a physical attraction between the two women, in addition to praises of elegance, beauty, and wit. The significant feature of Sor Juana's erotic poetry is not that it is between women but, as Octavio Paz has seen, that the physical sexual attraction between the two is transcended to obtain a sense of personal identity through the eyes of the loved one.

There are also many love poems in which the sex of the absent lover is not explicit; the notable difference between this poetry and the poems to María Luisa is that in the former, the lover is a phantasm, a sign of absence, while in the latter the lover is present. The link between the two is the necessity of the other for the self, even if it should only be in the imagination:

> Hold still, shadow of my elusive love
> image of the enchantment that I most love
> beautiful illusion for whom I happily die
> sweet fiction for whom I painfully live.
> If the image of your grace, attraction
> serves my breast as obedient irons
> why do you enamour me flatterer?
> if you are but to mock me in flight?
> But boast you shall not in satisfaction
> that your tyranny triumphed over me
> that although mocked you leave the bond

that your fantasy's form held tight
it matters not to mock arms and breast
if my imagination imprisons you. (Poem 165, 1951)

Sor Juana's other has become the counterpart of the I.

Sor Juana's status in New Spain was anomalous; she did not fit into the established social structure. As the most gifted and intelligent writer of the time, she was clearly unsuited for normal married life for women at court. She was a woman in a society that had only four roles for women: legal wife, concubine, prostitute, or nun. She chose the religious life, although she never expressed any religious vocation, as the lesser of evils. As an illegitimate daughter of a couple who never married, she had no name or status that would have enabled her to negotiate a platonic marriage, and as a young woman with no dowry she could aspire neither to marriage nor to the convent unless she could secure a rich benefactor. She found her benefactors, among them María Luisa, the vicereine and her closest friend.

Sor Juana has been characterized by several biographers as having masculine traits in spite of the fact that all the documents from the period demonstrate that she behaved like any charming and gregarious young woman, save in one respect: she was an intellectually brilliant autodidact who had only one Latin teacher for fewer than twenty lessons and who at twenty was the astonishment of the Spanish-speaking world because of her learning. This social misfit was the personification of a number of contradictions: she was a scholar and she was a woman, she was a lay poet and she was a nun, she was allowed to write under viceregal patronage and she was silenced because she wrote. She was the very work of the devil in the eyes of the archbishop of Mexico, a strong-willed intelligent poet and brilliant intellectual in the body of a beautiful woman. This social anomaly was able to write for twenty-one years because of the protection of the viceroy and because of her financial shrewdness and political skill. But there was also a price to be paid for these years of accomplishment: alienation, solitude, and death before she was forty-seven.

Sor Juana's philosophical views on life and society must be examined within the context of her status in the social structure of seventeenth-century New Spain. Her library and learning were limited to a neo-Thomistic concept of the universe wherein the church fathers were the highest authority because their learning was based on revealed truth of the scriptures rather than on experimental science or rational inquiry.[9] Sor Juana had only a vague notion of the revolution in science that was raging in Europe, and she was most probably unaware of the writings of Descartes (1596–1650), which would have given her valuable intellectual support. She was nonetheless a Cartesian thinker. She was a rebel against blind authority imposed on society in the name of God. Her thinking led in the following direction: the human being is the creation of divine providence and is endowed with free will. There can be no justification for punishment and reward for one's acts if there is no free will. Once the concept of free will is accepted, individuals cannot use the excuse of external forces driving them to commit acts. If there is free will, then the only valid authority among men and women is the consistent use of reason to convince one and the other of their respective differences. Sor Juana turned to the church fathers and argued that there is no basis in revealed scripture to justify the exclusion of women from education and there is, above all, no rational argument for keeping women ignorant. This deistic rational philosophy, had she been able to develop it more fully, would have led her in the direction of her contemporary Descartes and perhaps even Voltaire. The direction of her thought also led her, of course, up against the Holy Office of the Inquisition and against the formidable opposition of the Jesuits. Her argument for a divine providence indifferent to the acts of humanity represented a deistic search for liberation from the subordination of women imposed by church and state. What must be kept in mind is that because she was a woman, her pursuit of learning and knowledge was a transgression of the social code under which she lived. If a woman committed a crime such as theft, or even murder, she was condemned just as a man would have been, but this social structure had no way of dealing with a female intellectual except to force her into a situation where her sex became the issue. She was attacked because her critique of the Jesuit Antonio de Vieyra suggested a deistic philosophy, but she was condemned not for what she wrote but for what she represented: a female intellectual. The bishop of Puebla enunciated words of severe censure: "What a pity that so great an intellect should lower itself in such a way by unworthy notice of the Earth that it have no desire to penetrate what transpires in Heaven; and, since it be already lowered to the ground, that it not descend further, to consider what transpires in Hell" (Peden, 2).

Sor Juana's *Answer to Sor Filotea de la Cruz* is a courageous autobiographical self-defense. She argues with vehemence for her right to seek knowledge and, at the same time, recognizes the limitations of human learning, including that of her detractors. She insists throughout that the soul has no sex, that sex is an aspect of the body and of worldly existence; thus if women have immortal souls as well as men there can be no sexual distinction in spiritual matters, and if study and learning are not transgressions of God's will, why should they be transgressions for women? Octavio Paz proposed that Sor Juana's defense and her surrender two years later were a form of martyrdom for the cause of women's liberation. She never recanted, creating a silence that is deafening even at a distance of three hundred years.

Electa Arenal has called Sor Juana's *Primero sueño* the delineation of a feminist epistemology (1991, 137). Certainly, Sor Juana stands with Santa Teresa of Avila as a brilliant female intellectual in a misogynistic society. Paz observes acutely that her awareness of her status as a woman undoubtedly was an essential part of Sor Juana's life and writing. As a young girl she wanted to go to the university. At twenty-one she entered the convent in order to be able to pursue a life of learning, and as a mature woman she repeatedly stated that understanding is not a sexual attribute. As a writer she searched for role models in antiquity and among Christian women. She looked toward Isis, goddess of knowledge, as well as among Christian women, of whom her favorite was Saint Catalina of Alexandria, a learned woman, virgin, and martyr. Sor Juana's choice of these role models may provide the single most important clue to understanding both her reasons for entering the convent and her mode of fighting the censure she received for her audacity. She entered the convent as a form of liberation in a patriarchal closed society. She fought against her adversaries first by responding to the best of her ability as a writer and then by the nonviolent protest of silence, or martyrdom, as Paz suggests, for she never recanted the life of the mind that she so ardently espoused.

Sor Juana knew that being a woman was not a natural impediment but rather a social obstacle to her wish and need to study and write. She had learned of sexist injustice first hand with the example of her mother. As an uneducated woman and as an unmarried woman living with a man, she was denied social status, yet after the death of her second partner, she demonstrated her skill and intelligence in running the *hacienda*.

There will continue to be much speculation about Sor Juana's motives for maintaining silence from 1692 to 1695; however, a close reading of her debate on the Jesuit Vieyra will show that her silence was much more than capitulation to church authority. In fact, it was an attack on the archbishop of Mexico, Aguiar y Seijas, and the patriarchal system of discrimination against women. When she writes, "God has called an ignorant woman to humble the arrogant," she refers to all those who claim to speak in God's name in order to impose their will on women. The struggle between Sor Juana and the clergy is one of ideology, a struggle for liberation.[10] The archbishop went into a rage, and the institutional apparatus of the church responded by falsifying documents to the extent that they were able to do it. They would have tried her for heresy, and not false pride, if they had been able to produce the witnesses. The evidence of her writing and the openness of her critique and defense could not be suppressed entirely, however, and time has served Sor Juana well. The argument in her favor as an advocate for the liberation of women is compelling.

A deep current of thought on the human body runs throughout Sor Juana's writings that is demonstrated in her almost obsessive fascination with mirrors and her own figure captured in portraits. This is much more than the narcissism of a vain woman. The human body as she looks upon it is never the projection of her soul; on the contrary, she feels that the soul is the interiorization of the outside. This face, this woman, is body and object, and as such it is of the world, but this worldly singularity is evidence of the whole of her universe. Sor Juana does not see her represented image as a doubling, but rather as a doubling of the other, the one others see and know. The image in a portrait is therefore not the reproduction of herself as she knows herself, but a repetition of the external woman known to others. She ponders on this non-self which is the one others know and on the possibility for limitless copies of it. The stark distinction between these selves attests to the uniqueness and the nonrepeatable essence of herself. Poem after poem delights in the baroque play of images between the model and the portrait, the image reflected in the mirror and the person who is looking into it; in short, the play of reality and appearance. That which must be taken as material reality, however—the body—is but appearance and that which is not apparent at all is consciousness. The self that she is to herself is not on the outside. But this does not mean that the one who is seen by others is not involved in the interior of the thinking person. This exterior self who belongs to others remains outside as long as the model does not look at it, but when she looks upon her external image, it becomes interiorized. Sor Juana's poems about this double encapsulate the play between the interior and the exterior, and thus these poems represent yet another form of doubling.

There is an overwhelming sense of an encounter with a desire to *be* when one reads Sor Juana's writing. She uses literary and poetic conventions like so many disguises with which she appears to her readers. The obviousness of the convention suggests that disguise does not, for Sor Juana, involve being hidden. Rather, the lyric voice's use of disguise enacts the playing of a game. It is the game whereby desire to be is translated into a plurality of situations without jeopardizing the unity of the self. Moreover, a subtle but powerful idea emerges: the attempt to be represented by one and the same persona—which in writing would involve the fabrication of a completely false alter ego, a kind of super ego that would indeed eclipse the self. All of this play of disguise by the lyric voice is united by the same desire: to be many and one at the same time. This apparent paradox is the root of her insatiable curiosity and thirst for knowledge, as well as her despair in *Primero sueño* at not being able to encompass it all under the magical name of knowledge. Sor Juana's despair is turned around at the end of *Primero sueño*, when the lyric voice finally emerges from the endless alternation of loss and gain. The lyric voice's reflection through poetry, the poem itself, is a form of reappropriating the world. She cannot know all, but she can imagine.

Whatever differences one encounters among the numerous biographers of Sor Juana, and there are many profound differences of interpretations, all agree that fundamental to any explanation of this extraordinary woman is the fact that her life was a constant battle to prove the intellectual equality of women and men. The battle was completely without hope of victory. She was in the wrong place at the wrong time. She was quite alone in a society and a period in history that was totally controlled by men. She fought not out of some quixotic ideal, but from the visceral necessity of a person who, even as a child, knew herself to be superior in intelligence and knowledge to her contemporaries and yet was denied because not only was she a woman, she was also illegitimate and born a *criolla* in a colonial empire.

She took on viceregal Mexico and the Spanish empire on their own man-made terms. She pursued rational inquiry in every avenue that opened to her, taking the language of men and mastering it in order to surpass them. She wrote better, more lucid prose and verse than any contemporary in the second half of the seventeenth century. One cannot overstate the remarkable courage she must have had to challenge all comers to do intellectual battle. As long as she had viceregal protection and she avoided issues pertaining to theology and politics, she was relatively safe. But as in a Greek tragedy, her strength hid her weakness. The open challenge to debate all men on equal scholarly and rational grounds led her to be persuaded to enter the tilting fields of theology. The fact that her views were well within orthodox opinion was of no avail; her enemies used the opportunity to accuse her of intellectual pride. It is not that Sor Juana did not uphold the authority of the king and the church. Further, it is not that her deistic position could not have been accommodated by church doctrine: the Thomistic principle that reason is a God-given gift to humanity rendered her position theologically "legal." Sor Juana's relation to authority was not one of subversion, but rather, transgression. Her case demonstrates that the authority that ultimately destroyed her was irrational, completely lacking intelligence, and imposed arbitrarily and violently, in clear contradiction to the cornerstone of counter-reformation Catholicism, which holds that divine grace must be supported by the actions of women *and* men, both of whom are endowed with free will.

Sor Juana won the debate but paid for it with abdication of the life she most valued. This visceral feminism has now come down to an age where the denial of basic rights to women has been challenged with some success. As more of

Sor Juana's thought becomes accessible outside the Spanish-speaking world, it is possible that a greater understanding of the colonial heritage of Latin America will be brought into focus in discussions of feminist thinking. One of the blind spots of first world feminism has been a certain ahistorical approach to the third world.

Five	**Questions of Female Identity**

Rosario Castellanos, Luisa Josefina Hernández, and María Luisa Puga

Fictional characters in literary works of art can be described as configurative representations of self or aspects of self in the text/reader interaction. In the experience of readers, they are at first the subjects of the narrator's discourse but, ultimately, as the reading of the text begins to take on the fuller dimensions of a narrative world, characters change from virtual persons to become figurative variations of past and present identities of real persons. Eventually, if they inhabit distinctive narrative worlds, they become fictive persons. We know Emma Bovary, Anna Karenina, and, closer to home, Fortunata and Doña Bárbara, but what is striking in portrayals of female fictive persons by male novelists is that the identity of these characters is shaped by forces external to their will. Their self-awareness as fictive persons is not generated from a strong or weak concept of self but rather is imposed on them. From Moll Flanders to Nana, social forces are determinate. With Fortunata and Doña Bárbara there is biological instinct as well as social convention.

It is not that such fictive persons as Dorothea Brooke or Lily Briscoe are more complete, consistent, or profound configurations of the female than those of Flaubert, Tolstoi, Zola, and Pérez Galdós. Even a weak suggestion of such gender-related novelistic ability cannot be supported by critical commentary. As a group, women writers are neither better nor worse than male writers. What I shall attempt to present in this chapter is that women writers add a dimension usually absent in the configurations of female fictive persons by male authors, without denying that there are notable exceptions like Clarín yesterday and Fuentes, Kundera, or Fowles today. The added dimension is a more ambiguous, unpredictable, more open identity, for the fictive persona. George Eliot's narrator may liken Dorothea to Saint Teresa, but there is a deference to the complexity of consciousness. She, of course, was writing within a tradition that had no qualms about the widespread use of female stereotypes. If there was a nineteenth-century reluctance to impose moral or social closure on characters, this came primarily from Russian and French characterizations. Virginia Woolf has expressed this added dimension succinctly: "It is no use trying to sum people up. One must follow hints, not exactly what is said, nor yet entirely what is done" (1976, 29 and again on 153). I am not proposing another variation on feminist essentialism; as I have argued in the introduction, feminist criticism must be open to the fictive making of narrativity whatever the sex of the writer. What I am suggesting, as an initial generalization, is that women's characterization of the fictive person moves away from a center of consciousness that is strong, clear, and unitary (with or without psychological development), and in its place expresses a subtle, necessarily incomplete, and fundamentally indeterminate glimpse of a person in a social process. Nancy Miller offers this useful description: "The subject in this model is not fixed in time or space, but suspended in a continual moment of fabrication" (270).

On the topic of the self in moral space, the Canadian philosopher Charles Taylor writes: "A language only exists and is maintained within a language community . . . one is self only among other selves. A self can never be described without reference to those who surround it" (35). My argument is that the fictive self can be drawn out only in a fictive space, and this fictive space can be relatively broad or constrained. The fictive space given to female literary characters in the work of such major novelists as Pérez Galdós is far more limited than in the work of his contemporary, Emilia Pardo Bazán. This is not because of any lack of skill, experience, or sensibility, but rather because inscribed meanings that are transmitted with only minor changes are fully dependent on a priori shared judgments in the community. The dominant shared judgments about women in most communities are concepts of limitation of possible action, behavior, comportment, and, of course, thought. In other words, women in fiction are far more likely to be conditioned creatures. Male fictive characters have also been socially conditioned, but the possibility for radical action, whether of genius or madman, has always been present. Innovation within a common language community thus has appeared to be a male prerogative. A fictional character cannot be a fictive self on his or her own. The character is a self only in relation to his or her others.

If we turn to Mexican literature, there is a dearth of memorable female fictive characters, by either men or women, until we come to the most recent literature. Put another way, why is it that major writers like Azuela or Yáñez have not created distinctive female fictive selves?[1] Surely it is not because of a lack of talent or interest. If we examine more recent work, for example, Gustavo Sainz's *Gazapo* and Fernando del Paso's *Palinuro de México* (1977; Palinuro of Mexico), and, especially, *Noticias del imperio* (1987; News of the empire), there is an almost obsessive focalization on the female, but these female fictive selves are dressed in the color of the male's desires, to paraphrase Octavio Paz. When we reflect on these characters, we see that they are quite alien to the encounter with women who join us in our lives as one of so many future virtual selves with which we make our world, and this is so primarily because these female characters are overdetermined, that is to say, they are not fictive selves; they are the necessary female other to the male configuration of the world. In Mexican literature, Jesusa Palancares is one of the first memorable female fictive persons. But a simple juxtaposition of male and female writers is not of much use, nor is Elena Poniatowska the lone or even the first of women novelists to create effective female fictive selves.

I am concerned with the creation of what Taylor calls the moral space for the configuration of female fictive selves. There are a few women novelists in the earlier part of the twentieth century, such as Nellie Campobello, but they wrote only a few minor works.[2] In Mexico the major production of women writing fiction and theater can be said to begin in earnest with Rosario Castellanos and Luisa Josefina Hernández; it is with their work that we will begin our commentary.[3]

What I mean by "fictive person" instead of the more generic "fictional character" is that fictive persons are not just imaginative constructs of persons we have met in life or even composite portraits of such persons. A fictive person is a center of consciousness in a textual relationship we have helped to make in our reading. These persons carry the fragments of our world that we have given them, but they are also different and independent of our purpose and design, and can confront our values, opinions, and conventions; at the most unexpected moments, they can respond in ways that anger and alienate whatever sympathy we had bestowed on them. These female fictive persons are never contained or constrained by the immediate material circumstances in which we have met them. They are both of our viewpoint and opposed to it. Their world is both familiar and unknown. And this dialectic of mine and not mine is so because their identity depends on the constant fluctuation between the known and the unknown.

I have argued for a feminist literary sociocriticism that recognizes the redescriptive power of literature in the making of social narrativity. The philosopher Richard Rorty has come closest to making this argument within the philosophical mainstream of the United States:

The drama of an individual human life, or of the history of humanity as a whole, is not one in which a pre-existent goal is triumphantly reached or tragically not reached. Neither a constant, external reality, nor an unfailing interior source of inspiration forms a background for such dramas. Instead, to see one's life, or the life of one's community, as a dramatic narrative is to see it as a process of Nietzschean self-overcoming. The paradigm of such a narrative is the life of the genius who can say of the relevant portion of the past "Thus I willed it," because she has found a way to describe that past which the past never knew, and thereby found a self to be which her precursors never knew was possible. (29)

Some eight pages later he adds:

Another way of making this point is to say that the social process of literalizing a metaphor is duplicated in the fantasy life of an individual. We call something "fantasy" rather than "poetry" or "philosophy" when it revolves around metaphors which do not catch on with other people—that is, around ways of speaking or acting which the rest of us cannot find a use for. (37)

There are in the works of these women writers female fictive persons who are alienated from the society in which they live. These women have come to reject the role set out for them because it does not fulfill their aspirations as social persons. This denial of place and purpose, a crisis of identity, is commonplace for a female in a male-dominated society. The inquiry by fictive women into who we are becomes an open question in which all women in Mexico are involved, a question that requires radical rethinking of our usual understanding of personal and social identity: the process of self-overcoming that Rorty recognizes.

In this chapter I shall comment on the character identified as woman #4, a voice in the farce El eterno femenino (The eternal feminine) by Rosario Castellanos, then turn my attention to Maria Antonia, a secondary character in the play "La fiesta del mulato" (The mulatto's orgy) by Luisa Josefina Hernández, and, finally, I shall look at the unnamed narrator of María Luisa Puga's "Inmóvil sol secreto" (Secret and immobile sun). Of the three, only the narrator of María Luisa Puga's story is central to the text and a center of consciousness, but all three together can give us some direction in our analysis of the crisis of identity of the female eunuch in Mexican society.

Rosario Castellanos (1925–1974) wrote poetry, short stories, essays, plays, and two celebrated novels, Balún Canán (Nine guardians, 1957) and Oficio de tinieblas (Ritual of darkness, 1962).[4] Her prose style yields an uncomplicated, clear, and direct exposition of narrative situations that have to do with both the rural Mexico of her native Chiapas and the general condition of being a woman in Mexico. There is a powerful sense of social conscience in her writing, but she expresses her critique of Mexican society through the textual situation of interethnic relations rather than through an authoritative narrative voice. Naomi Lindstrom observes that it is through the creation of individual fictional selves that Castellanos overcomes the traditional failure of composite ethnic characterization (135). This characteristic of her literary works may explain why she has been described as a woman writer of social conscience but not a feminist. It seems that Mexican critics equate feminism with overt advocacy and cannot recognize that creating situations characterized by social compromise is the literary alternative to direct argumentation. Rosario Castellanos died tragically while in her prime as a writer and at a time when the feminist movement was beginning to come forward in Mexico as a political force for women's rights.

Shortly before she left for Tel Aviv in 1971 as Mexican ambassador, Castellanos gave a speech which marked a new period of feminist politicization, and three years later, a short month before her death in 1974, she completed *El eterno femenino* (The eternal feminine), a farce in three acts which also marked the coming of a new era; both texts are turning points. In this chapter I want to examine in detail the third act of the farce, but before I turn to the play, I translate a fragment of the lecture Castellanos gave in Mexico City in 1971 on the eve of her departure for Israel:

It is not equitable, and therefore not legitimate, that one of a married couple can aspire to receive nothing in return for what she puts into the marriage.

It is not equitable, and therefore not legitimate, that only one of the married couple has the opportunity to form himself intellectually and the other not have another alternative but remain submerged in ignorance.

It is not equitable, and therefore not legitimate, that one member of a married couple find in his work not only a source of enrichment but also the satisfaction of knowing that he is a useful participant in the life of his community through his work, while the other performs tasks that are not worthy of remuneration, tasks that barely mitigate the superficiality and isolation that she must suffer, work that by its very nature can never be considered complete or finished.

It is not equitable, and therefore against the spirit of our laws, that one member of a married couple have full liberty of movement while the other be reduced to paralysis.

It is not equitable, and therefore it is not legal, that one member of a married couple be master over his own body and do with it as he pleases while the other must reserve her body not for her own aims, but in order to comply with purposes separate from her will.

The relationship between men and women is not equitable in Mexico.[5]

These are words of a feminist who has taken a clear political position with regard to the status of women. The difference between this position and one of social conscience, which she always held, is that there is now a specific sense of purpose: a feminist revolution.

The play *The Eternal Feminine* has three acts structured on a decreasing scale of caricature and an intensifying scale of ideological direction. The setting for the play is a beauty shop where a young woman, Lupita, is having her hair done on the day of her wedding. The shop's owner has just installed a gadget into the hair dryer that will induce pleasant dreams in clients as they doze off.

The first act consists of Lupita's dreams of the wedding night, the first month of marriage (which includes visits from her overbearing mother), her married life (which includes her husband's infidelity and her killing him), her dialogue with her double, and, finally, her submergence into gross consumerism. The caricature is heavy handed; the only sense of direction comes with the dialogue which unfolds between Lupita and her double on the relative advantages of being married as against being a single woman.

The second act is another dream sequence. This time Lupita finds herself in a fair and enters a sideshow where she is treated to a parody of Genesis with Adam, Eve, and the serpent. She is shocked at Eve's confrontation with the patriarchal God of the Old Testament. She comes out of the scene and finds herself in a museum where a series of famous women of Mexican history come alive, including Sor Juana Inés de la Cruz, Doña Josefa (of the War of Independence), Carlota, Malinche, Rosario (the lyric addressee of Manuel Acuña's romantic poetry), and the *soldadera* (camp follower) of the Mexican revolution, Adelita. The humor is sharp edged but the tone of caricature continues.

The third act is the climax both in the framing story and in the thematic development of the play. There has been a power failure and Lupita's hair will not be done in time for her wedding. In this desperate situation, the hairdresser suggests that she try on a wig. She does, and each wig, with its particular hairstyle, gives her a flash of the imagination into a different female life-style. This is a radical change from the first two acts, where Lupita retained her identity and her way of life, for now she adapts to a variety of different ways of living. With the first wig she becomes the unmarried school teacher, office, or hospital worker; the second wig transforms her into a prostitute; a third wig is tried and she sees herself as the mistress of her former employer; a fourth wig makes her take on the role of a reporter doing interviews of famous and not-so-famous people. The last wig, which is labeled "the cutting edge," changes her into a drawing-room intellectual giving a course, "Culture Is in Fashion This Year," to upper middle class women. The five scenes are explicitly theatrical.

In all the life situations in which Lupita, the protagonist, finds herself, she is a newcomer and must be informed about the rules by which the game is played, and, in each, she discovers that this potential role for a woman is undesirable and rejects it. Since she is also rejecting the wig she has tried on, at the end she finds that she has run out of possibilities for having her hair done in time. She is beside herself and does not know what to do; the owner of the beauty shop tells her that that is *her* problem. Lupita turns to the audience and cries: "My problem? My problem? Damn!"

One by one, the five situations present five alternatives to marriage that will be recognized by the audience as verisimilar. In the first scene, as a middle class single woman, she can be a primary school teacher, but it is clear that she does so only because she has not received a marriage proposal. She has no interest or vocation. The social pressures on her as woman have drained all vocational sparks from the time of adolescence when she passed from being a serious student to being a typical middle class Mexican woman, waiting to get married. The prognosis of this life-style is emptiness. The same comes forth as she sees herself as an unmarried secretary or nurse. The future holds only the embittered face of the spinster.

In the second scene, she is dressed like a prostitute. She is immediately informed that she must have a pimp and a territory in which to sell herself, and that she must hand over part if not all of her earnings to him. An experienced whore takes her aside to advise her on methods, telling her that the most important part of her job is to sell herself to her customers as a victim of some man and to never suggest that she is a prostitute by choice. Men want to feel superior to the woman they have sexual intercourse with, the prostitute explains, for most of them would not be able to get aroused unless they felt that they were ravaging a poor defenseless creature. The experienced professional tells Lupita that this job demands payment in advance. "After they have unloaded on you, they don't want to know you." The psychology of *machismo* is, of course, the basis for the scene.[6]

The third scene begins with Lupita lying in bed listening to her own voice on a tape recording. It is a letter she plans to send to a newspaper advice column for the lovelorn. The recorded letter is based on a collection of empty, rhetorical circumlocutions and cliche-ridden pink prose taken from "True Confessions." Lupita's real situation comes out in her dialogue with her maid. She is living in a well-appointed prison, having nothing to look forward to, knowing that eventually she will be cast out in favor of a younger woman. She is isolated, bored, and, most of all, anxious. She has learned to live a life of pretense which she tries desperately to believe in. The language of "True Confessions" supplies her with the means, but reality keeps intruding. Her lover first visits every day, then every other day, then once a week. Then he begins to cancel.

The reporter of the fourth situation has been assigned to interview prominent women in public life. She finds, to her dismay, that they are all manipulated and dominated by men. None of them can begin to think for themselves.

The last scene unfolds after Lupita tries on the last wig, "the cutting edge." She is giving a lecture to a group of chic women who are interested in acquiring a little culture in the same way that they want to try on the latest fashion from Paris or New York. Lupita is a model of elegance as she prepares to give her lecture, but it is evident that this is the act of a pseudo-intellectual who would drop everything at the slightest possibility of marriage within her social and economic class. She begins her lecture announcing that the topic planned for that day will be postponed because there is a more pressing and urgent matter: there has been an attack on the traditional values of Mexican womanhood. Lupita tells her four students (who are identified by number) that the attack is specific and is directed against the holy abnegation of Mexican mothers; against the virtue of wives; against the chastity of brides; in other words, against all of the proverbial virtues of Mexican women, virtues on which the most solid institutions are founded—the family, the church, and the nation.

The only student to respond is #4, who says that it must not be so important since it has not been prohibited by government censorship. Lupita responds that this is so because Mexico is a democratic nation and respects freedom of expression.

Lupita goes on to identify the offending piece as *The Eternal Feminine*, a play written by the shameless Rosario Castellanos, who is not only not married, but is also divorced. Lupita makes a call for action. Out of the sometimes senseless discussion, slowly, a thought emerges that perhaps they ought to form a political party in order to defend Mexican women. When one of them suggests that they ought to demonstrate for women to get the right to vote, Lupita informs her student that Mexican women have had the right to vote for the last twenty-six years, since 1946. In practice, the right to vote was not extended to Mexican women until 1953.[7] It is at this point that woman #4, who has been silent most of the time, begins to take on the role of political leader for the discussion. Her statements, taken together, make up a Mexican feminist manifesto. The farce has become pointed with direct political commentary.

In the context of the political status of women in Mexico, woman #4 says that with or without the right to vote, Mexican women continue to be oppressed. Now clearly in control of the discussion, she launches her challenge; whatever order one takes, it all adds up to the same result: the uselessness of women in present society. Lupita, who is desperately trying to regain some authority, challenges her to come up with an alternative, suggesting that perhaps she wants to propose a Kingdom of Amazons. But woman #4 responds with irony that in Mexico's environment, the structure of the beehive would be more appropriate. Amidst the pandemonium that reigns, a number of political structures are thrust forward. First is, of course, the patriarchal structure with its authority grounded in the Bible. Again #4 counters: "The Bible is a very beautiful book that one should read, that one should enjoy, but that one doesn't have to take literally. According to Engels in his treatise *The Origin of the Family, Private Property and the State*, woman's condition is nothing more than a superstructure of the economic system and of the way wealth is distributed" (355). Lupita, trying to regain the initiative, adds: "And Bachofen proves the historical existence of matriarchy."[8] The superficiality of Lupita's remark is fully exposed by #4.

She takes Lupita's remark of pseudo-learning and turns it to decisive advantage: What else is the Mexican family? she argues. *Machismo* is the mask of our society behind which Tonantzin (the Nahuatl goddess associated with the Virgin of Guadalupe) acts by deceit. Mexican males dominate society, and Mexican women lie, cheat, and manipulate men in order to share in the spoils. She argues: "Bad faith, in the Sartrean sense of the term, is what makes our backbone so flexible" (355). The idea that the natural order of human evolution passes from matriarchy in ancient times to patriarchy in modern times, argues #4, has been turned into the foundation of a society of deceit and manipulation—in brief, the present, the epitome of bad faith that is the Mexican family. Lupita, astonished, asks #4 if she has seen the play; she responds that she does not have to see the play to be able to think for herself.

Not seeking to continue in an adversarial position, #4 retorts that it is time to act. After hearing out a number of proposals, including the Christian Family Movement and U.S. feminism, #4 inquires if there is not another way, a third way that is not traditional patriarchy or made in the United States. The third way has to reach to the heart of the problem. It's not enough to adapt to a society that changes superficially, while its roots remain the same. It's not good enough to imitate the models proposed for us that are answers to circumstances other than our own. It isn't even enough to discover who we are. We have to invent ourselves.

In this dialogue, the discussion develops from the simple-minded structure of a bifurcated society of masters and slaves to a glimpse of a sick society of bad faith where men exploit women and women cheat and manipulate men. Castellanos understands that the social and cultural climate of Mexico has some elements in common with patriarchal social structures everywhere, but that it also shares common characteristics of underdevelopment and national servility with other third world countries. But the unique configuration of Mexican society and its ills, Castellanos asserts, calls for an autochthonous response, and that response, she says, is nothing less than inventing a new Mexican woman.

The parody and satire of the play has given way to direct exposition. On the whole, the play has made fun of men and women in the roles they play, and the mutual deceit with which they live. The third act serves to sum up the entire play and to give it direction; thus it is that in this act we hear women discussing the reality of women's compliance with their portrayal as sex objects, the never-too-often-repeated admonition that maternity is the sacred duty and primary function of a Mexican woman, that the family structure depends on woman's abnegation, that this is her most important role in society. We are also made aware of the economic and social power which perpetuates a master/slave relationship between men and women. The dialogue brings forward a number of models taken from history, anthropology, discourses on nature, and, of course, the Bible. Through all of this debate there is a growing critique of the malaise of Mexican society and a call for a plan of action. The conclusion is the radical one of making a new Mexican woman in response to the particular circumstances of Mexico. If we read the play, or see it presented, against the background of the author's declaration of feminist principles, we can understand why Rosario Castellanos was a leading voice in the Mexican feminist movement and, after her untimely death in 1974, why she has become recognized as its first modern writer.

In *The Eternal Feminine* there is a crisis of female identity because the social image through which women are to establish their social identity is bogus. It was made by men, for their convenience and pleasure. No woman who reflects on her own aspirations within society can find herself in it. There is no way that the female fictive person can realize her social self in this patriarchal objectification of women. She is either presented from the outside in terms of the waves she creates, or metafictionally, as playing a role in the script the social system has given her in order to survive. But what is it that survives? Where can one find a female fictive person in the sense of being a center of consciousness who belongs to society as a free participant?

Luisa Josefina Hernández (1928–) has proven to be one of Mexico's leading female writers and a major exponent of woman's reality.[9] She vehemently objects to being considered a feminist; she sees feminism as a fashionable attempt to solve a problem which is inherent in the feminine condition. According to her, women have always had to find ways to assert their rightful place in society without destroying it. Although her work is not recognized outside of Mexican professional theater circles, she insists that she does not have any professional constraints that can in any way be attributed to the fact that she is a woman. She has published both plays and novels continuously at a pace that makes her one of the most prolific writers of Mexico.

La fiesta del mulato (The mulatto's orgy; written in 1966 but not published in Spanish until 1979; English translation 1971) is a play that depends on rapid changes of scenery, lighting effects, dance, and, above all, music to make its dramatic statement. The reader of the play must compensate for the absence of the performance experience through a careful reading and mental enactment of the stage directions.

The play is set in the mining city of Guanajuato in 1799, that is, about a decade before the beginning of the Mexican movement for independence from Spain. The ineffective colonial structure of civil and religious authority serves as a background. The cast includes sixteen characters, but only one is eventually given a specific name: in the beginning of the play, she is merely the mulatto's wife or the *mestiza*, but as the play progresses she is called by name, María Antonia. In the ensuing play-within-the-play, she plays the part of the Marquesa de Cruilles, whose portrait is part of the dramatic situation. The mulatto and his wife become the central focus of the play, but the *indio*, the mulatto's servant, and his new-found friend, the friar, are the "focalizers." It is through their eyes that we see the dramatic action; the *indio* is gregarious, and the friar, who represents the viceroy, has to be won over.

In total there are twenty separate scenes set in two different time sequences: first, the fiesta and the incidents leading up to it, and second, the trial of the mulatto and his wife by the mayor, as representative of civil authority, and the two priests, who represent the church. There are also twenty separate interventions by the focalizers (the *indio*, who also takes part in the dramatic action, and the friar, who is both audience to the dramatic action and commentator on it). The play ends when the focalizers merge with the dramatic action.

The dramatic action centers on the sexual fantasy that is played out by the mulatto and his wife and the trial they undergo before the civil and religious authorities, which comes as a consequence of their week-long performance. The play opens with the chance encounter of the friar by the *indio* servant of the mulatto. The lights dim, and the voice of the *indio* narrates, but the narrative begins to unfold as dramatic action when the narrative characters become dramatic personae. The *indio* takes up his persona with the dramatic action, leaving his role as commentator and narrator, but switching back when the friar wishes to discuss what has been represented in the play-within-the-play. The dramatic action moves back and forth among the scenes of the mulatto's fiesta, the preparation for his trial, and the trial itself.

The action begins when the *indio* seeks out the mulatto to inform him that the richest vein of gold yet discovered has been found in the Mari Sánchez mine, which the mulatto owns with two partners from Mexico City. The mulatto immediately orders a week-long fiesta to be held at the entrance of the mine. Nothing is to be spared; there must be musicians and servants to serve all the food and drink that the workers from the mine and the townspeople can consume. But for himself he asks only to make love to the Marquesa de Cruilles. He knows her from a painting that hangs in the mayor's palace. The *indio*, as *mayordomo* (butler) of his master the mulatto, sees to it that all is done as he has been instructed: that the musicians and servants are hired, the food and wine are purchased, the fiesta is organized and begins at once, and, most important of all, that the Marquesa goes to the mulatto. The *indio*'s solution to this problem is very simple; his mistress, the mulatto's wife, is extraordinarily beautiful and strongly resembles the woman in the painting. Thus, he asks her to dress up like the marquesa. She willingly obliges without losing sight either of the requirements of acting or the demands of the part she is to play; that is, she becomes an actress. The *indio* takes her to the mulatto dressed up like the marquesa, wearing a dress that is identical to the one in the painting. The resemblance is so remarkable that the painting appears to have come to life. The mulatto receives his wife as if she were the marquesa. He is not surprised; he is overjoyed. The polite conversation between them evokes a stylized image of an aristocratic lady courted by the mulatto in Venice; Desdemona is being greeted by Othello. The acting gives way to their sexual desire. He reminds her of their actual situation in Guanajuato and calls her by name, María Antonia, before they make love.

The scene changes to the city hall; the woman stands on trial accused of imitating the marquesa, that is, of pretending to be another person; the mayor and the priests are judge and jury. She replies that she is the legitimate wife of the mulatto and that it is no sin for husband and wife to have sexual intercourse even if it is out in the woods and not in their own bedroom. One of the priests persists: why did she willingly put on the dress similar to the one in the painting and adopt the personality of another woman? Her reply is direct: she did it so that the mulatto would want to make love to her. The priests cannot understand sexual fantasy and accuse her of being bewitched into thinking she was another person. She protests vehemently. She insists that she has always known who she is, the mulatto's woman. The mayor leaps up and asks her to swear that on the Bible. She replies that she will willingly swear that she has always known that she was herself and not anyone else. The mulatto is brought into the courtroom. When he sees her, he addresses her by name, María Antonia, but as soon as he does, she begins to play the part of the marquesa. The mayor triumphantly declares to the mulatto that this woman, who is dressed like the Marquesa de Cruilles, wife of the old viceroy of New Spain, is in fact his wife and that her impersonation has been a masquerade. The mulatto and his wife look into each other's eyes, and when she is asked to swear before God who she is, she responds that she is the Marquesa de Cruilles and that she belongs, body and soul, to the mulatto. Amidst all the shouting and clamor of the priests and the mayor, the mulatto calmly and firmly tells her: "Thank you, María Antonia" (326).

The scene switches back to the time of the mulatto's fiesta. The *indio* assists his mistress in the daily sojourn from the city house to the site of the fiesta near the mine so that she can once again make love to the mulatto as the marquesa. In their conversation, María Antonia confesses to the *indio* that in order to play her part better, she has convinced herself that she is the marquesa; when she is not actually playing the part, she tells him, she thinks of nothing else, and her identification with the marquesa has become so powerful that she has taken the painting from the mayor's palace. At the end of each night of celebration outside the mine, María Antonia takes leave and returns to her home in the city, escorted by the *indio*. There she rests throughout the day in order to resume the fiesta at sunset. During each of these days and nights of the fiesta, María Antonia and the mulatto have gained a sense of each other as their necessary complements; they both now feel that they are each other's indispensable other half and that only when they are together are they complete. In other words, that their identity is intimately tied up with their physical and spiritual union with the other. The play ends when the friar, the commentator on the performance that has been staged for his benefit by the *indio*, intervenes with the authority of the viceroy to overrule the mayor and the priests and to free the mulatto and his wife after months of imprisonment.

The play develops a central issue of feminist psychoanalytic thinking: the relationship between woman's identity as an individual and as a social persona. The central question as posed by feminist psychoanalysts like Luce Irigaray (*This Sex Which Is Not One*) is: what reality, independent of her reproductive function, can a woman respond to? Women's individual and social personae are contradictory in a profound way. Women as individuals are an equal to men and, in some not-too-distant future, may even enjoy the same economic, social, and political rights as men. But as social personae, women must preserve and maintain the social code of femininity. The social value placed on woman as a persona is directly tied to her maternal and to her seductress roles, that is, to her so-called femininity. In other words, in the social order, women are objects, products that have been produced and packaged, through extensive effort and expense, to be used and exchanged by men. As merchandise, as commodities, as subjects, women have had no authority in the social order.

This aspect of the identity crisis of María Antonia as herself and María Antonia as the marquesa is developed in the play and is highlighted by such expressions as "I only did it so that he would want me" (235) and "I belong body and soul to this man" (326). Clearly this is the language of woman as sexual commodity. When the Holy Office of the Inquisition questioned her about her impersonation of the marquesa, María Antonia could not understand their concern. After all, what could be more commonplace than a woman dressing up to play a part in the sexual fantasy of a man? As a woman, this is what she has learned to do in a life where the roles she plays are those designated by the central casting of patriarchal society. Women always play parts that they have been given and there is no question of creating their own. Mexican women in the colonial period, and to a large extent in the contemporary Mexican social order, have three ages, each involving contradictory social roles to play: as an adolescent she is a dutiful daughter and a nubile virgin, but she is also the siren seductress; as married woman she is the obedient servant of her husband as lover and housekeeper, and has become the sole custodian of his honor because other men desire to possess her more than ever; as mother, she is the venerated giver of life to her husband's children, and as such, must become sexless for them and, at the same time, continue to be a wife to her husband. The script of these parts is inscribed in the entire discourse of interpersonal relations. María Antonia can quite openly say: what is all the commotion about? I played a part to please my husband. Patriarchal social institutions of church and state are devoid of logic, and even of common sense, because the discourse of this society is not rational; it is the discourse of power and domination.

María Antonia is alienated not because she does not know who she is; indeed, she knows very well that she is a miner's wife and that she must play the part of seductress to keep him. It is the social order of church and state that alienates her from society by throwing her in prison because she is doing what she must in order to survive in the male-dominated world in which she lives. She can identify with the part she is playing just as the marquesa, as a woman, also had to act her role. The release from prison does not signify any degree of comprehension of the woman's split identity, but is merely a way to reward the wife for a part well played. We have to look elsewhere for an introspective view into female identity.

María Luisa Puga's (1944–) "Inmóvil sol secreto" (Secret and immobile sun) was published in 1979.[10] The story, written in the form of a diary (but without dates), is narrated in the first person by an unnamed young woman. There are fifty-four paragraphs in the narrative, most of them short (some as short as one or two lines), with a few long descriptive or introspective passages. The narrative time consists of less than three full months. The place is the village of Fiskhardo, located on the northern point of the Greek island of Cephalonia, one of the largest islands in the Ionian group. The legendary Ithaca is visible to the east. The plot is simple and direct: a young woman and a man go to spend some time on the island in order to renew their relationship and so that he can write. The idea is to escape from the turbulence of life in cities like Mexico City or Buenos Aires. Enrique has ambitions to be a novelist; the narrator, who does not give her name, has no specific plans. Most of all, she is dissatisfied, and agrees to join Enrique in this escape to break the pattern of her life. She also goes because she feels guilty for having hurt him, even though she has never loved him or promised him anything. They were lovers before, but she left him for another man. She lets herself be taken in by the lie that they can leave the past behind and begin their relationship anew, letting herself believe that the important objective now is to find peace and thereby a new relationship. She admits to herself that she cannot avoid the feeling of guilt for having caused him such grief before. The feeling of guilt is chained in a causal relationship with his jealousy. If he is jealous of her, it must be because she is guilty of betrayal. She observes him closely, trying in vain to see behind his mannerisms, gestures, and speech. Slowly, from this continuous search for herself in him, she begins to think about her need of him and about guilt and betrayal. The story takes a decisive shift when she decides that she will write an account of their stay on the island. She tells herself, and now us as her readers, that she decided she must do something to occupy herself while he reads and writes notes for the book he is going to write.

She takes the routine of their activities as the narrative pattern of her discourse. The narrator begins with description, but slowly moves into introspection. Somehow the writing itself has become a kind of self-analysis. Conscious that she is writing for readers about what she sees, does, and thinks, she is only vaguely aware of the fact that her writing is taking her deeper and deeper into questioning her feelings of guilt. The couple remain on the island for almost three months, long enough to establish a way of life, and they develop a delicate balance, sharing their lives in almost complete isolation from society. The narrator records her own thoughts and speculates about her partner's thoughts. When she tells Enrique of her intention to write about their experience on the island, he becomes violent; she is surprised to find that his silence was not the inner peace she had taken it to signify. The narrator describes their routine as a sad resignation in which both of them have given up trying to understand each other and are just swimming with the inertia of time, which takes them from the house to the beach, from the beach to the café, and then to bed.

After Enrique gets over his tantrum, he admits that she might well be able to write, but adds, ironically, that now in addition to being unfaithful, she will also be an intellectual. The final break between the couple comes in the third month, when she receives a postcard from her other lover, Enrique's rival. Enrique locks himself up in a hard, remorseless shell of antagonism. She now just waits for him to announce the end. But why must she wait for the man to act in order to react? Is it possible that this is the only meaning of guilt? As a sexual object, she has to wait for men to act, and then she is responsible in some unarticulated way for their action. She is the lure, the bait, and, therefore, the cause. Not fully grasping the significance of her feelings, she gets up from the table in the cafe where she has gone to write and walks over to the table of the gringo with "the dark eyes" who has been her unacknowledged admirer from the day they arrived in the village, and goes off with him. From him she goes to make love with Enrique; she describes making love for the last time with Enrique as the first time it was good. The next day they go their separate ways.

The plot is simple linear development from the time they arrive on the island until they leave. There are no flashbacks to their lives before; nor are there other stories for the characters that surround them in the island village. The tight concentration on her thought process is indicative of the linguistic as well as cultural isolation in which they live. The climax to the plot comes with the delivery of the postcard from her previous lover. The structure is entirely determined by time and self-analysis, since space and characters are reduced to the bare minimum. The narrator's discourse divides into two parts in a smooth temporal flow of specific moments punctuated by generalized descriptions of routine. The temporal sequence is linear and is divided into six units, three in each part.

The first half is dominated by the first person-plural and describes the place, the action, and the actors. The second is almost entirely introspective and is written in the first-person singular. The first unit of time takes us to the arrival of the couple to the village and covers the first impressions as recalled by the narrator. The second unit recalls a specific moment of their first day and emphasizes the sense of fear and isolation; the third unit has an explicit time frame; it is the recapitulation of their routine, established during the first two weeks in the village. The narrator insists on the importance of the first-person plural for what she has narrated. She feels deeply involved with her other and finds happiness in spite of the dim awareness that the *we* she so highly values is false; for the moment, though, she does not care to probe deeper.

The second part begins with her decision to write and the direct reference to her activity as a writer; the time span is one day in the second month. The discourse has now changed and the *we* has become the singular *I*. The fifth unit of time covers her solitary experiences at the beginning of the third month, culminating with the arrival of the postcard. The last unit of time is a narrative summary of their conflictive relationship, which culminates in her going off with another man and making love with Enrique before separating on the last day.

In this highly concentrated story about a woman and her lovers, there is a subtle development of a fictive self who begins to write, first about herself and Enrique as a couple; gradually, she is drawn to look quite closely at him and slowly begins to examine herself through her writing. She becomes aware of why she insists on writing in the first-person plural and records her intimate responses in a discourse that is completely devoid of sentimentality. She questions why it is that she feels she needs Enrique so much, and recognizes the moments of genuine intimacy as the reason for putting up with his adolescent attitudes, male theatricality, and, above all, his evasion of reality, which he calls "forgetting." The simple structure in six units of time, three narrated as *we* and three as *I*, establishes a tight pattern of ideological disclosure. Her discourse begins with full acceptance of the social system and reflects the very value network that has made her as woman gratuitously guilty.

The first unit, the longest, establishes the narrative situation. The man and woman find themselves alone and isolated in this remote corner of the world. Instead of finding one of those beautiful villages depicted by travel agency folders or the lyrical books on the Greek isles, they arrive at a poor, dusty village, with unbearable heat and a squalid room to live in. There are no distractions, so they cannot help but to be involved with each other constantly.

The two most significant passages are paragraphs 12 and 20. In the first, the narrator describes a dog tied to a tree next to the house:

There is a dog tied to one of the olive trees; he runs around the tree tirelessly until he is completely wound up round the tree and then he begins to run in the contrary direction. When he gets bored with this exercise he jumps up into a tree branch and there appears to meditate for the longest time, barking from time to time without any special purpose. He has been there for six years. (367)

There is no comment by the narrator; that will come much later. In paragraph 20 she writes: "I saw, or for a second time discovered in him, after having unforgivably forgotten him, his enviable and suspicious calmness, his desire to live his way" (368). But why is it that the narrator has to be forgiven for having forgotten Enrique? What sort of betrayal is it to have not loved someone who wants you?

The second temporal unit establishes the personal and interpersonal situation of two people in isolation. The existential situation is presented: "Enrique spoke of a thousand things, he kept speaking, empty talk, about syncretism and alternation, which he loved to bring out and he vehemently simulated a certain naturalness, and we both played the game of pretending to be in a cafe anywhere in the world. At that moment we were afraid, both of us" (369). They are isolated in a remote place without a common language with others to communicate basic thoughts. She thinks this situation is due to his being so jealous and her feeling guilty for provoking the jealousy.

The third unit establishes the new pattern of life they have made for themselves. They eat, sleep, talk, and move about in each other's company. There are few couples in any society who could survive such a test if they were not already totally interdependent. She feels utterly alone in this total silence under the blast furnace sun and thinks that she cannot survive without him. Her discourse in this third unit begins as *we* and gradually slips into *I*:

We are immersed in the island . . . We drag ourselves over the cool tiles looking for a corner . . . I feel hopelessly alone, I suffer imagining Enrique fried to death under the sun somewhere . . . My abandoned lover, my nostalgia is a threat that besieges me and that I cannot accept, not in this heat . . . How comforting the plural we is to me. I know that there is a lie there somewhere, and I don't care. (370–372)

The routine and the shared circumstances have given the narrator a sense of belonging to a minuscule unit of two; she has temporarily exiled fear and anguish and holds on to this feeling even if it is not true.

The second part of the text is exclusively her first-person observation of her partner. She observes Enrique's theatricality, the movements of someone who has been in front of the mirror, practicing how to smile. She also recognizes the social roots of this acting as a male code of self-importance called honor. There are moments, however, when Enrique sets aside his role and permits himself to make real contact with her as another person. She takes care to describe his reaction to her telling him that she plans to write about their experience on the island together. The incongruity of her guilt is striking:

Today I told Enrique that I was thinking of writing about what had happened between us. He got angry. He suddenly let loose all the fury he had been holding back these last few months . . . It surprised me that his silence was not the peace I thought to have noted, but rather a growing rancour that finally exploded almost with pleasure. I would like to be able to explain to him that I want to exorcise my nostalgia which is getting out of proportion, that I have to translate to a cold and tangible language that will make it real and vulnerable to time. . . . For the first time I felt how much I had hurt him. I saw his wounded pride on his face and I understood that it was unbearable and suddenly I heard myself speaking as if I were a convalescent who begins to get her spirits up. . . . I see his pain without feeling mine. It is the first time, and the compassion I feel for him is unbearable. I understand that to be sorry does not signify much more than a polite word we give to another and I would like to give him something now. I would give him my unfaithful love as he calls it, but it's clear that won't help him one bit. Nor proof either, proof of what? That I wish I had not loved another? (372–373)

Her observation of Enrique's reactions and the sense of guilt in her are directly tied to her irrational sense of remorse for having been the object of attention of a man she did not love. Slowly her inquiry leads her into the full question of identity and freedom. She presses the examination forward. The notable change to the first-person discourse initiates the gradual disclosure:

I am not sexually attracted by him and he knows it. I make love with him, looking for a way to find him, the same way I do everything else with him alone. I think that he also looks for me, but no, he is looking for something else, not me. In his frantic insistence on always touching me or talking to me all the time, or just that I be there for him to look at me, he is searching for the distinction of another presence. With wariness, with total passivity, an energy that has been over used, I understand that he only wants to know that he has won. . . . It is not me he defends, it is not me he is looking for but only his self-image that he wants to remake. I am his battlefield. (374)

Through the close observation of Enrique in the restricted situation and circumstances of isolation, the narrator, through her writing, slowly gains access to the meaning of their relationship, but she is also on the verge of self-analysis at a deeper level. Because she does not love Enrique, and has sexual relations with him in order to share herself with him—the way she does everything else—she feels terribly alone, even when she is making love. She keeps asking herself what he is looking for in her. Gradually she begins to understand that what he wants is to possess her, like private property, in order to eliminate the remaining presence of her former lover. Patiently, cautiously, he puts all of his effort into one goal: to win, to own her, not for any worth she may have as a person, but only as an object to be possessed. This is the cure for his wounded male pride; such is the nature of self-love and male vanity. She is only the means through which he will remake his shattered male self-image. What, then, she asks, is her role in being a cause for his suffering and her inevitable feeling of guilt? The pattern of introspection is not one of direct confrontation with an alienating social structure but, rather, a subtle process of analysis and inquiry into her relationship with Enrique, which contains, encapsulated, the problems of participation in her society as a whole. The ideology of her world shows up every time she looks closely at her lover.

The fifth unit of the story is a tight first-person narrative of five paragraphs entirely devoted to self-analysis. She is now writing in earnest. Every morning, almost as if to remind herself that she has presence outside of Enrique's tyrannical possessiveness, she goes to the cafe to see if the gringo is still fascinated by her. Comforted by this desire, she can go back to the room to write. The climax of the relationship comes with the delivery of the postcard and Enrique's rage in having to face the fact that he won only temporarily. If she is to him but the cause of this obsessive wounded pride, what is she to herself? she questions. The image of the dog running around the tree is evoked in her description of their routine. She is trapped like the dog.

The last unit of the story consists of six paragraphs, four extremely short ones and two with more elaborate discourse. The sense of disclosure by the fictive person is fully achieved. The male theatricality, of both Enrique and the gringo, gives her the impetus to probe into the meaning of her guilt. The narrator has had three male lovers. The one she had previous to the beginning of the story lingers in her memory as nostalgia for what is past. Ironically, it is his continuing interest in her that comes to end her efforts for making her present lover, Enrique, into more than the man with whom she lives and makes love. The third lover, the gringo, is the silent admirer that she uses to break with Enrique. The most significant part of these three relationships is that the narrator feels guilt only with respect to Enrique. There is no sense of guilt or remorse at having abandoned the sender of the postcard, and there is only a feeling of sadness in taking the gringo as a lover. Yet, in the case of Enrique, she is plagued with a sense of guilt for having left him before, for not being in love with him now, for having wounded his pride, for being other than what he wants her to be. This sense of gratuitous guilt is based entirely on the social condition that denies a woman the right to be herself and imposes a sense of ideological transgression if she is not what the male wants her to be. Of course, she can never be what every male wants her to be (his object, his possession) so she is con-demned to always be guilty of not being the possession of the men who have desired to own her. The objectification of the female in the patriarchal social structure has created the obligation of the woman to be what the man wants her to be. The long tradition of unrequited love poetry which decries the cru-elty of the woman for not becoming the sole possession of the man embodied by the lyric voice is the historical intertext of her ideological self-accusation. But the woman who gives herself to her lovers is castigated even more as the fallen woman. Lacan puts it this way: "One lack is superimposed upon the other. The dialectic of the objects of desire, insofar as it creates the link be-tween the desire of the subject and the desire of the Other . . . now passes through the fact that the desire is not replied to directly" (215).

She has lived with and made love to the adolescent-minded Enrique for three months, in virtual isolation, and yet she can feel guilt because she receives a postcard from a man to whom she has not written or even given her address. The sense of absurdity of the situation is with us only momentarily before we recall the hatred heaped upon women because an unrequited lover has killed himself. The logical impossibility of being able to be the sole possession of all the males who covet her is the absurdity which derives from patriarchal ob-jectification. Women as objects of desire are, of course, incompatible with women as social persons. Patriarchal ideology has denied women access to es-tablished avenues of taking their place in society as persons. When the narrator finally understands her situation, she knows that she is guilty because of the very fact that she is a woman and that Enrique is jealous because he is a man, and that is the condition to which their society has chained them. In order to break the chains of her gratuitous guilt, she must clearly and openly transgress her status as property. She breaks the bonds of guilt that have kept her tied to Enrique by getting up from the table in the cafe and taking up her third lover. The conclusion of the story is almost telegraphic in its brevity, but very full in its implications. When she returns to the room she is able to make love with Enrique for the first time without restraint or falseness because she is no longer his possession. There is no guilt if there is no broken obligation. She has an obligation to herself, and that obligation is incompatible with her becoming the object or possession of anyone.

María Luisa Puga took the title of her story from *The Labyrinth of Solitude* by Octavio Paz. In chapter 2, "Mexican Masks," the Mexican poet describes the sexual role Mexican tradition has given women. They are the unmoved movers. Woman awaits disdainfully as the male cavorts around her. She is the center of this universe, a magnetic passive polar force. She attracts and pas-sively receives; she does not seek and at the center of her magnetic force is her hidden passive sexuality: "It is a secret and immobile sun" (38). The narrator persona of Puga's story understands her cosmological analogy, rejects it, and breaks with it by taking the gringo as her lover. Her action breaks with her ideological role.

A sociofeminist interpretation of this short story is distinguishable from other readings insofar as this interpretation examines the creative tension of the text from the point of view of being a woman in the social world. In my project, the issue is the problem of identity for the female in a social system that has objectified woman as private property. The fictive self of this story has discovered the sense of liberation that comes only with transgression of the social, alias, moral code.

The three women I have discussed—woman #4 in *The Eternal Feminine*, María Antonia/marquesa in "The Mulatto's Orgy," and the narrator in "Secret and Immobile Sun"—are three fictive selves who are conscious of their status in society and who seek through whatever means possible to gain a social identity. Woman #4, as a feminist, calls for a new paradigm of female/male relations. María Antonia finds a place for herself in her lover's eyes, but only by trickery; she must play the part of another woman. She must, paradoxically, be another woman in order to be the woman her lover wants. The narrator of *"Secret and Immobile Sun"* seeks herself in her lover and finds that she is nothing more than compassion and gratuitous guilt until she transgresses her role as woman, object of desire. These three fictive women are all involved in the crisis of self-identity as social persons. They all have roles assigned to them because of their sex and not because of their own needs or skills. Whether as a wealthy married woman going to a fashionable session with the frustrated pseudo-intellectual Lupita, or as the wife of a miner who wants above all to be appealing to her husband, or as a young woman running off to a Greek island in search of herself and to work off her sense of guilt for being an objectified woman, they are all faced with the same reality: if they are to achieve any degree of personal fulfilment, they must subvert their roles, and if they are ever to find any meaning in their place in society, they must transgress the social code, as they all do in one way or another.

Woman #4 rebels openly against the system in words, but she knows that is not enough; she must act. María Antonia makes love dressed up like the marquesa because she wants her husband to want her; she is aware that she is playing a part, but she knows that is what she must do as a woman in her society; she plays the part asked of her but she plays it for advantage. She has been imprisoned for impersonation of another woman; the difference between this act and her normal condition as a woman escapes her. She cannot be herself; she must always be someone else in order to comply with her role. The young woman of "Secret and Immobile Sun" gains an understanding of the alienation she endures as a woman who is always an objectified other in society. Her transgression is calculated to free her and gain her own identity. She is able to make love openly only after she has broken with her otherness of gratuitous guilt.

The three fictional representations are very different. Only that of María Luisa Puga's story can be said to be a female fictive self in the sense of being a center of consciousness. All three women are from different periods, and, most importantly, in spite of the differences of time, space, and representation, all three express aspects of the problem of self-identity of Mexican women. Each in her own way embodies a principle of Mexican life. The way of living they represent is always a compound of negative and positive forces pulling them, one way or another, but always in a situation of alienation from their own society. They seek to belong and participate in society; they want to do what is expected of them, and they want to be appreciated as individuals.

I began this chapter with the open question of why there are so few female fictive selves in Mexican literature. The relative absence of these centers of consciousness is not a matter of a lack of talent or interest among the principal male writers; nor is it a matter of specific formal configuration. It is primarily a question of the ideological process of world-making. Writers use language to construct their particular perspectives of reality, and male writers consequently start from a worldview which they assume to be general, but which is strongly conditioned by male values. Even when they openly seek to question or challenge these values, as Carlos Fuentes does admirably in his short novel "Mother's Day," they can deconstruct the monolithic mirage of patriarchal supremacy, but they do not create a woman's sense of space, a female center of consciousness.

It takes more than being female, and having talent, to produce female fictive selves; there must also be a climate of reception that can recognize the validity of a woman's center of consciousness. It is in a female literate population that the configuration of women's space will be found. The woeful statistics of literacy and lack of higher education for women in Mexico are the hard factual truths underlying the absence of the woman's perspective in Mexican literature.

Verbal discourse is, above all, a social phenomenon, and every society imposes belief systems on what is appropriate and what is inappropriate for women, but restricts males only on the basis of criminal activity. It follows that there is a recognizable woman's sense of world which is determined in large measure by the social structure. It is from within this space, where women are at home, that they inhabit reality, create fictional worlds, and, ultimately, challenge the ideological constraints that limit what they can include in this female space.

The development of a female fictive self comes about as women participate actively in the world-making process. The creation of an androgynous neutral space is impossible because it does not account for the power of the social structure; the escapist pink ghetto of a closed world is equally false, since men and women continue to share, albeit unevenly, the reality of social interaction. The significance of the female fictive self is that it is a center of consciousness from which the process of world-making takes place for women. In Mexico it is entirely a question of infusing this woman's space with freedom.

Six

Identity and the Other as Myself

Elena Poniatowska

Testimonial literature involves direct use of a subject's experience and the narrative structuring of the subject's story.[1] There are, of course, a number of historical novels and not a few biographies and autobiographies that qualify for inclusion in a general way. There is, however, a stricter use of the term in which the subject's testimony is clearly differentiated and stands as one voice in a world not chosen by the speaking subject yet is a voice that is clearly responsive to social forces beyond the individual. Only a few novels have had this testimonial voice in full context, and usually this has been accomplished by the skillful use of first-person and third-person narrative voices. Testimonial literature also encompasses a direct historicity of the testimony such as that we find in well-researched biography. Several examples of biography make extensive use of the subject's own views.[2] In this case, the biographer provides the context and the contributing subject provides the testimony. This is without a doubt a hybrid genre in which the storytelling, world-making skills of the biographer are closely related to the subject's testimony.

This hybrid genre of testimonial biography in recent years has developed rapidly and has become a major source for breaking the silence in which women, especially illiterate women, have lived for centuries in Latin America. Traditionally, state and church authorities considered the written word, quite correctly, as an issue of *entitlement*. As long as women did not write—or at least did not read—their orbit of effective action, even for the most extraordinary, was extremely restricted. Because the colonial economy depended on a large disenfranchised sector of the population as a source of labor, those in power discouraged literacy, and both ecclesiastic and civil authorities declared that it was detrimental to the welfare of society for women to learn to write. Of course, the racial and class structures of Mexico also functioned as rigid societal forces that controlled the population. The point I am making is that irrespective of social class and race, the females constituted the service sector for the males—a service sector that was largely unremunerated and completely disenfranchised (see Francesca Miller, 35–67, esp. 39).

Although these social structures were developed during the colonial centuries of Spanish and Portuguese rule, they have persisted into our time. Paradoxically, when women of the upper classes became literate in the early nineteenth century, they rapidly became the dominant sector of the reading public, so that by 1840 a novelist or poet in Latin America could expect to address an audience that was made up primarily of women. In the Mexico of the mid-twentieth century, there was still a clear differentiation between the sexes in education. Higher education was for men since they were to be the "bread winners" and protectors of their women. Young women of the upper and middle classes were essentially being trained for marriage, going from their father's domain to that of the husband's. Women of the lower classes could aspire to serving their own families and in the homes of the middle and upper classes. Thus, theirs was a double servitude.

The second half of the twentieth century has been a time of growing emancipation for women in all of Latin America, and part of that emancipation has been the entitlement of the written word. This emancipation began differently throughout Spanish-speaking America. In Argentina and Chile, it was born from outrage at gross violation of human rights. In Guatemala, it was a response to genocide; in Bolivia and Mexico, a response to centuries of social injustice. But in all cases, it was because there was a new generation of women who began to write, as reporters or as university faculty, and by the 1970s books by more than a token few began to appear throughout Latin America. Their numbers were very small,—some would say minute—but they had found that the key to having a public voice was writing in the daily newspaper.

Testimonial fiction by Latin American women transformed testimonial biography, and a new configuration of a hybrid genre was born out of necessity when two women pushed back the boundaries of illiteracy, the orality of life stories, the oppression of sexism, and created a symbiotic relationship of narrator and subject. A cross section of this writing can be introduced by examining the following four landmark texts. First, Jesusa Palancares and Elena Poniatowska's *Hasta no verte, Jesús mío* (1969; Until we meet again) presents the point of view of a woman of the lower classes in her struggle for survival during most of Mexico's tumultuous twentieth century. Jesusa tells her extraordinary life story as revolutionary, servant, and, finally, washerwoman in the barrios of

Mexico City. Second, there is Domitila Barrios de Chungara and her narrator Moema Viezzer's testimonial *Si me permiten hablar* . . . (1978; Let me speak . . .). This is the testimony of a Bolivian miner's wife, who speaks with simplicity of her life and the harsh realities of exploitation.[3] Third, we have Rigoberta Menchú and her collaborator Elizabeth Burgos-Debray's *Me llamo Rigoberta Menchú y así me nació la conciencia* (1983; I Rigoberta Menchú: An Indian woman in Guatemala), which narrates the story of a people's struggle for survival; Rigoberta is a Quiché native of Guatemala. As she tells her life story, she relates her account of military atrocities against her people, and she pleads for justice and her people's right to existence.[4] Fourth, there is Hebe de Bonafini and her narrator Matilde Sánchez's *Historias de vida* (1985; Stories of life), which speaks with eloquent simplicity about human dignity in the face of unspeakable cruelty by the military. Hebe de Bonafini is one of the founders of the Mothers of the Plaza de Mayo in Argentina, and this is her story of abuse of power and the tragic loss of her two sons and daughter-in-law at the hands of the Argentine military.[5]

Hasta no verte, Jesús mío (1969) was the text that opened up the genre of testimonial fiction; it exemplified the efficacy of two women working in collaboration. It has historical significance, but it is also a remarkable narrative work of art. This is a breakthrough text because it bridges the oral tradition with the literate mainstream of present-day Mexico. Its strength lies in that it is testimonial and not well-intentioned condescension and it has given women like Jesusa a public voice. Cynthia Steele's study of *Hasta no verte, Jesús mío* has provided us a close analysis of the nature and the extent to which a deep spirit of collaboration developed between the two women. The life, language, and personality of Jesusa Palancares were drawn from a year-long series of interviews Jesusa gave Elena Poniatowska; they developed a "close but difficult dynamics" (31). Steele, working from Poniatowska's notes, reconstructs the difficult process through which these two women eventually overcame the obvious differences of social class, education, economic status, and age, which Steele calls "the complex pattern of approach-avoidance, of trust and respect alternating with rebellion, that Poniatowska describes in the older woman's behavior toward her" (32).

But how important is it for these women of the lower classes to have gained access to the written word? Just what is it that I mean when I say that writing by women in Latin America is synonymous with entitlement? The function of narrativity is nothing less than the shaping of our temporal experience, and written narrativity, because it is released from the circumstances of production, can become an instrument of unlimited creativity or distortion in service of a discourse of power. Both testimonial fiction and the pre-aesthetic decorative arts (see Introduction) are genres that cross the boundaries between fact and fiction, between utilitarian need and imaginative configuration, because they both exceed the limits of established paradigms of representation. A woman's life can be narrated in as many different ways as writers can devise, but a woman's life as narrated in testimonial fiction is both a bearing witness and a sympathetic construction of the contexts for the story. It reads like fiction, has the imaginative structure of fiction and the dramatic reenactment of events, but it is also steeped in the personal history of the subject, for there is at stake much more than the narration of another life story; there is, above all, the construction of a woman's space in a world that has exiled her from having a public space and that has fixed, prescribed circumstances for her activity: the kitchen, the bedroom, the hospital as nurse, the primary school as teacher, the convent, or the brothel. The crossing of boundaries serves to break with traditional genres but, of more consequence, to map out a woman's space that is hers and not that prescribed by society.

Carlos Fuentes' subversion of the social narrative codes opens up the issue, but female identity can be realized only within a woman's space, and this is above all the achievement of Elena Poniatowska. First in *Hasta no verte, Jesús mío* (1969) and, subsequently, in *Querido Diego, te abraza Quiela* (1978; Dear Diego, 1986) and *La "Flor de lis"* (1988), this prolific writer has given us one of the richest configurations of women's space in Mexico.[6]

Elena Poniatowska was born in Paris in 1933 and has lived in her mother's native Mexico since 1942;[7] she has been writing since 1954 and is today the most successful woman writing in Mexico.[8] The narrating persona that is Jesusa Palancares in *Hasta no verte, Jesús mío* is neither an autobiographical narrator nor a fictional narrator but rather a hybrid enunciating voice that retains the language, point of view, and personality of the subject Jesusa, but that is at the same time a narrator who works through a well-structured stream of emplotment. Poniatowska's Jesusa retains her authenticity because she has all the characteristics of an author and yet expresses herself in her own idiom and with her unique sense of values and of the world. These characteristics of narration have the capacity to describe scenes and incidents, to narrate action, and to project opinion and judgment on the effects of the action.

Jesusa's voice has the expressive range of her social class and age. She uses language that hitherto had not appeared in literature, with the possible exception of limited dialogue of fictional characters in the work of Rulfo and others.[9] But the remarkable aspect of this text is that this old woman from Mexico's lowest social stratum is the narrator and she speaks directly to her implicit interlocutor, who in the reading experience becomes the reader herself or himself. This mode of speaking directly in the idiom of the *vecindad* (tenement) has been present in Mexico for more than forty years, but always within the very limited medium of popular comics and cinema, and never with the claim that this is valid testimony of the speaker's life story.[10] *Hasta no verte, Jesús mío* is just that: it is the life story of an old woman, born at the beginning of the century, who is now nearing seventy years of age. She recounts her story directly to the reader in the relaxed manner of family narrative. This is a mode of speaking and listening familiar to everyone in her audience, and it maintains all of the detours, sudden moves, flashes of memory, as well as deliberate recounting of specific incidents, all colored by her constant evaluation, opinions, and generalizations of her past, and those who have been part of it.

The book has twenty-nine chapter-like segments which indicate the sequential telling of the story and not the life incidents themselves, although there is a general movement from childhood to youth, adulthood, and old age. The position from which the story is told is that of old age remembering, assessing, and summing up what life means to her.

The story opens with a recounting of Jesusa's escapism through spiritualism and the idea of reincarnation, and it ends some three hundred pages later with an indigenous approximation of Zoroastrian pantheistic values. She claims she does not want a Christian burial, not even a burial; she wants her body to be consumed by vultures in the fields and her remains to become part of the natural cycle of life. She does not believe in the basic goodness of the human being; her view of life is one of a constant struggle for survival. She admires courage and strength of character, but has only scorn for the weak who do not fight back, especially women. Jesusa does not condemn men for being womanizers and abusive; after all, she says, they are only animals. Women have an innate capacity for values higher than mere survival, but they are constantly in a state of slavery and do not know how to break free.

Jesusa recalls the fear her husband instilled in her from the beginning of their marriage. She never looked him in the face and was subject to constant flogging at the slightest provocation or gossip about her. So as not to be seen as an abusive husband, on the pretense of having her wash his clothes, he would take her away from the camp where the army was quartered. Once they were in an isolated place, she would assume an oval position seated on the ground with her arms around her head to protect her face and head from the blows. The lashes poured down on her back and arms until he tired. She often passed out from the beatings. On one particular day when he once again ordered her to go wash his clothes, she hid a pistol and bullets in her pockets. This time he was punishing her because a woman said that Jesusa had sexual intercourse with the paymaster, a man she had never seen. But this time Jesusa rebelled; she pulled out her loaded gun and told him: "Now I am armed, now pull out your weapon and we will settle this" (99). This was the first time she had ever raised her voice to him, the first time she looked him in the face. Frightened, he tried to convince her. She ordered him to walk ahead of her and took him to the woman who had gossiped about her, firing the gun at her feet. Jesusa's husband went through a radical change in his relations with her; he could no longer abuse her.

Some of the most interesting aspects of Jesusa's language are the coded social values. For example, we can examine the words *good* and *bad* when applied to a girl and a woman. A good girl is quiet, obedient, and submissive and does not question her superiors. A bad girl, by contrast, questions, discusses, and does not follow instructions until she is told why she has been ordered to do something. In other words, a good girl is a docile servant of her father and brothers, only to be replaced by the husband and in later life her adult sons. Jesusa says that after the shooting incident she became bad and Pedro good, meaning that he was no longer able to treat her like a submissive woman and she had broken the constraints of her sex. She relates that when Pedro drove her to rebel, she told herself: "I'll defend myself or die trying." This is what Jesusa calls being a bad woman: "If I were not bad I would have allowed Pedro to go on until he killed me from beatings" (101).

The narrative development of this powerful personality is subtle; Jesusa's strong opinions on all aspects of her life are constantly mixed with her eyewitness report of historical events as well as careful descriptions of the participants. She colors everything she describes with rich detail, never showing signs of trying to present herself in an attractive manner: "I was not pretty, that is the least I had and have had" (70). What is more, she demonstrates extraordinary candor about her physical appearance, her lack of education, and the almost complete lack of love in her life: "I am not a loving person, I do not like people. I am cold-natured. I never got attached to anyone" (282). Her approach to sex is animalistic and she denies ever having had any pleasure from sexual activity. It is just what a woman must give a man and that is that: "When Pedro was in the midst of campaign and there were no women there, he did use me . . . I never took off my pants, just pushed them down when he used me" (86).

In chapter 10, Jesusa describes her husband Pedro as a remarkably skillful womanizer who had a woman in every town and as many as he wanted. She does not blame him; she says that it was the women who sought him out, and he obviously could give them something they didn't get from their husbands. They were constantly offering themselves to him and what was he to do "but be a man" who "has no choice but 'cumplirles,' give them the satisfaction they seek" (105). Turning to the question of why he married her, she says that she never gave him affection, never allowed him to kiss her, and never allowed him to treat her with affection or speak to her in the manner of a lover. "I am not used to kissing, for Judas kissed Jesus, and see what came out of it. What nonsense that all is. Let them do what they have the urge to do and let them stop trying to dress it up" (108). Pedro had a good body, but with her there was no sexual foreplay; she would not allow it. He could take his due when she was in bed, but nothing else. She would not even embrace him. She states directly: "This is why I don't know what love is, I have never had love or felt in love, I have not felt anything and I don't think Pedro has either" (108). Her *macho* view of sexual relations as a merely physical act expresses her overwhelming suspicion of all relations with men. Jesusa admires raw courage, strength, and toughness, and all the rest is simple bodily function. In women she despises the weak and submissive but also scorns the sexually active; the former are beasts of burden; the latter bitches in heat.

She portrays herself as a loveless, tough, resilient survivor who thoroughly enjoyed going into combat as the only woman in the cavalry. She fought alongside Pedro and says: "I was never afraid . . . Fear does not exist for me, fear of what? I only fear God. He is the only one who has to turn us to dust. But fear of people in the world, what's fear? If it is one's turn, it is one's turn. It's all the same. That's the way things are" (110).

Her description of battle in the northern campaigns of the Mexican revolution are barbarously simple: you just go out there to kill the others and you try not to get killed yourself. There is absolutely no sign of cause or purpose, just trying to kill those distant figures you know are the enemy in this battle: "All you see are these little figures on horseback. Some are coming, some are going, all are shooting on both sides. If you don't have good aim you miss, but if you do there it is. The little figure on the other side drops. Pedro was a good shot" (110).

As the narrative unfolds, the reader is drawn into a personal relationship with the narrating persona. Jesusa carries her life experiences with her like so many outer coats a clochard would have to remove before the natural form would be visible. Her relations with others and her always strong opinions about the world build up a personality that is clearly rooted in her social and cultural reality. The only other work that I know that has the same kind of social persona interaction is the Brazilian novel *Grande Sertão: Veredas* by João Guimarães Rosa, published in 1956. The notable difference between the two works is that Guimarães Rosa created the language of his narrator from an amalgam of the dialect of Minas Gerais and the particular speech patterns of a number of individuals talking about the devil. In *Hasta no verte, Jesús mío*, the language is the idiom of the lowest class of migrants from rural to urban Mexico at the end of the Mexican revolution (1910–1921), yet the sense of individual appropriation of the idiom is particularly intense in Jesusa's discussion of affection.

She obviously likes animals and likes to care for them. Throughout her story the constant reference to the domestic animals she has nurtured is as close as she ever gets to saying something that does not have the ever-present rock-like cover she has developed for her emotional protection. But since the animals are all killed or leave her, there are always bitter statements even in these remembrances. Jesusa particularly remembers her coyote, "Coyota," that a colonel shot because the animal came to Jesusa's defense. She says: "I dreamed about her. I missed her very much. I needed her . . . I'll never care for animals again. What for? So that someone can kill them?" (117).

Without a doubt, one of the most remarkable aspects of Jesusa's narrative is the uncompromising portrayal of her own shortcomings. In chapter 11 she recalls when the regiment is ordered to set up camp in San Antonio Arenales, in the north of Mexico. In the evenings Pedro would read to the illiterate Jesusa to her great pleasure, but he would not allow her to be a passive listener; he would stop reading and ask her questions, and if she did not understand, he would explain the passage and then reread. And then, she says, "I would understand him much better even though I would still say all the stupid things that came into my head and it is that he never taught me to talk properly, and now all of a sudden he started asking me to explain what I had understood" (115). Jesusa continually refers to herself as *burra*, an ass. She says that years later, in the early 1940s, she thought she had an opportunity to be taught to read and write; she was working in a hospital. There was a national campaign to extend education to those who did not have any. But she ran up against teachers who wanted to talk about nature rather than teach reading to the hospital workers. As usual, Jesusa rebelled: "I'm fed up. If you're not interested in teaching me [to read] tas, tas, cross me off the list. I have to earn my living and don't have the time to lose on the bullshit your graces administer. So you can go and shove it" (202). One learns from what Jesusa says about the instruction given that it is what we would call basic biology at about the second- or third-grade level of primary school. She concludes: "And so I remained ignorant but happy. It is better to bray than to play the part of the dummy" (202). Once again, the aggressiveness and fighting spirit of Jesusa come forth. It is this same character trait that will surface in her opinion on all social issues.

Jesusa Palancares presents a worldview that has all the characteristics of her background and age, but what is constant is her refusal to submit to physical or mental abuse. She will not be taken for granted. No one can take advantage of her with impunity. This generalized attitude is especially noteworthy in her narration of political circumstances and of her relationship with men. On the political front, Jesusa distrusts all political authority in Mexico. She recalls the revolutionary leaders she has met, including Emiliano Zapata and Pancho Villa. She respects the memory of Zapata as a leader who rejected the presidency; she despises Villa for the needless cruelty he inflicted on civilians. But it is her encounter with Lázaro Cárdenas that offers the clearest sense of distrust: she knew him as a soldier and then saw him again as president of Mexico (1934–40). She does not trust anyone in authority, including Cárdenas, because she believes that the only motive that matters in politics is self-interest, and that the political leader will act only when he thinks there is personal advantage to be had.

What unites Jesusa's value judgments on all matters, her prescriptive talk of what should be done or ought to have been done, on the one hand, and her description and recollection of what happened to her, on the other? In this text, the dynamics of the story telling itself mediate the past remembered and the present judgments imposed on that past. The narration of *Hasta no verte, Jesús mío* unfolds a textual world of its own, with a unique admixture of historical truth claims and highly personalized responses. This world, as seen through the memory and opinion of the narrator, has a viable status of another's experience in the reader's own sense of world.

As readers, the major obstacle to overcome is our culturally inscribed bias toward conventional plots and the sense of completeness that they impart. Life itself, it has been said by Paul Ricoeur and others, is a narrative full of inconsistencies and, of course, always radically incomplete for the person who lives it. All versions of one's own life story are a dialectic of remembrance and anticipation of future action. This is the kind of plot we find in *Hasta no verte, Jesús mío*. The narrator is in her last years of life, but she is far from dead. She can remember, assess, judge, and consider tomorrow. She has, in a word, appropriated her past by narrating the story; in a very real sense, order, direction, and identity are the results of the story telling. Jesusa Palancares and her collaborator, Elena Poniatowska, have resurrected what Walter Benjamin called the oral storyteller's art of exchanging experiences. In *Oneself as Another*, Ricoeur comments on Benjamin's views:

He means not scientific observation but the popular exercise of practical wisdom. This wisdom never fails to include estimations, evaluations that fall under the teleological and deontological categories . . . in the exchange of experiences which the narrative performs, actions are always subject to approval or disapproval and agents to praise or blame. (164)

What, we may ask, is the reader's response to Jesusa and to her story, and to both of them together? She is certainly an unsettling storyteller, not only because of her idiom, which is that of the rural Mexicans who migrate to Mexico City, but also because of her powerful personal viewpoint on ethical questions. The reader's response is to take her as an individual and not as a fictional construct. There is a strong implicit personal encounter between the reader and Jesusa. In response to our question of who is speaking, we are confronted with a defiant answer: "Here I am whether you like me or not; you can't ignore me."

Each incident that is narrated rings authentic, whether it is the battlefields of the revolution or her work as a servant of the wealthy in Mexico City. Jesusa considers the Mexican wealthy to be the most abusive employers known to her; she says that women of other cultures give orders and want as much work done for as little pay, but they do not treat their servants like mangy dogs:

That is why when I would inquire about work, I would say: "If it is with Mexicans don't even give me the address, because I am not going." They are my fellow countrymen, but frankly, I can't get on well with them. It is not that foreigners do not command, but they do it in a different way; they are less tyrannical and do not meddle in one's life. (245)

The point I have been stressing is that the very act of narration, of telling this story, is both the mediation between giving an opinion and describing, and a transgression, a subversion of authority. This is not the kind of a story that relates great accomplishments, and this is certainly not the kind of a narrator whose authority is predicated on social or economic status. But still Jesusa goes on and tells her story in her way, in her language. Slowly, the disparate islands of memory are linked together in the telling itself. Jesusa is creating her story, giving it a sense of order instead of merely having distinct memories of one incident or another. The story telling, then, is the story of this text. For, by giving Jesusa a narrative voice, Poniatowska has in fact given her entitlement as a literary persona—not as a fictional character whose many attributes and characteristics are subject to the limitations of the author's imagination and the expansion of the reader's imagination. Jesusa's persona is not constrained as the product of one mind, but the reader is constrained in what he or she may make of Jesusa. For Jesusa is a testimonial persona, and is, thus, as subject to all the factors of life in her time and place as the reader is in hers or his. Yet she, like every human being, has the capacity for reflection, thought, invention, and remembrance.

The testimonial persona is much closer to the autobiographical persona, but with the essential difference that in true autobiography, the narrator needs no mediator. Pseudo- autobiography of celebrities is not being addressed here.

The telling of Jesusa Palancares' life story was the first time a woman of her social class and age was given a voice in Latin America. Others have followed and have been every bit as successful. I mention only Rigoberta Menchú, Domitila Barrios, and Hebe de Bonafini as outstanding examples. These testimonial personae are granted an entitlement to active participation in their respective communities.

In a world of ever-increasing demands on a reader's time, with so many books on diverse topics of art, literature, and science, one might well ask why one should be interested in the life story of an illiterate woman from the lower social classes of Mexico—especially one who is so full of opinion, spiritualist escapism, and narrow interpretations of both historical and domestic incidents. She was not heroic (except, perhaps, for surviving in a very hostile world). Nor is the reason for her significance to be found in the claim that she represents the millions of Mexicans, the majority of the nation, of her social class. She is neither representative nor typical. Jesusa is a unique individual with a strong personal identity notwithstanding some shared cultural traits that are immediately recognizable.

Jesusa's story is important because the reader, by listening to a voice that expresses a a worldview that is neither the dominant ideological one nor an intellectualized rebellion from the lower classes, is exposed to social reality in a very direct way. Jesusa's story represents the entitlement to speak as a person and to be heard as a person who has lived through the most climactic events of Mexican history in the twentieth century. Her story telling draws particular views of life from her language and the notions that this language carries. One of the most notable is the peculiar sense of male honor that demands that if a woman offers herself sexually, a man cannot refuse her, or he will be judged as lacking in virility and manhood. This *macho* code of the male sexual performance is part of the community: "I immediately understood that it was not his fault; he fulfilled his obligations as a man because women were after him for a purpose" (104).

Not only does Jesusa's narrating persona break new ground as a female voice from the lower social classes of Mexico, but also, as a testimonial narrator engaged in the social realities of present-day Mexican life, she confronts readers with personal observations and opinions to which they otherwise would never have had access. It is a reading experience that syntactically and structurally is based on a dialogical situation. The reading of *Hasta no verte, Jesús mío* approaches and hovers very close to the experience of being in conversation. The sequentiality of the narration openly takes on the movement of a free-wheeling conversation.

Jesusa approached many topics defensively because she had been rejected or abandoned by persons whom she had grown to value. Perhaps one of her more explicit rejections of modes of identification comes when she expresses her disdain for the ever-present sentiment of Mexican nationalism and patriotism, which is summed up in the slogan, "There is no other country like Mexico." Jesusa says: "After all is said and done, I don't have a country. I'm like the gypsies, from nowhere. I don't feel that I am a Mexican and I don't recognize a Mexican nationality. Here nothing else matters than personal interests and advantage. If I had money, I would be a Mexican" (218). This statement reflects a remarkable degree of alienation, especially in a culture that was so thoroughly dominated by propaganda based on sentimentalist patriotism. Unquestionably, any critical assessment of Mexican culture must go beyond the statistical analysis of a culture of poverty or appraisal of one of the richest artistic traditions of the world. The concept of Mexico from below is also an essential part of this mosaic, and yet it was circumscribed and limited in the narrative discourse of Mexico until the publication of this work.[11]

Jesusa's values, fears, and biases are all expressed in the vivid language of the lower classes. They are expressed as personal opinion, but they are always expressed in the specific context of incidents and dialogue, and it is in these situations, with the specific details of wounded pride, disappointment, and personal offenses that we encounter Jesusa's generalizations. She has limited knowledge of the mechanisms of the economy, politics, or social developments and because she cannot read, her knowledge is limited to her own experiences and what she has been told. Thus it is that we have a highly subjective persona with limited capacity to understand her world in any comprehensive manner. Yet it is this narrative persona who makes a significant contribution to the readers' own redescription of the present-day Mexican nation, for Jesusa's is a response to the power of the Mexican dominant class in terms that can only be defined as universal demands for human dignity and the right to work with self-respect. Others, like Domitila Barrios de Chungara and Rigoberta Menchú, have followed, but Jesusa and her collaborator, Elena Poniatowska, were the first to break ground in this process of creating testimonial literature. It is, therefore, not in the personal expression of pained reactions that Jesusa's truth claims confront the reader, but rather as a collective rejection of abusive civil authority. This response is, of course, not limited to Jesusa's class and her Mexico; we can hear the same kind of reaction from New York City to Los Angeles in the United States, if we care to listen.

Jesusa's indictment is that the affluent social class that rules Mexico (about 5 percent of the population) operates under norms that are racist, abusive, and, through a barely disguised slave trade, exploitative of the massive underclass. She speaks from this subsistence level underclass of the uneducated majority who have heretofore been denied a voice. Others have spoken in their name with or without their interests in mind. The Mexican underclass has vented its rejection through revolution or, more recently, urban violence. Jesusa gives this worldview a voice.

It is because of the dialogical structure of this text that the reader gets involved in the life story, but it is the anger and direct opposition to the operative Mexican stereotypes that challenge the reader. Jesusa does not accept her societal roles as a woman or as a Mexican: "I have never wished to have children, what for? It is enough trouble to take care of myself" (312). She would prefer to be a man because the male, she says, has more freedom:

All women would be better off being men, sure; it is more fun, one has more freedom and nobody mocks one. On the one hand, being a woman, one is never respected no matter the age, if young one is tricked and if old one is ridiculed, one is taken as a joke because of age. On the other hand, a male dressed as a man goes and comes; or goes and does not come and since he is a man nobody stops him. A thousand times better to be a man than a woman! (186)

She would rather be a wandering nomad than a Mexican because she will never submit to being a submissive slave to the affluent Mexicans.

As I have argued in my introduction, if we accept the idea that a text is a literary text because the reading experience has the power to provoke reflection in the reader, a reflection that opens up the possibility of a redescription of the reader's own world, then certainly *Hasta no verte, Jesús mío* is a significant literary text, a testimonial literary text. In the social context of Mexican female identity, we are speaking about the self-image with which women of all ages and all social classes have had to live in this nation with a population of ninety million. The diversity is overwhelming, but so are the polarities. Therefore, in every case, any consensus description would necessarily fit only in part when applied to the individual women of Mexico. Engaging in the game of generalization is to play the game of fools, but on a deeper level it is the perpetuation of the social stereotypes that verge on racist and sexist reduction of the other.

Thus far, we have looked at three aspects of female identity: (1) the social stereotype institutionally created and supported to this day and the subversion of this stereotype in literature like that of Carlos Fuentes; (2) the transgression of the social codes Sor Juana Inés de la Cruz exemplifies; and (3) the dialogic nature of an identity that is at once true to oneself and is functional in one's society.

Decades ago, some U.S. feminists were calling for female literary characters that would serve as role models for female readers (see Chapter 1). The absurdity of such proposals comes from not understanding either the nature of literature or the social function of literature. The reading of the literary text is a dynamic process of world-making in which the reader is the key agent. Like all dynamic processes, the development can be tracked but it cannot be predicted. The social function of literature is to provide countless levels of narrativity from which the individual worldviews of the members of the community draw their emplotment.

What are we to understand by literary characters like Emma Bovary or Anna Karenina? In what sense does the term *character* possess both a descriptive and an emblematic value? The mere fact that I can name these two well-known characters in a book on Mexican literature certainly attests to their emblematic capacity. But let me press further. What is conveyed by the emblem of Emma or Anna? Is it that as transgressors of the social codes, they became fallen women and paid for the transgression with their lives? The mention of their names also brings forth specific descriptions of their world, values, and comportment for those who have read the novels. Thus they are emblematic in a general way, and they are also descriptive of a specific time, place, and social structure.

If we turn to characters who narrate their own story, like Mariana of *La "Flor de lis"* and Jesusa of *Hasta no verte, Jesús mío*, we encounter a further twist to our consideration of literary characters, for these characters add a verbal self-identity to the identity of the individual. The assumed continuity of the identity of the individual who acts is now both an empirical truth claim and a playing of a part in society. The self-identity of the character as narrator betrays itself in so far as she is aware that in this process of self-presentation, she is creating an image of herself, the image we know as the social persona. The individual who narrates is thus immersed in a tensional relationship between the hard core of sameness and the social projection that is forthcoming through the narration.

Poniatowska's narrative characters lose a great deal of the emblematic power of the great literary characters of the past because they are not the product of an independent point of view; rather, they come to us, like all first-person characterizations, as limited and highly subjective self-presentations. If we add that these texts are structured dialogically, like some of Faulkner's finest works or Guimarães Rosa's great novel, we can see that we have female characters who have a bifurcated tensional identity; there is the individual as source, the enunciating voice with all of the attributes of individual continuity, of sameness, but there is also the social persona they themselves project about themselves. Their identity as characters comes forth in the tension between the sameness of the narrator and the variability and volatility of the persona.

Insofar as the reader is concerned, this tensional relationship discloses the deepest core of our own sense of identity, because we are reflective individuals who play parts in the community in which these parts, or, as Wittgenstein called them, forms of life, come prescribed with greater or lesser flexibility in terms of how we can play the part. Therefore, characters who function under the same forces as readers become complex dialogical partners with their readers.

The female identity of Mexican women, like that of persons everywhere, comes forth from their dialogic involvement with the world. The significance of Poniatowska's characters' identity is that it becomes a means for disclosing our own identity as a reflection of the text-reader relationship that we have created in our reading.

If *Hasta no verte, Jesús mío* is testimonial literature, which is closely allied to biography based on interviews, *La "Flor de lis"* of 1988 is much closer to autobiography and to the specific subgenre of diary. As with all narrative texts, there is a structured organization of details; this text features an explicit historicity of Paris and, especially, Mexico City, from 1938 to the 1950s. Because the text records the coming of age of a young woman, the reader shares in her first encounters with the world beyond her protective home. Her quest for control over her life is tied to her search for her identity in the world. The salient truth claim that emerges is that her own identity is dominated by her apprenticeship in being able to look at herself as an other; specifically, as the other of the persons who share in her life. The discovery of "myself as an other" is slow in coming and always painful, for there are powerful ideological forces that rule her world which she neither understands nor controls. These are ways of living which are inscribed in this community, but they are ways she cannot accept merely out of the obedience expected of her. In brief, the ideology of her world is the territory she must traverse if her social persona is to be reconciled with her willed individual identity.

This highly readable first-person narration departs from the genre of the mimetic novel and even the subgenre of the confessional novel because of its system of narrative filters.[12] All except one of the twenty-eight chapters are narrated from the first-person singular point of view in the present tense. Since the novel covers approximately fourteen years in the childhood and adolescence of the narrator, the present-tense focalizations must be a recovery of the past and its actualization into a present of the enunciation. Thus the scene and the details presented are those elements from the past that have remained in the memory of the protagonist as the key markers for remaking the past. These are the filters of remembrance, selection, and enunciation. The text opens with the following lines:

I see her open an antique wardrobe; she is wearing a long white nightgown and she has on her head one of those hats for sleeping that appear in the illustrations of the pink library of the Countess of Segur, on closing the wardrobe door my mother hits herself and pinches her nose. The fear of doors will never leave me. Doors are always pinching something, separating, excluding me. (13)

The year is 1938, during the months before the terrible year of 1939 when France fell to Nazi Germany, and the narrator, Mariana, is between her sixth and seventh birthday. Mariana lives in Paris, where she was born, with her aristocratic parents and her sister, who is one year younger. She is surrounded by uncles, aunts, grandparents, and servants. The narrative focalization has a double focal point, like a telescope. If you look into it in the direction in which it is aimed, you will see the figures enlarged in the present, but you can also look into it in the other direction; in this view you can also distinguish figures, but they appear small and remote. In the sixth entry, we read this telling evocation:

Around the trees of rue Berton, all along, down to the Seine, they have installed little gratings. I do not remember the Seine itself until much later, what is very clear is that rue Berton goes down to the Seine and I like that very much: I can run with all my might to the corner where I have to wait for mademoiselle and my sister. "Vous avez encore marche sur une crotte." That's what the problem is with the streets, they are full of dog turds which stick onto your shoes, that's why the French always say "merde." (18)

This is neither the language of an adult nor the language of a child; rather, it is the literary reenactment of the past in the present of the enunciation we are reading. This novel is a sociopsychological cross section of Mexican women of the dominant social class demonstrating the blindness, simple-mindedness, and insignificance of the lives of affluent upper class women. The period of 1942 to 1955 in Mexico City was a time of rapid change in Mexican life and the time of adolescence for the narrator of this diary. This is a novel whose point of view depends not only upon who is describing, but also upon what is being described. The scene-narrator relationship is a symbiotic one in which each is making the other. Point of view is determined not only by the first-person sensibility of an adolescent girl from the upper class of Mexico City, but also by the events and action being described and the way of life of this social class.

In general, we judge the behavior of fictional characters in novels not only by the personal characteristics usually provided by the narrator, but also, and I would say primarily, by the context in which these characteristics are presented. The motivation we attribute to a character's action is usually our response to the way the character's personal traits develop in the specific context of action being described. In this novel, all the characteristics of the fictional characters, including the narrator herself, are the highly particularized versions that a young girl in that situation would give. The narration is not merely the distanced viewpoint of an older, mature narrator looking back; nor is it just an inscribed eye-witness report of an adolescent's diary. Elena Poniatowksa's technical achievement has been to capture the act of remembering and recreating the past. The remarkable result in this novel, one that separates it from merely being another novel in a diary format, is that there is in evidence, throughout, the ideological question mark of the narrator's point of view upon the object of description. This object of description, the women of a specific social class at a particular time, is witnessed by an adolescent, and this testimony is organized as a diary, written in the present tense with numerous breaks, separations, interruptions, some extended intervals, interpolated popular songs of the day, advertising jingles, and numerous epigraphs; all of this is written with a fine irony that lays the ground for the progressive identification of the narrator's own ideological position.

It would be difficult, if not impossible, to pursue textual commentary if the ideological context of the period were not clearly set forth. The modernization of social consciousness in Mexico has produced two contrary but equally negative attitudes. The first is a nostalgia for the integrative symbols of the past, the preconquest Quetzalcoatl and the colonial Virgin of Guadalupe, which has resulted in a symbolic traditionalism that defensively uses these images to propagate an ideology of nationalism that is the external face of a political system of exploitation. This nationalism is fundamentally reactionary since its prime objective is to retain economic and political power in the hands of the few who have reached the top. The discourse of this nationalism is filled with rhetoric of exaltation, with slogans of the purported social justice won by the Mexican revolution, and with the two integrative symbols as the axial centers for a national unity.

The social models of rationalistic individuality which had served as the social code of the economically dominant social class before the revolution were altered when the upper class had to make way for lower class military and political figures. The new social code was that of the *macho* who takes all he can get and tramples anyone who gets in his way. The counterpart to the macho is the *pendejo*, a combination of loser and fool.

Mariana and her family are quite alien to the social models of Mexico. Her parents are accepted into the upper class because of their wealth and the prestige of their European aristocracy. However, the upper class no longer has control over society. They have had to yield to the new class of the revolutionary rich. Thus, her world is marginal to political power. There are new faces at the top who must be accommodated, and there is a wall of corruption which Mariana's father finds impossible to break through. The modernization of social consciousness has produced a retrograde class, the elite of the old system, and a new class of rapacious rich, who have neither the style of the old guard nor the same models; their images of value are not European but made in the United States. This shift in value structures is at its highest intensity in the 1940s and 1950s.

But there is also a second response to the modernization of contemporary Mexico. It is the *macho-pendejo* syndrome taken to its antisocial extreme of wanton destruction of anything with an explicit social value. This viewpoint rejects all traditionalism, and its followers like to think of themselves as being modern. Its popular manifestations are in contemporary youth culture and the antisocial *nacos*. We must not lose sight of the fact that Mexico is a country where 60 percent of the population lacks even the basic functional education the first world considers primary, and that any discussion of the modernization of social consciousness deals with the discourse of a small percentage of the population. Large sectors were in the past manipulated through religious, marxist, or revolutionary rhetoric. The sole unifying thread which ties the various manifestations of antisocial behavior is the violent opposition to all forms of constraint. The message is simple, whether blasted out in a rock performance or in graffiti—you've got to discover the real you by letting go, breaking the rules, and so on.

The ideas of one of the characters, the French priest Jacques Teufel, are not Mexican in origin, but they feed into the antisocial movement which was in its beginning in the 1950s and which matured into an oppressive social phenomenon decades later. Teufel's message presages the later antisocial nihilism. His vague utopian notions are tied to a powerful rejection of customs and constraints, especially on sexual relations. He asserts that women, especially girls, must discover their true naked selves by rebelling against their families and having children at random with men of all social classes, thereby destroying inequality and ending exploitation. The sexual revolution of the 1960s and 1970s did not, however, deliver the promised liberation. In Mariana's Mexico, there is still an elite based on family wealth, but there is also a new class of rich, the politicians of the postrevolutionary power struggle. There is also a nihilistic response to traditionalism. Corruption is the means to buy stability for the rapid modernization of the new Mexico.

In the Mexico of the 1960s and 1970s—that is, not the Mexico of Mariana but that of Elena Poniatowska—the traditionalism of the past has become the ideological foundation of the governing Party of the Institutionalized Revolution (PRI) and its own potent discourse of power. The counterculture is either the rampant vandalism of the *naco* or a fashionable import, like a punk hair-style, for the entertainment of the youth of all social classes. But the reality of life for the vast majority of Mexicans is the relentless continuation of poverty, ignorance, and exploitation and the struggle for survival.

There are, of course, Mexicans who strive for a pluralistic and free society, a system with social justice, but those who pursue these lines of action face over-whelming obstacles in a society that has become increasingly more corrupt with each new administration since 1940. The present situation, the one of the writer and not the narrator, stands behind the narration. In the diary, there is the reenactment of a false world that is gone; in the text which we read, there is a world inherited from the past that is a net of holes, to use José Emilio Pacheco's preconquest metaphor, where the main tie between individuals is abuse: you are either inflicting abuse or trying to defend yourself against it. Violence and abuse are institutionalized. The system rewards audacity and ra-pacious greed and is indifferent to intelligence, training, productive labor, and talent. Some claim that the beginning of this decline from rationalistic patri-archy to social warfare goes back to the conquest; others pinpoint the revolu-tion. I would argue, though, that the origins of the malaise of contemporary Mexico lie in the process of modernization which developed during the presi-dencies of Avila Camacho (1940–1946), Miguel Alemán (1946–1952), and Ruíz Cortines (1952–1958), a period of rapid industrialization and the transforma-tion of an agricultural society into a modern economic satellite of U.S. capital-ism. This is the period described in La *"Flor de lis,"* but the point of view is from the most sheltered corner of Mexican life, the diary of the adolescent daughter of an affluent family.

Mexican presidents from Avila Camacho (1940–1946) to Zedillo (1994–) have always made public claims that they represent the common interest of the Mexican people; indeed, in their more impassioned rhetorical moments, they claim to incarnate the common good. Yet the undeniable fact of life is that this political structure is dependent on repressive organized force; it is a power pyramid of self-enrichment made up of the government, its supporters, and the military which rests on the base of the millions of exploited men and women of Mexico. This political structure is realized in the novel as the hidden reality which the narrator comes to know only indirectly. She is as unaware of the meaning of corruption as any sheltered wealthy young girl would be, but this is the reality the priest Teufel constantly refers to in his harangues on social classes and social justice. Mariana hears about it from her father, who does not know how to cope, and it is behind the subtle irony that comes out of her reflections.

The other salient characteristic of Mexican life is the wide, virtually unbridgeable moral and ethical distance between family life and political reality. It is in the attempt to accommodate these two structures, one based on custom and personal ties, the other on exploitation and repression, that we discover the reality of everyday life in Mexico. Mariana reflects introspectively on her family's insistence on etiquette and what it reveals to her now:

How does one put the spoon into the mouth, how does one sit, how does one wipe one's lips on the table napkin; these are the forms that irrigate our brain, not ideas. Still today it is practically impossible for me to free myself from the first impression of appearances; to set the height to which one raises the elbow when one picks up a glass is for me a conditioned reflex. Further, it furnishes and fills my spirit, this perception of the other makes me think that I have exercised a critical and analytic task; this fact finding occupies a place in my mind and stops me from moving on to other spaces. (257)

There the introspection ends and we flash back to the present of the young Mariana shortly before the end of the novel: "Mama, I think we are a very cruel family. It's cruel the way we do charity, our little closed world is cruel, we here, they . . ." (257). It is into the midst of this schizophrenic world that the French priest Jacques Teufel enters, and it is in the wake of the turbulence he creates that Mariana matures into womanhood, not without nostalgia for her lost innocence. Teufel's ideas of social reform in this society are little more than a fashionable way for the young to rebel, but then, eventually, to join the system.

The text is a highly controlled system of observation sometimes touched with irony and sometimes leading into reflective introspection but, throughout, the first-person narration is devoid of affectation or simulation. The narrative flow is in a present time of visualization. What is perceived is perceived from the singular viewpoint of the young female narrator. This is a novel about a girl becoming a woman; a wealthy, privileged member of the social elite becoming a woman in a country in which she was not born but now considers hers, with all of its problems of poverty and social inequality.

The fact that the diary is replete with autobiographical details from the author's life, not the least of which is the personal chronology of adolescence, leads the reader not only to the normal suspension of disbelief, indicative of all mimetic fiction, but also to the much more powerful granting of authority to the experience of testimony, hearing a witness's report of the intimate thoughts and reflections of coming of age in the decade of the 1950s. The sequentiality of passages is one of spatial and visual order and not of plot. The reenactment of scenes pertinent to the narrator's adolescence is the organizing principle. The use of montage as well as the constant present of perception make the structure of this novel explicitly cinematographic. But it is more than the mere transposition of cinematographic technique to narrative; La "Flor de lis" is a novel where the visual images flash before the reader only to vanish into the recesses of consciousness.

The textuality of this novel is significant, one that I can only touch upon here, but which merits close study. There are forty different emblems. The most often used are the pyramid, associated with Mexico; the fleur de lis, with France; the daisy, with Luz, Mariana's mother; the five-pointed star within a circle, used on military aircraft and associated with her father; the heart, which represents talk about love, sex, and marriage; the fern, which is used to introduce other members of the family (that is, others besides her mother, father, and sister); and finally, a number of variations on the star and on the cross to mark introspective entries. The cross of Malta is used only to introduce epigraphs in Latin from religious exercises. There are also several pictographs—telephone, bus, automobile, airplane, envelope, and a hand writing to announce the presence of the represented object in the fragment. Tamales and tostadas, popular Mexican food, are used symbolically to represent the Mexico of the lower social classes.

Other notable textual features are the numerous interpolated documents, ranging from advertisements to spiritual exercises. The frontispiece to the novel is the advertisement for a very typical Mexican restaurant named "La flor de lis," which can be read as a metaphor for the narrator, protagonist, and the author herself, who is Mexican in all save her last name and place of birth. The diary itself is framed by two quotations from the comics character "Little Lulu," an intrepid little girl in a red dress. The first serves as an opening to the reenactment of the fragments. It is dated "Special issue, January 1954;" the second is a play on the first, using names of the narrator's family and acquaintances, and is ascribed to the narrator herself. It is dated "Fall issue, 1955," that is, twenty-two months after the first. It is precisely during these months that Mariana goes through the maturing process and crisis that take her from adolescence to maturity, approximately between her seventeenth and nineteenth years. These twenty-two months comprise the second half of the novel—from the time she goes to a spiritual retreat and meets the French priest, Father Jacques Teufel, to the end of the diary, just after he leaves Mexico and returns to France. It is also worth noting that Latin lines from the spiritual exercises of the retreat and the girls' reading are interspersed through this part of the text. There are other interpolated passages such as advertising jingles heard over the radio, popular songs of the day in Spanish, French, and English, and, most important of all, five long sections from Luz's diary, for Mariana's mother also kept an intimate record of her life, and the narrator has access to it.

Throughout the entire novel, the narrator sees and evaluates the world through the lens of her social status. This is the particularly limited point of view of a young upper class girl who enjoys the comforts of affluence in a country where the gulf separating the rich from the poor is extreme and obvious. She knows only what she has been allowed to know about Mexico; she has a scale of values that is representative of both her social class in Mexico and her specific family ties to France. It is a sheltered, self-indulgent worldview, but when she begins to question her world, she does so from the reflective evaluation of the emptiness of women's lives in her social class. She has to mature beyond the ideological constraints of her environment; she is still quite childish in her late teens. When she asks her mother whether she will one day be a saint, Luz responds: "You, dear, are a little frog bloated with pride" (241). Her favorite reading is still the comic strip "Little Lulu," the little girl who never grows up but who outwits adults at their own games of life. Mariana is virtually unaware of the meaning of living in poverty, of violence, or even the nature of sexual relations beyond the moral instruction she gets from the nuns. She is taught from the time she enters school that her purpose in life must be to marry, have children, and establish a family. Hers is a world of innocence and fantasy, much like that of her comic strip heroine. This little world is not threatened when she is sent to a religious boarding school for young ladies in Philadelphia. The irony of her reenactment is clear: "In the convent no one speaks of poverty. Latin America is a banana garden" (98). Her gradual realization of the falseness of her world emerges in the diary:

No place has as much democracy as the United States; the level of excellence is the highest here, and free enterprise is always encouraged. That is why we, the little girls of means, the chosen ones, the ones who will always be on top have been sent to the United States to receive the last coat of polish, the protective coat against whatever contingencies life may bring in these changing times. It is only fair that only the best survive and we are here because we are the top of the top, the crème de la crème, the cherry on top, the owners of the emporium. (99)

The interpolations from her mother's diary are key factors in the liberation of Mariana, who has idealized her mother from her earliest memories. Luz has been the epitome of everything a woman should be. She is beautiful, elegant, attractive to men, in full control of her household, a loving wife and mother. Mariana's happiest childhood memories are being in bed with her mother surrounded by her warmth, her scent, and her beauty. Mariana feels that she can never be like her beautiful mother; she lacks all the grace, talent, and beauty her mother displays so naturally. The break with the mother's psychological hold on Mariana will be the inner and real crisis of the traumatic relationship with the French priest. As long as she feels inadequate next to her mother, she will unconsciously seek to continue her childish innocence. She does not want to know reality because she fears that she will always be unable to be a woman in her mother's image.

Luz's diary entries refer to her attraction to the charismatic Jacques Teufel and her repulsion at his excesses. His charisma inheres in his passion for social reform, which brings excitement into her empty life and does not really challenge her social status. The poor are still them and the rich are still us. But Teufel's sinister violence and eventually his sexuality frighten her to the point that he becomes terrifying to her, the devil incarnate.[13] Although Luz is a woman of some experience, she does not know how to deal with this situation. She is powerless when faced with the personal magnetism of this man; his domination of her reaches almost pathological proportions. The great attraction has been the erotic excitement of doing something, of filling her days with purpose together with a man who admires her physical beauty. This safe outlet breaks down when he attempts to have sexual intercourse with her sister Francisca, is rejected, and has a paranoic attack when he is on an outing with the girl scouts.

Two significant ideological factors are at work here; one is the priest's use of the clergy's traditional domination of Mexican women to gain access to power. Women like Luz and Francisca are fascinated with an excitement that for all its revolutionary rhetoric does not threaten their social status; the other main ideological factor is that by reading her mother's diary, Mariana becomes aware of her mother's vulnerability and her emptiness. Mariana's determination to be independent of this tradition of female limitation is the beginning of her liberation.

If we return to the beginning of the novel and outline the nature of the narrative emplotment, the ideological organization of the novel will become clear. The novel consists of twenty-eight unnumbered chapters written in the diary format of fragments—232 in the entire text—following a chronological development which mirrors Elena Poniatowska's own childhood, adolescence, and maturity. The novel covers the time from 1938 to 1955, with more than half of the text devoted to the last twenty-two months. This is the period of Mariana's adolescent crisis, brought on by her relationship with the French priest. Mariana's world consists of her mother Luz, a Mexican woman of wealth married to a European aristocrat; her sister, Sofía, one year younger than Mariana but in most ways the more worldly and daring of the two; and her little brother Fabián, fourteen years younger than Mariana, born in 1947.

The first two chapters depict Mariana's childhood in France, the beginning of the war, and the family's emigration; the father remains in France as part of the French resistance movement. Mariana and the rest of the family go to Mexico, her mother's place of birth. They arrive in 1942, and Luz begins a new life of adjustment to a different social structure. Mariana is European but also part Mexican. The long absence of her father during this time of acculturation draws her even closer to her mother than she had been in France. Her father returns from the war in 1946, her brother Fabian is born the next year, and in 1948 Mariana and Sofia are sent to a Catholic boarding school in Philadelphia. Her adolescence is permeated by the sense of class isolation in a country she barely knows. She is told repeatedly that in the natural order of peoples, some are on top and others have to carry the burden for all. The girls return to Mexico in 1950 to engage in the typical life of unmarried young women of the upper class in Mexico. Mariana is about sixteen and Sofia fifteen; they busy themselves with dance lessons, piano lessons, riding instruction, teaching catechism to youngsters on Sunday mornings, going to dances, and, in general, participating in a whirlwind of social activities. The next two years mark a separation of the two sisters; Sofia leaves childhood behind and begins to take her place in the life-style for which they have been educated. Mariana, in contrast, does not mature and continues to think and act like the childish sheltered young girl she was at fourteen, in spite of the fact that she is the elder sister and is nearing eighteen. She gives numerous indications of her resistance to becoming a woman and having to compare herself with her mother. She admires her sister but idealizes her mother.

In the midst of this extended adolescence, Mariana goes alone, without Sofia, who is too busy with her fiancé, to a spiritual retreat sponsored by the French church in Mexico. She meets Jacques Teufel. The major part of the novel follows her experiences with this charismatic and unbalanced priest. He preaches social change in Mexico through the banishment of all social and sexual repression. He stresses that Christ was the poorest of the poor, using images of Christ befriending the prostitute Mary Magdalene and washing the feet of the poor; yet for all his radical pronouncements, Teufel is careful not to question the social structure itself. His attack on social elitism in Mexico never goes beyond the surface of the social system, but it does offer young girls the opportunity to visualize themselves as saints and martyrs for Christ's cause. Teufel fascinates Mariana: she can finally be an individual, she thinks, and take her place in the world as a martyr; she will be part of his army of heroic women, who will change society by living with the lower classes.

She convinces her mother to invite him to dinner; he goes to dinner and ends up living with them. His stay in Mariana's house is traumatic, reaching a critical point when he tries to have sexual intercourse with Mariana's aunt. To the women of the house, he is a combination of redeeming prophet and devil.

Mariana's father sees him as a Rasputin-like figure who has extraordinary power over women. Luz asks him to leave, and shortly thereafter he suffers a breakdown. After a brief period of hospitalization, he returns to France. The effects on Luz as recorded in her diary and demonstrated in her own breakdown have a profound effect on Mariana. She finally breaks the hold her mother had on her, and as the novel ends, she determines to make her own way in the world.

This brief summary of the story reveals that Poniatowska's strategy of emplotment is, as I stated at the outset, fundamentally ideological, consisting of five clearly defined psychological phases. The first consists of the reenactment of childhood. The experience of the change from one world, living as an aristocratic child in France, to a new life in Mexico, is linked to the prolonged absence of the father, and moves Mariana to idealize her mother and see herself only in her shadow. The second phase is the period of adolescence and Mariana's emerging awareness that her worldview is false. The third is the extended adolescence of Mariana; this is marked by her childishness and reluctance to become an adult, resulting from her fear that she will never be like her mother. The fourth phase is traumatic: she finds that her mother is not larger than life, that she is a woman plagued with a sense of emptiness. The fifth and final phase comes only in the last entries of the diary, as Mariana recognizes the falseness of her individual situation as well as her social viewpoint and is determined to make her own way and be her own person. The year is 1955, about the time and age when Elena Poniatowska began to work as a journalist.

The five phases of psychological development of the narrator are plotted in a sequential manner. The first nine chapters consist of the first eighty-eight entries of Mariana's diary, in which she reenacts her childhood. The themes that run through these entries—those fine narrative threads that tie the novel together—are the dominant image of the mother, the return of the absent father, a constant comparison between France and Mexico, and three significant instances of introspection. The second phase, that of a normal adolescence, is limited to two chapters (10 and 11). A broad range of themes is presented. Aside from the powerful mother image, there are the first signs of sexuality as well as the sentimental thoughts of love and marriage. The intensity of the introspection grows, and the influence of religion appears. The third phase of the extended adolescence is represented in chapters 10 to 25. These are the critical months of 1954 and 1955, from the time Mariana goes to the spiritual retreat to the time Teufel is asked to leave her house. The character's discourse changes markedly in these fifteen chapters. The formerly dominant image of the mother as an ideal figure begins to change into that of a rival. Mariana now embarks on the fantasy of religious heroism and begins to develop a capacity for self-examination. The latter is especially evident in chapters 21 to 25. The fourth phase, one of crisis, is covered in chapters 26 and 27, when Mariana's image of her mother is finally brought down, together with the destruction of her heroic self-image as a martyr in Teufel's service. The liberation from the shadow of the mother is the critical point; the themes here are only the mother and Teufel. The final phase comes as the novel ends in chapter 28. The degree of introspection is at its highest here. After reading her mother's diary, the narrator begins to pull away, gaining momentum in entries 229 to 231 and culminating in 232, appropriately titled "Accipe sal sapientiae" (take the salt of wisdom)—words spoken by the Roman Catholic priest in the baptismal liturgy when he touches salt to the infant's lips. The theme is herself as a woman, making her own way and leaving behind her the heritage of superficiality and emptiness that enslaves the women of her family.

When Mariana meets Jacques Teufel at the spiritual retreat, he provokes her, causing her childish feelings of inadequacy to burst into flames. In a personal interview with her, he asks her what she believes in, and she responds that she believes in good breeding, polite manners, and, in short, tradition. He becomes violent and confronts her in a manner she has never experienced. He attacks every social grace, every value she has been taught to admire. He asks her to become a martyr for a new society of Christ's justice on earth. She is overwhelmed with joy; someone, a man, is paying attention to her. She is no longer insignificant; she can be important as herself; she will be a hero and martyr for him. This is the first time in her life that Mariana can imagine herself in a situation where she will not be compared to her mother and found lacking.

The passage that follows is central for understanding the reasons for Mariana's extended adolescence as well as the ideological superficiality of the paranoic priest:

—In the present world, men have the absolute obligation of breaking with social class distinction.

—How?

—What you have just told me, Blanca [the name Teufel has given Mariana], is decadent. It tastes rancid, rotten, of prejudice; simply it doesn't make sense. Life itself takes us along other ways. You yourself, my child, are much broader in outlook, much greater than what you think you are. Life will see to it that you recognize it. The society to which you belong must be destroyed, tear it to pieces with its prejudices, its vanity, its moral and physical impotence (146). . . .

—Yes, yes, I want to give myself, I want to, of course I want to, anything except pass unnoticed. (147)

Mariana ardently desires to be herself. The voice of a man enunciates the challenge to the powerful influences of family and upbringing which keep her from becoming herself. She is ready to expand beyond the family into which she was born. She is ready to make her own way in the world. Such are the thoughts of exuberant adolescence. It is necessary to relinquish her parents, and especially her mother, as the primary objects of love. The mother, to Mariana the blissful comfort of the womb, has been idealized into a larger-than-life image of beauty, charm, good breeding, and self-esteem. This separation erupts as she turns her love from the mother to the opposite sex in the person of Jacques Teufel.

Mariana's life and that of her family is completely uprooted by the presence of the mercurial Teufel. All the women of the family fall under his spell, but the two intimate viewpoints we have—the diary entries of Mariana and those of Luz, her mother—reveal significant differences. Luz feels alive in Teufel's company; she becomes his assistant, taking him wherever he commands in the city. She is in awe of his passion for changing the very social structure which has provided the only sense of order she has ever known. In her most intimate moments she looks into the bottom of the well of her existence and finds an emptiness that the excitement of Teufel helps her evade. She writes in her diary, as reported by Mariana, the following thoughts: "'We women are always waiting, I believe, we allow life to live us, we are not taught to make decisions, we spin, we turn around, we return to the point from which we began, I don't know how to ask, I'm ambiguous'" (207). It is this terrible emptiness that Teufel's mission has temporarily banished. If Luz's response to Teufel has been a frantic excitement seeking to hide a sense of emptiness, Mariana's is the typical symptom of adolescence, an aroused sexuality together with a renewed need for independence and self-esteem. She now takes delight in her appearance and in her woman's body. Mariana writes in her diary: "My hair filled me with a strange pleasure. I'm important. I give off light, I repeated to myself. . . . And, in bed, I could not sleep and suddenly I find myself with both hands on my sex. I take them away. It's a sin. Nevertheless like elastic bands they return to the same place" (213).

When Jacques Teufel's paranoia increases to the point that he is hospitalized, Mariana finally is told about his background, his countless affairs with women, his attempt to have intercourse with her aunt, and his long history of mental problems. The shocking deflation of her heroic love leads her to renewed introspection: "My inconsistency is partly hereditary. Ever on the surface, being a child of wealth is defined as not being conscious. . . . What is it that I really wanted? What is it that one has to really want?" (233).

Mariana must overcome two interrelated aspects of false consciousness if she is to be free: one is her traditionalism, rooted in her status as a member of the social and economic elite of Mexican society; the other is her belief that the only true function of a woman in life is to have a family, a deeply entrenched belief that her mother and past generations of women in her family have passed on to her. The fact that Mariana's family are members of the Mexican elite and at the same time outsiders sharpens her introspective questioning of self-identity. Thus, a critical detachment is inherent in Mariana's participation in social life. Another distinctive aspect of Mariana's psychological development is her prolonged adolescence, which lasts until she meets Teufel, and which is in great measure owing to her attachment to her mother and her fear of comparing herself to her. The political discourse that Teufel preaches is nominally a response to Mexico's social situation, but it is primarily a form of safe revolutionary discourse used as a means of exorcising the speaker's personal demons; at the same time it serves to ignite Mariana's fantasy of religious heroism.

The final break with her past comes when Mariana goes to see Teufel for the last time. Her mother has told her that he is a womanizer, and for the first time in her life, she has seen her mother as another woman, not as the prototype of women. When Mariana is alone with Teufel, she launches, a bit self-consciously, into a bitter denunciation of his lies and hypocrisy. He responds: "—One must live and if you do not transgress, if you do not humble yourself, if you do not come near the swamp, you are not living. Sin is penitence, sin is the only true purification, if you do not sin, how are you going to save yourself?" (251). Finally, with this last circular argument, Mariana sees through Teufel's self-serving rhetoric. In fact, Teufel's outburst on the social ills of Mexico and the role of the affluent classes, far from being original with him or his situation as self-proclaimed reformer, has a long history, going back to the medieval rebellions of the *fratecelli* against social inequality and sexual repression.[14] This mixture of social rebellion and promiscuity has recurred from time to time when an individual's sexual repression becomes linked with the discourse of rage against social injustice. But the outrage, like the rhetoric, comes from European institutions of church and state, and these are the intimate demons of this priest. His outbursts have no potential for effecting positive social change in Mexico. Indeed, they have only a negative significance, for they help to strengthen acceptance of the view that institutional exploitation is natural; the church can portray his rebellion as sexual aberration of a priest who cannot live in a celibate state.

The last three entries of the text are climactic moments of introspection. Mariana has matured, but there is a lingering nostalgia for the loss of innocence, and at the same time a resolve to break out of her female inheritance. The only fragment in the text not written in the first person is a third-person description of Mariana herself. It is as if she has taken a position external to herself and observes and judges what she sees:

It is sufficient to close one's eyes to find Mariana in the depths of memory, young, unaware, innocent. Her very insipidness, her bewilderment are touching; the seed of her future solitude germinates in her confusion, the same seed that germinated in Luz, in Francis, in those women who are always strangers, who leave barely perceptible traces, bird prints made by slim and fragile ankles, easy to compress, blue veins exposed, my God, how fragile, what is to be done to keep creatures like that on earth, they are barely a piece of paper blowing in the wind. (259)

It soon becomes clear that Mariana has been addressing herself in the mirror, but she continues in the third person: "That is why Sofía is getting married. More than the other women in her family she wants to grab onto the hand of a man, enclose reality, belong" (259).

Mariana finally breaks out of the contemplation of herself as other; she understands and rebels:

Is this my inheritance, grandmother, great-grandmother, great-great-grandmother, is this the gift you left for me in addition to your features in the mirror, your inconclusive gestures? I can't stand your ineffective gestures, your indolence, your frustrations . . . No one will know who you were, just as you never knew yourselves. No one. Only I will invoke your name, only I who one day will forget myself—what rest!—only I shall know what you never were (260). I don't know what will become of me. . . . How many long hours we are alone looking out the window, mama? It is then that I ask you mama, my mother . . . the sadness that I feel, where do I put it? Where, mama? (260–261)

This passage carries a powerful echo of the words of despair that Mariana's mother recorded in her diary; in the present, they have become a protest against the limitation of what life offers women of her social class in Mexico. What can they look forward to, except to serve as adornments in the home of a man?

The liberation from the futile emptiness of being decorative art comes only with participation in society. Mariana has taken the first step toward knowing herself openly by encompassing the liberation of other women through her writing. In writing about herself and her others, she is also writing for and about women. The act of writing enables her to purge her ideological conditioning. The future is not a dream of happiness ever after, but, in complete contrast, a confrontation to be enacted through her participation as writer—as woman *and* writer, not as woman *or* writer. Her identity, therefore, is caught up in a narrative strategy of identity which opens up the narrator's world for others.

Both *Hasta no verte, Jesús mío* and *La "Flor de lis"* disclose a strategy for the making of identity which consists of several converging forces. The freedom of the individual is not some overt trait or situation; it is not self-evident; it can only be proposed for others if it is believed in by oneself. As women, these narrators can only begin speaking about another woman's freedom because they believe in their own freedom; that is, they are what they can do and they can do what they are. Freedom is realized not in itself, as a concept, but by what women do, what they produce, what they say. Both speak to their other with the affirmation that the other is as free as they are. This is the entanglement of you and I finding a way where each one can maintain her freedom without taking away the freedom of the other. Jesusa and Mariana achieve this end. How can the narrator's text liberate her and her other, her fellow women, and still offer freedom to him? This is the paradoxical nature of women's writing. When Poniatowska writes books like these, she writes for both women and men; her implied reader can be either. The way out of the paradox is to allow for another point of view in the process of world-making, that is, the reading of the text. What are the practical consequences of these strategies for an implied reader? Fierce disagreement, participation, and possibly appropriation, all of which hold out the possibility of new understanding. Let us rule out compromise and generalized agreement as utopic, but rather, as critical readers, we can recognize that there will be breakthrough moments in thinking which can trigger new ideas about the other's identity.

As a feminist sociocritic concerned with the redescriptive power of these texts, what is never out of view through all of the debate is that the textual strategies of creating female space are realized through the dialectic of a speaker and a listener/reader, both living in a woman's language of action—whatever the reader's gender may be. By living in this language, readers and critics alike are for a brief time close to the very source of female identity: the words with which we dress our soul, the narrativity with which we see our world.

The female identity of Jesusa or Mariana is neither a prescription of what ought to be nor a description of the idiosyncratic individual. These women define themselves in response to the roles they have been obliged to live, and they insist on creating their own identity as a dynamic process which is a tensional pull between the voluntary self and the social persona.

Seven   **The Hard Edge**

Cristina Pacheco

Contemporary literary theory has challenged some long-standing preconceptions about what constitutes a literary work of art. One of the most important challenges to the institutional concept of literature has been the dismissal of traditional generic distinctions as categories of literature. The lines between autobiography, reportage, and fiction have been blurred by writers as diverse in talent and ideology as Ricardo Pozas, Oscar Lewis, and Elena Poniatowska.

My premise is that a work of literature is any text whose reading brings about the reader's reflection on his or her world.[1] This redefinition of literature is especially significant for feminist critics. Until the 1950s, with a few notable exceptions, Mexican women's writing had been traditionally restricted to "sentimental" fiction and newspaper sections designated as "social pages." Since mid-century, a growing number of women in Mexico have broken these constraints and have been writing in the traditional genres, all aspects of journalism, and what we call testimonial literature, wherein the immediacy of journalism, combined with the imaginative power of fictional writing, induces an imaginative figuration by the reader.[2]

Cristina Pacheco (1941–), one of the most popular writers in Mexico today, bases her fiction on news documents rather than direct testimony.[3] Her short stories concentrate on the social, economic, and spiritual status of contemporary Mexico and especially, but not exclusively, on the poor in contemporary Mexico, the people ignored by the Mexican government and the advertising media. Constructing a fictionalized social document, Pacheco depicts the daily life of millions in the Mexican metropolis. The people of Mexico City are the protagonists of the nine books she has published to date. She has received numerous prizes, including the National Award for Distinction in Journalism in 1975, 1985, and 1986. The titles of her books published to date are *Para vivir aquí* (1983; In order to live here), *Sopita de fideo* (1984; Noodle soup), *Cuarto de azotea* (1985; Servant's room), *Zona de desastre* (1986; Disaster zone), *La última noche del 'tigre'* (1987; The 'tiger's' last night), *Para mirar a lo lejos* (1989; To see far away), *El corazón de la noche* (1989; Night's heart), *La rueda de la fortuna* (1993; Ferris wheel), and *Amores y desamores* (1996; Loves and loves lost). Two volumes of interviews have also been published: *La luz de México* (1988; Mexico's light) collected her interviews of Mexican painters and photographers, and *Los dueños de la noche* (1990; Masters of the night) is a collection of thirty-two interviews of celebrities from the popular and artistic media.

There are several notable examples of this genre, each of which provoked an awakening of conscience for the readers of its time. In Argentina, Roberto Arlt (1900–1942) chronicled the society of his time in Buenos Aires. In Peru, Ricardo Palma (1833–1919) wrote *Peruvian Traditions*, which depicted life in that country in the nineteenth century. In Mexico, it has been Cristina Pacheco who has moved readers to a painful awareness of life in present-day Mexico City. There are, of course, vast differences in aesthetic perspective between Palma's ironic mimetic, Arlt's urban testimonial, and Pacheco's documentary fiction. Cristina Pacheco writes in the tradition of the didactic aesthetics of the political cartoonist or José Guadalupe Posada's woodcuts.

The origin of Cristina Pacheco's mode of narration is explained in a brief note to her volume *Para vivir aquí* (1983; In order to live here):

To compensate for our extreme poverty, my mother used to tell us stories. Thanks to those narratives we understood who we were and what our circumstances were, as migrants from the countryside who, like so many other millions of Mexicans, struggled to adapt and survive in the city. Since then I learnt that, oral or written, tales not only entertain but also form our experience and allow us to broaden it with other experiences which we have never had. (11)[4]

Cristina Pacheco does not look for negative aspects of Mexico City's marginalized population, but describes what the newspaper reporter in her finds. Each tale's plot is a glimpse of life captured by Pacheco. The fact that this is a work of imaginative dramatization does not diminish its documental validity. This is documentary literature since there is an open direct line from the specific daily incidents occurring in Mexico City as reported in the daily newspapers and her tales. Pacheco's use of language is idiomatic, without any trace of a political discourse of denunciation. It is the ordinary speech of the city with touches of humor, wit, and jokes. Her characters are genuine voices but anonymous. Both women and men speak with the verisimilitude of daily life. Most of the stories have as protagonist a woman or a young girl who faces adversity with that enormous capacity the poor of Mexico have to endure pain. Pacheco has captured the sad childhood of the group Luis Buñuel called "the young and the damned" (los olvidados) in his memorable film. Pacheco's stories are set in the present in the poorest and most outlying sectors of the Mexican capital.

In this chapter I examine a selection of Cristina Pacheco's stories from the eight story collections published to date. In particular, I am concerned with examining the social symbol of the Mexican girl and woman in Mexico City's sectors of extreme urban poverty—what Oscar Lewis called the culture of poverty, that is, poverty not as a temporary condition but as a way of life for oneself and one's children and their children. First, I propose that we take a close look at Pacheco's stories about young girls and the ways in which they respond to cruelty and abuse. There is today a growing body of research into child abuse and the abuse syndrome showing that yesterday's abused child is today's abusive parent. In Mexico, children of the urban poor are generally malnourished and exploited by adults, but the specific relationship of the abused girl to the mature woman needs focused analysis. The girl as victim grows into the woman who is also a victim, while the boy as victim often grows into the man who abuses. Subsequently I will look into the stories that depict the plight of a number of mature women.

I want to begin by establishing the documental validity of Pacheco's fiction about young girls. Her work is not oral history, and my analysis is neither a sociological nor an anthropological study, but rather, feminist social literary criticism. Pacheco writes fiction based on the reporter's experience in the city, and I am searching in the narrativity of Mexican life for that elusive reality that we consider the collective identity of a community. How significant are these stories in the making of the collective identity of the contemporary Mexican woman? The young girls represented in Pacheco's stories are victims of a world they cannot alter; the change for a better world is in the hands of others. I have grouped the stories of this first section under three categories: enforced servitude, physical abuse, and sexual abuse.

It is not surprising that there is but scarce criticism on Pacheco's work, since these tales lack formal innovation and do not fit well into specific literary currents, whether domestic or foreign.[5] It is significant that the few commentaries published in Mexico do not accept the aesthetic premises of testimonial or documentary literature, as Marta Trueba called it (1982), but rather consider Pacheco's work from the restricted standpoint of European or U.S. mimetic norms (see Espinosa Rugarcía et al). This premise is not only derivative; it is also inappropriate for assessing writing that does not conform to certain culturally prescribed modes of representation. The mimetic aesthetic is not a mere imitation of visible reality; in western aesthetics since the Italian renaissance, the mimetic has been characterized as a remaking or refiguration of the world as perceived by the artist (Ricoeur, 1984, 52–54). Pacheco's documentary literature has its origins in the writings of anthropologists (see Pozas, Lewis). In this hybrid genre, a verbal description of action presents a social truth claim for the reader to consider. The critic searching for the psychological development of characters, as in Flaubert or the verbal mind games of Borges, might refuse to accept the character as a social symbol who displaces the moralizing function of an authoritative narrative voice. Readers of Pacheco's tales respond to the truth claims which the narrative offers and in so doing become involved in the ethical refiguration of their own sense of world and their values. Of course the narrative composition has an intentionality of denunciation, but what is of primary importance here is that readers, especially readers from Mexico City, find themselves faced with a situation with unmistakable aspects of the reality which is lived every day, and these readers must either stop reading or take ethical or moral positions. This literature is quite removed from the denunciations of Zola in *J'accuse* and closer to his *Germinal*.[6] Pacheco's work, like Zola's, offers a biting reflection for the reader who is willing to be part of this world. Some Mexican critics assume a comfortable pseudo-intellectualism which serves as a blindfold, and they refuse to consider documentary and testimonial fiction seriously.[7] The apparent simplicity of Pacheco's narrative does not present a fully delineated image but only a sketch which serves as a catalyst for the readers' or spectators' imagination and, at the same time, forces them to reflect on their values.

As I stated in Chapter 1, feminist social criticism concentrates on the process of world-making rather than the distinct products of individual interpreters. The interpretations of other critics are of little consequence to us unless we can understand the process that lies behind them. Equally, we have a profound distrust of all claims to full mastery over the text or the declaration of definitive interpretations. Practitioners of feminist social criticism are keenly aware of the difference between what is said ("all men are created equal") and what is meant ("all males are created equal") and, even more importantly, how something is said. The argument against Cristina Pacheco is a familiar one: the form is simple; there are no elaborate metaphors; there is no linguistic elaboration; the stories are journalistic reductions of complex social problems (see, e.g., Ruiz de Velasco). The same terms can be used without exception to characterize Picasso's *Guernica*—but there is no longer an ideological reason for rejecting his work. Academic literary studies in Mexico continue to reject feminist criticism and, even more emphatically, feminist social criticism. Therefore, it is not surprising that nothing of consequence has been published on Cristina Pacheco in Mexico in spite of the overwhelming popularity of her writing. This lack of critical attention to her work is an effort to keep the political embarrassment of the testimonial disclosure of Cristina Pacheco out of the critical debate, an attempt that has failed because ideas have no borders. Outside of Franco's Spain, Picasso's stark black, white, and gray angular and heavy lines and the harshness of representational distortion have been recognized by art critics as the artistic means for creating *Guernica*'s message of violence. Cristina Pacheco's short narratives are constructed with the same economy and the same discipline. As in the case of Picasso's painting, the artistic design is not one of static representation of an allegorical symbol depicting the event. In both Picasso's studies for *Guernica* and Pacheco's fiction, it is the very act of destruction that is being reenacted again and again and again as long as there are persons to look at the canvas or to read the text. Franco's Spain opposed the painting's ideological meaning but chose to dismiss it on aesthetic grounds; so it is with Cristina Pacheco's stories in Mexico. But perhaps the harsh images of Cristina Pacheco's young girls and women have a more striking analogy in the painting of objectivist German painters who were persecuted by the Nazis after they came to power in 1933. I refer to the work of Otto Dix, George Grosz, and Max Beckmann. The palpable reality they depict in their paintings has a hard edge. Despite attention to detail, this art is not realistic, for there is a powerful undercurrent of social criticism that eschews sentimentalism for a pictorial language of color and space that displaces and sets off the subject matter. The Nazis branded these paintings as degenerate art; we might call them works of participation in a higher morality. The same quality of artistic merit and political condemnation attend today to the relentless Cristina Pacheco.

Pacheco's documentary literature is solidly fastened in what Ricoeur calls the precomprehension of the world that all readers have:

The intelligibility engendered by emplotment finds a first anchorage in our competence to utilize in a significant manner the conceptual network that structurally distinguishes the domain of action from that of physical movement. . . . Actions imply goals, the anticipation of which is not confused with some foreseen or predicted result, but which commit the one on whom the action depends. Actions, moreover, refer to motives, which explain why someone does or did something . . . As a result, these agents can be held responsible for certain consequences of their actions. (1984, 54–55)

There is no doubt that Pacheco's work has as its aesthetic principle the goal of moving the reader to consider *goals* and *motives*.

The question "why was it done?" is not incompatible with the question "who has done it?" To identify an agent and to recognize the motives involved in the action are complementary operations. We also know that these characters act and suffer in circumstances beyond their control and that they nevertheless belong to the practical world of every day, because they must respond to the world as they find it. In their intervention as historical agents, fictional characters anchored in the specific reality of Mexico City today follow a temporal sequence of physical events and therefore offer the reader a role as a participant in the favorable or unfavorable situation occasioned by the action.

Characters in Pacheco's stories act as social symbols, for they synthesize the social action of intrahistorical protagonists.[8] The structures of Pacheco's stories are more descriptive than introspective. The stories involve the reader in a certain sequence of events that occurs in the daily reality of the Mexican capital, but this sequence of events may not be what the reader might consider the norm. This is a world of contingencies. This literature's aesthetic strength lies in its capacity to force itself into the reader's world.[9]

The exploitation of young girls who work as household domestics from the age of five in conditions which can only be described as slavery and which effectively exclude them from normal childhood development and from school is tragically commonplace in the poorest sectors of Mexico. The alarming growth of the disproportion of wealth between the different sectors of the national population has created a demographic time bomb which threatens the country's future. Mexico is a country of young people who have survived malnutrition, abandonment, and exploitation, and who are growing up in the midst of ignorance and illiteracy.[10]

The exploitation of young girls in household jobs is not only the result of poverty (in their provincial home states, only 20 percent normally receive adequate nourishment), but also the result of social class bias, which reinforces the idea that girls from Mexico's native population are accustomed to substandard living conditions. The most alarming statistics reported by physicians on the precarious existence of half of Mexico's young population cannot be ignored. The figures show that more than 50 percent of Mexican children of preschool age at present suffer some degree of mental retardation due to malnutrition.[11] Therefore, the enslavement of young girls in household jobs has to be examined not as isolated extreme incidents, but as part of a national inequity in a society which has paid its external debt at the expense of its children.

The first of the three topics I have selected which Pacheco portrays in her stories dealing with young girls is that of enforced servitude. Pacheco's stories feature hard-edged descriptions of principal characters. In the five stories we examine on this topic, these girls are all very young and live in Mexico City.

Sonia is about five years old and is the guide in the story "Four Blind Men and an Angel" (in *Para vivir aquí* [In order to live here], 107–110). She is described as being very small, with a strangely deformed head; her mouth is toothless and she wears a dirty dress. The blind musicians she guides go from one restaurant to another playing their music at the door while the child goes in to collect donations. Sonia enters a restaurant and is fascinated at the sight of a glass of cafe au lait. She asks the waitress whether she can have one too. The owner, joking with his customers, orders that she be served. Talking with her, he learns that she has never drunk milk; her only beverages are water and *atole* (Mexican drink made of corn). When he asks her jokingly if the mouse took away her teeth, Sonia, not understanding, says she did not see a mouse, but that she does remember the blows—"the violence which accelerated the course of nature usually observed elsewhere" (109). After just two bites to the biscuit and a few sips of milk, Sonia feels full and almost faints. The state of malnutrition she lives in has become obvious.[12]

In "The Child Elvira" (in *Cuarto de azotea* [Servant's room], 15–17), Elvira is in first grade. All that is mentioned of her physical appearance is that her hands hurt, chapped from the December cold; she is abused both physically and mentally by her parents. Her chores include carrying water in pails far too heavy for her, washing dishes, and doing household work for neighbors. When she shows her unhappiness at being sent to work instead of school, her mother tells her: "Just to show you, I am going to take you out of school, anyway it hasn't done you any good" (16).[13]

In "Slavery" (in *Cuarto de azotea*, 97–99), Alicia is an indigenous child from Oaxaca for whom her Mexico City "employers" paid two thousand pesos. They insult and beat her: "'Wretched *india*, you are good for nothing, but to gulp food down' . . . trembling with fury, doña Luisa takes the hot iron and tries to burn the child's face. To protect herself, Alicia raises her arm and covers her face" (57). She manages to escape from her employer, and it is the newspaper vendor woman who tries to lessen her pain.[14]

Jesusa is another child brought from Oaxaca to Mexico City, where she has become "The Prisoner" (in *Zona de desastre* [Disaster Zone], 97–99). The 1985 earthquake destroys the house she was living in, but she survives because she is tied to a pole in the middle of the house's patio. She has spent three years, since she was six years old, working in this house, being tortured and living tied up to a pole. The narrative voice observes: "Since Jesusa arrived to live in the yellow house nobody had quiet nights because suddenly, like a gust of wind, horrible screams rang in through the doors and windows" (98).[15]

Another child saved by the earthquake is Chelina in the story "The Shade of a Tree" (in *El corazón de la noche* [The night's heart], 75–79). Her father dies when the house caves in, but because he has chained Chelina to a tree, the girl survives. The neighbors used to hear her scream when her father beat her or when he left her without food, but afraid of reprisals, they never denounced him. The girl lived chained to the tree since she was very young. Her pastime was to clang one piece of chain against another, and she had made a ditch around the tree, going round and round like a chained dog. When the neighbors saw Chelina's condition, they called an ambulance and she was taken away. But after some time, she comes back to the side of the tree where she has always lived.

There have always been children who are victims of perverse parents or other abusive elements of society. Abuse of children is an international crime, as prevalent in the first world as in the impoverished third world. However, society's response to the abuse of children differs from one country to another. In Mexico, the second paragraph of article 211 of the criminal code affirms that corporal punishment to children is considered an offense only when the victim takes fifteen days to recuperate (see Bernal).

In September 1989, the Commission on Childhood of the National Council of the Mexican Women's National Union (UNMM) proposed a "Legal Code for the Rights of Minors." Part of this commission's declaration states that "children have become a subject of abuse, they have been drawn into the traffic of narcotics, are subject to sexual abuse and are even used for the sale of their vital organs." These facts are further aggravated because "there is no government budget line designated for their protection; the expenditures that the government assigns to Social Security have been constantly reduced, from 19.8 percent assigned in 1978 it was reduced to 10.56 percent in 1982" (Hernández Téllez, 42). Further, it is stated that out of every two million annual births in Mexico, one hundred thousand infants die before the age of five, and one million of those who survive have physical and mental defects (43) [16]—all victims of a society which pretends to have the well-being of its children as a priority.

The topic of physical and mental abuse is found in the following five stories by Cristina Pacheco.

Josefina, the small protagonist of "Noodle Soup" (in *Sopita de fideo* [Noodle soup], 113–115), is the oldest of six children. Her mother sends her with a dinner pail full of noodle soup to her father's workplace. The narrator states that the child is happy to do this because there is food in the house, even though only noodle soup and beans; it is understood that there are days where not even this is had. Even though she is a child, it is stated that she must walk along the gutter to avoid the hands of men who are drinking down the street; she cannot escape hearing what they call out to her. In the subway, the tumultuous hubbub of those getting off makes her lose her balance and the soup is spilled. The child gets off, embarrassed, sad, and fearful of the severe punishment she will receive.

In "Offering" (in *Cuarto de azotea*, 91–93), Rosario and her two brothers do not understand why their mother buys food only for the offering to their dead father on the upcoming Day of the Dead. One night the mother listens to the questions that her children ask each other: do dead people have a mouth, a stomach, and a place "to keep food." Next day they all go to the cemetery and the mother asks permission from the deceased to feed the children at least with the chicken broth and not wait until the Day of the Dead. Although the mother suffers to see her children go hungry, it is evident that beliefs weigh more heavily than her children's hunger.

"Joela" (in *La última noche del "Tigre"* [The 'tiger's' last night], 107–110) is the eldest child; she is ten years old, and all day long from waking to going to bed she is doing household work or errands. Her only privilege is being allowed to go to school, even though she has no time out of school to even open a book. Joela is immersed in sadness and asks herself if it is because she is so tired. She fears her father: "The most terrifying thing for Joela was the sight of her father . . . he is always ready to scold and punish her" (109). The teacher who knows of her life and reads the compositions she writes in school is burdened with the weight of the injustice.

The narrator of "The Bottom of the Glass" (in *La última noche del "Tigre"*, 118–121) is one of so many of Pacheco's stories of children who are victims of an alcoholic father. The emotional suffering, bitter experiences at mealtime, bad nights, lack of freedom, shame, and terror that these children suffer is described bluntly:

My father's disappearance, notwithstanding the terror it gave us, offered us a period of grace: it postponed the moment we would have to hear his sick monologue, his curses, his obscenities. Whilst he was away we were free because we knew that upon his return we would have to move about on tiptoes, keep the windows closed, and have to face our neighbors' pitying looks or cruel comments. (119) [17]

In "I Love My Teacher" (in *Para mirar a lo lejos* [To look far away], 19–21), the narrator asks openly where her teacher gets the strength to face the knowledge she has of the abuse, violence, hunger, and loneliness suffered by her young pupils: "Many times the cause of a pupil's absence from school was the clue to the brutal punishment imposed by parents or brothers. . . . Sometimes falling asleep in class was explained in simple direct phrases describing a common fact: 'I didn't have any breakfast and can't keep awake'" (20–21).

In Mexico, as in many other countries, there is a deep social contradiction: the society professes to have an enormous respect for women and at the same time fosters the idea that any female youngster can be considered an object of lust. Female street vendors in Mexico City begin to work at age four, and by fifteen they are mothers.[18] Typically between thirteen and fifteen, they are initiated into prostitution, usually through their partner. For women, life is precarious on the streets and in the slums of Mexico City; authorities calculate that there are about ninety thousand women raped annually in Mexico—one every eight minutes.[19] Less than 5 percent of the rapists are brought to trial, and an even smaller percentage are incarcerated. More than half of the rapists have an authoritative relationship to the victim; that is, they are fathers, uncles, teachers, or police officers. The rape victim usually knows her aggressor; studies have demonstrated that the majority of rapists in Mexico have repeated the offense at least five times. There are many instances of children like Adriana Nava, seven years old, of Chimalhuacan, who was raped by two men who were not taken to court because of the authorities' failure to act (see Barranco and Rodríguez).

What is there in Mexican society which promotes violence against women and moves the authorities to ignore these crimes or side with the aggressors? Cristina Pacheco says that one of the main reasons is the prevalent image of women as sexual objects and the all-too-common psychological scapegoat syndrome of the oppressed who look for someone weaker to abuse. There is no human being more inoffensive and helpless than a seven-year-old, and there are few human beings as oppressed as the young men in the impoverished sectors of Mexico.

In "The Man, the Girl, and the Saint" (in *Para vivir aquí*, 99–102), Clotilde is the terrified child, not yet twelve years old, who has been kidnapped by a man who for three weeks has forced her to be his woman; the saint is the image of the Christ child the man has above his bed. The man "offers him a reward" if the image will help him to keep the girl, but the girl offers the image a dozen to help her escape. She gets away.

In "The Sleeping Woman" (in *Cuarto de azotea*, 65–67), Epifania goes out every morning with a heavy sack of sunflower seeds, nuts, candies, and fruit to sell. But she falls asleep as soon as she finishes arranging her merchandise on the sidewalk. She only manages to make from ten to twelve pesos, which she hands over every night to an angry mother who scolds, beats, and, finally, threatens to throw her out if she does not sell at least twenty pesos' worth. Epifania fears being thrown out and tries to sell her wares, but her weakness inevitably causes her to fall asleep. She is so exhausted that "she does not notice the stares the fire-eater casts her way between clouds of black smoke; nor has she noticed the young cafe-drifter who observes her with the same lust every time he passes by her" (66).

In "Fifteenth Birthday" (in *Cuarto de azotea*, 123–126), Gloria's party ends in tragedy because her drunken father, who thinks that every male is intent on having sexual relations, shoots his daughter's date when the couple go out to the patio.

In "Justice" (in *La última noche del "Tigre"*, 79–82), Estela, eleven years old, is gang-raped. Her father repeatedly goes to the police and to a lawyer's office looking for justice, but all he gets are remarks like the following:

In order to take the action you want we need you to bring witnesses that confirm how and by whom the girl was attacked. It is also necessary to know if Estela had a relationship with any of those boys . . . maybe it is not the case of your kid but sometimes women incite, get into a mess and when they do not know how to get out of it claim they were forced. (79)

In "The Orbit of the Stars" (in *Para mirar a lo lejos*, 21–24), a twelve-year-old girl, Estrella, has developed physically at a very early age: "She matured all of a sudden. Her face did not change, only her body: well-endowed." She likes to sing, does it well, and can imitate popular singers: "Estrella went to all the performances where she was called by Johnny, 'a producer and agent of stars.' But she never came back with a contract" (22). Johnny prostituted her but Estrella went on dreaming, changing costumes according to the popular singer she was imitating at the moment. After several years, she returned home mentally unbalanced.

The purpose of this review of fifteen stories by Cristina Pacheco has been to outline the documentary basis of her writing. These stories, as a whole, create a social symbol of victimized young girls. The plot of each two- or three-page story is a small descriptive statement about injustice. The strength of the documentary story is to initiate the re-creation of the action in the reader's imagination.

Up to this point I have been developing the clear parallel between Pacheco's stories and the empirical data on life for young girls in Mexico City. Now I would like to offer some critical analysis of her stories as short stories as well as manifestations of her Zola-like didactic aesthetic. I will focus on stories from *Cuarto de azotea*. This section will examine (1) the formal features of Pacheco's narrative technique, (2) the emplotment, (3) the reading experience, and (4) the stories as documentary stories.

Documentary stories as realized by Pacheco impose a strict discipline on the writer. On the one hand, the situation of the character must be made clear and fully accessible to the reader in only a few pages, but on the other hand, the third-person narrative voice must not intrude, must not offer opinion, and, most of all, must not qualify the situation. This narrative observer must be a transparent window that does not add or subtract anything from the character's situation.

Dialogue is also restrained in the documental short story. There cannot be any hint of the rich dialectic of communication between two articulate speakers who respect each other and whose language is free of constraints. Pacheco's documentary dialogue represents the speakers in all their limitations and deficiencies; at times they approach being inarticulate. The only exchanges of characters in *Cuarto de azotea* which approach full dialogue are in letters presented without commentary in "No más porque no ha llovido" (Only because it hasn't rained, 73–76) and "Al pie de la letra" (In the spirit of the letter, 137–140).

Pacheco uses the first-person narrator's voice extensively, but again with extraordinary discipline, for her characters range from the poorest victims of abuse to the educated women of the last two stories I will discuss. The ability to speak freely and to express personal feelings in a language of social interaction is, of course, the mark of only a select few among Pacheco's women. Yet it is noteworthy that highly articulate, intelligent speech does not necessarily lead to understanding on the part of the person spoken to, for there are ideological barriers which are as great or greater than any limitation on the part of the woman speaking. In summary, Pacheco's narrative technique consists of a highly disciplined use of the characters' narrating voices as well as a third-person narrative voice. The art of her documentary literary technique is achieved through rigorous control of the narrative situation, which must belong to the characters and not to the narrative voice; it must be self-evident and devoid of any generalizing or moralizing commentary; and, most important of all, it must read as authentic speech to Mexican readers rather than the well-intentioned but false worldview of an educated and cultured author. Table 1 shows a schematic organization of the formal features of Cristina Pacheco's documentary stories. It is intended as a summary of the entire collection of short stories. The verisimilitude of the character's speech is, of course, necessary but the strict control of the third-person narrative voice is the basis for the transparency of her narrative technique.

The combination of narrating voices in Pacheco's short stories achieves a thematic unity that functions as a denunciation of social injustice. The stories establish the presence of their female characters, and they always articulate the frustration of women who try to participate in their community and who are denied access.

Table One   Narratological Aspects of Documentary Fiction

NARRATING VOICES	CHARACTER'S FIRST-PERSON SPEECH	CHARACTERS IN DIALOGUE	THIRD-PERSON NARRATIVE VOICE
Narrative capacity	Capacity limited to the scope of the character's world-view/means of self-expression	Verbalization of private thoughts in exceptional cases can become an exchange	Observer who describes without qualifying
Narrative function	Representation of the character in the social context	Character's participation in the social context	Establish basis for action
Narrative truth claim	Sincerity	Attempted participation	Situate characters in their world
Documental function	Presence	Frustrated participation	Bear witness to characters

In order of frequency of presentation, women's concerns are poverty, *machismo*, and love. The first two concerns are attended by a series of sub-themes which are derivative from the main statement. Thus, in conjunction with poverty, the stories feature a long list of social practices and problems which have become commonplace, such as back-alley abortion; rape victims treated as criminals; the economic enslavement of young girls as domestics and adult women in sweatshops; and illiteracy, hunger, lack of medical services, police corruption, and fear of violence and robbery. *Machismo* as a major social concern of Mexican society is not restricted to the population living at the lowest economic range of this third world country (see Chapter 1).[20]

Cristina Pacheco's treatment of sexuality is noteworthy. She is a highly effective observer who depicts sex as a natural part of life. Her material is both psychophysical and psychosocial. She does not treat either the religious issues of sexual taboos or the history of sexual relations. To fictionalize either subject would require more than the space she allows herself for each story. Her narrative point of view treats sexuality as a natural phenomenon with neither of the prurient filters of prudery or pornography. She deals with sexual frustrations and alienation through their effects on the male and the result in his treatment of the female.

The most disturbing aspect of human sexuality in the stories of Pacheco is that it has become a form of revenge by the male on life itself as embodied in the female. Tenderness is reserved for the female's relations with her children and is absent in sexual relations among adults. The egoistic search for self-gratification in the male is but the initial motive of male sexuality, for it is the male's self-image that is at stake. The sex act becomes degraded to the level of physical relief and limited to actual intercourse, with no foreplay. Mutual satisfaction is almost completely absent. The demonization of male sexuality is the extreme dehumanization of sex into a form of retribution for poverty and hopelessness. Sexual intercourse for the *macho* is a rapid physical release which cannot be elevated to the level of pleasure and which is often tied to a psychological drive to inflict pain on the woman. There is no sense of getting or giving pleasure, but only of release. Pacheco's stories do not deal with sexual love between women and men but only with sexual violence on the one hand and nonsexual love on the other.

The third theme is women's capacity for love. This includes love and nurturing of others at all the stages of life from youth to old age. In this society, love is a virtue that is exclusive to women, since men are taught to interpret tenderness and kindness as signs of weakness. Thus, all of the natural manifestations of human affection are presented as feminine traits. Women can forgive and can go without because their loved ones have become part of their being. Pacheco presents women as victims of a society in which they have managed for the most part to keep the fundamental human capacity for love alive. The *macho* is distorted as a human being because he has lost his capacity for love and in his abuse of women has become an emotional cripple.

The story "Esposa y mártir" (Wife and martyr, 33–36) is divided into three parts. The narrator is limited to a few lines. The story consists of dialogue and monologue. The brief first part sets the scene; Elisa regains consciousness in a hospital room where she has been for the last ten days. The woman in the next bed engages her in conversation. The dialogical situation is that of Elisa telling her story and doña Refugio interpreting it as the blessing of an all-merciful God. Elisa has been wounded with knives her husband threw at her. The narrative voice summarizes the scene rapidly.

The second part is entirely a first-person narration by Elisa of her family background. The third and last parts open with a one-line observation by the narrative voice. Elisa feels better and she needs to talk to someone. The rest of the story is dialogue between the two women. The dialogue develops the central incident of the story: Abundio comes home from work much earlier than usual, and before Elisa can inquire about his day, he tells her that he has been fired from his job as a night watchman because the owner found him shooting his gun at cans rather than making his rounds. Abundio is in a rage and Elisa tries to calm him down, asking him not to yell or he will awaken the children. He responds that they should be awakened because he wants to play target practice with them. Elisa responds that he can do what he wants with her, but that he is not to touch the children. He throws several knives at a plate she holds out, but in his unstable condition, he misses, and in his rage he throws the next three knives at her. One of the knives just misses the heart. Doña Refugio responds that she has to give thanks to the Christ of Miracles when she gets out of the hospital. The story's structure is exemplary of dramatic power and economy. There is not a single extra word in the less than four pages of the story. The combination of succinct third-person narrative voice setting the scene, the first-person narration of background, and the dialogue unfolding the dramatic action establishes a tension between tranquillity and violence and at a more profound level an ironic tension between a simple description by Elisa of Abundio's brutal violence, a pious acceptance of his inhumanity by Doña Refugio, and the reader's outrage.

The story "La esclavitud" (Slavery, 57–59), which I discussed briefly in the first part of this chapter, is about a young girl from Oaxaca who has been purchased from her family for two thousand pesos to work as a domestic servant in Mexico City. The story concentrates on the build-up to the sadistic burning of the youngster's arm because she comes back from the local tortilla merchant with the news that they ran out before it was her turn. Her situation is that of a domestic slave at the mercy of the couple that brought her to Mexico City. The narration is a combination of a narrative voice that reports on the action and dialogue. First, between Luisa and Sixto, the torturers of Alicia, and subsequently the halting broken dialogue between doña Julia, the newspaper vendor, and Alicia. Alicia presents a wretched picture: a young girl about twelve years old, barefoot, unwashed, dressed in rags, half-starved, her body covered with cuts, burns, and bruises, and her right arm now in extreme pain.

With the next story, we turn from the Mexican lower social classes and marginalized native population to the urban lower middle class. The story entitled "Los trabajos perdidos" (Lost labor, 61–64) is about Adela, a middle class housewife. The entire story, with the exception of the concluding paragraph, consists of the dialogue of a domestic argument. The husband Rogelio returns home from work, asking his wife Adela why the telephone is not working. He is a foul-mouthed lout whose sexist abuse of his wife is so powerful that it has permeated her view of herself. Rogelio's attack begins because she has forgotten to pay the telephone bill, but it becomes apparent that the interruption of telephone service is only an excuse for Rogelio to insult, belittle, and scorn his wife as useless. Although she puts up a defense of the value of her work, it is clear that all of the things that Rogelio takes for granted, such as meals, a well-kept home, clean clothes, and caring for the children are his rights, and the one who has to get them done is a non-entity. The climax comes in the last paragraph, with Adela's thoughts: "From self-pity she goes to rage when she realizes that she has begun to ask herself, 'Am I really as useless as Rogelio says?'"

The fourth story, "El hombre de la casa" (Man of the house, 94–101), centers on an upper middle class couple. They are both professionals, successful and highly visible as a modern couple. He is an architect, and she is head of her department in a large corporation. The husband arrives home and finds his wife in the last stages of dressing for a formal invitation that is very important to her professionally and personally—the inauguration ceremony of the new corporate offices. The ceremony will be in her domain, the place where she is known and important and where he is merely her husband. Such a situation is routine for wives of professional men, but it represents a reversal of the traditional pattern, and rebellion ensues: he refuses to accompany his wife. He claims that he is tired, that he has a headache, that he has forgotten about the engagement. She pleads with him, tries logic, argues fair play, affection, but all to no avail. Gradually, the truth emerges. He feels that his masculinity will be diminished if he is seen in the company of his successful wife at her place of work. This short story brings out the deeply rooted cultural connection which equates financial success with masculinity and servility with femininity. The ending of the story demonstrates that both husband and wife are conditioned by this ideology: Marcela's reflection in the mirror shows up her reddened face and she sees only the latent feeling of guilt that would beset her if she went to the inauguration without her husband. She thinks of excuses as she goes to the telephone, something that will be compatible with her image of being a dynamic, independent, successful woman who is full of self-confidence.

The last short story selected, "La dicha conyugal" (Conjugal bliss, 127–130), deals with the upper middle class of contemporary Mexico. Martha is a well-educated woman who has the advantages that wealth and social position offer a woman of her class. Now in her middle years, she is restless and yearns to be able to do something that is hers, to accomplish something as an intelligent, educated person. She is going through a mid-life crisis similar to that of women of her class in other parts of the world, and in keeping with her situation, she seeks the advice of a friend from her university days, Joel, who has become a distinguished neurologist. He greets her with the cordial friendship and familiarity of years. The dialogue that ensues between the two friends is cordial; he is solicitous of her confidence, and she does not hesitate in telling him that the reason she has asked to see him is that she feels life has passed her by, that she is unfulfilled as a person, that she wants more out of life than the future that awaits her. His response is friendly but without any sign of understanding that she aspires to the same sense of accomplishment that he takes for granted. He tells her to stop feeling guilty and enjoy her affluence. She says: "You do not understand me. This is not the time for me to sit back and do nothing." Her friend does not want to grasp the full significance of her words; she recognizes it in his look of disbelief. Joel, the narrator tells us, does not want to understand because her situation reminds him uncomfortably of that of his wife. He tells Martha that what she wants is impossible: "Time stops you, you cannot just decide to start out at mid-life." This story is unique in the stories of Pacheco, for this woman has the courage to say "no"; she does not accept her role in society, and she has the means to do something about it. The ending is ambiguous but has a glimmer of freedom. Martha states: "I do not accept it," and walks out.

What is literature? and, what is social history? These related questions have been asked and answered innumerable times, but they return to haunt us every time we engage a literary text as relevant to the world of action of both readers and writers. The nature of literature will remain an enigma as long as critics are tied to a subject-object mindset in their approach to texts. As a feminist social critic, I question the hegemony of the so-called real world. I find that all social realities are overladen with narrativity—a narrativity through which each of us thinks she makes up what she thinks is her own world, but which in fact is her father's world. Liberation from the preconceptions of our male-dominated social group does not consist in making up our own woman's language, for that would in fact chain us to reflex-action sexuality. Liberation comes only through knowledge and unmasking the role of social narrativity in sexist domination. Literary texts are not controlled by their authors, and much less by the social institutions that begot them; rather, literature is a personal, intimate, and sometimes threatening experience of reading that belongs to all who read these texts.[21] I make clear distinctions between reading and criticism. For one thing, a literary text exists as a virtual entity, that is, its potentiality for reading. The actual reading of a text is an individualized working out of the text's potential; it is always a private affair. Commentary about this private experience, by contrast, involves entry into the public sphere.

In my social literary criticism, I want above all to engage the reader in a discussion about what has happened to me in reading. I want to talk about the experience because "talking" about it completes it for me. But also I want to share, discuss, disagree, and agree with others about the world the text has given me because I know that my world is also part of my reader's world. Insofar as certain texts provide a space for the rethinking of one's own world, they are the creative force of the community. This room of one's own, to use Virginia Woolf's apt metaphor, is the right of every reader and especially those readers who have been marginalized by society. And, in my view, the social function of the critic is to have an open house at her room. This means that feminist socio-criticism is not in any way constrained to texts written by women or about women, but rather, it is always concerned with the woman's room, which has been the reading of the text in question.

Cristina Pacheco's short stories are literary texts of provocation which can lead the reader to rethink his or her values; it is primarily because of this provocation, which challenges the comfortable cliché-ridden superficiality of the dominant social group, that they are dismissed as advocacy by some and held out as popular literature by others. For feminist social critics, these stories provide that very special space for unmasking the deception of the social group's language, which seeks to keep women subjugated chattels in a male club, to honor and serve but not to think, speak, or create. Cristina Pacheco's literature has the enormous value of raising the consciousness of her readers. Her stories provide us with a powerful rush of sociocultural reality in our pursuit of the collective identity of Mexican women.

Eight   Poetry from the Margins

Sandra Cisneros

I n 1984 a Chicana writer from Chicago, Sandra Cisneros (1954–),[1] published *The House on Mango Street*, a postmodern novel which weaves a tapestry of apparently isolated vignettes into a poetic unity. Almost ten years later to the day, Elena Poniatowska's translation, *La casa en Mango Street*, was published; its reception should be revealing. There are a number of significant issues to be discussed concerning *The House on Mango Street*, but I believe that the most pressing issue is the ideological question of a poetics of identity in the double marginalization of a Chicana and the public response to this issue.[2]

Cisneros' literary persona, Esperanza, is the lyric narrative voice to whom the reader responds and whom the reader eventually knows.[3] The sensibility and feeling that the narrator captures from her experiences governs her relations with her world and its people, and is part of the long tradition of literature of the coming of age. As an aesthetic process, the apprehension of the world of Mango Street becomes a metaphor for identity. The consequence of this aesthetic process is that the reader is directed less toward the singularity of the places, events, and persons of Mango Street than toward the eye/I that writes them. The protagonist, Esperanza, probes into her world, discovers herself, and comes to embody the two most basic needs of all human beings: freedom and belonging.

The following passage from an article by Ricoeur will serve as an intellectual paradigm for my commentary on Chicana identity as a part of the reading experience. Ricoeur writes:

What we want to understand is not something hidden behind the text, but something disclosed in front of it. What has to be understood is not the initial situation of discourse, but what points toward a possible world. . . . To understand a text is to follow its movement from sense to reference, from what it says, to what it talks about. ("Model of the Text," 218)

The main semantic focus of Cisneros' text is the presentation of the narrating self. My commentary is aimed at establishing a historically based critical model of reading for the presentation of this self. The narrating presence is a composite of a poetic enunciating voice and a narrative voice, and this presence can best be described as a formal function within the literary structure who as a speaker is knowable only as a storyteller in her response to the extratextual, societal and historical, determinate referents. Notions of self or voice are implicitly controlled by the spectrum of the world of action as known to the reader, and notions of character are explicitly linked to the notions of person in the world. The union of the self and person is the hallmark of the lyrical text. If voice or self is an impulse toward the world, person or character is a social structure of dispositions and traits. In brief, the text in *The House on Mango Street* presents the exterior and the interior of living in the world.

The narrative situation is a familiar one: a sensitive young girl's reflections of her struggle between what she is and what she would like to be. The sense of alienation is compounded because ethnically she is a Mexican, although culturally a Mexican American; she is a young girl surrounded by examples of abused, defeated, worn-out women, but the woman she wants to be must be free. The reflections of one crucial year in her life are narrated in the present of a first-person point of view. This was the year of the passage from preadolescence to adolescence, when she discovered the meaning of being female and Mexican living in Chicago, but, most of all, this was the year she discovered herself through writing. The girl who did not want to belong to her social reality learns that she belongs to herself, to her others, and not to a place.

The frame for the series of narratives is simple but highly effective. The family has been wandering from place to place, always dreaming of the promised land of a house of their own. When they finally arrive at the house on Mango Street, which is at last their own house, it is not the promised land of their dreams. The parents overcome their dejection by saying that this is not the end of their moving, that it is only a temporary stop before going on to the promised house. The narrator knows better. The conflict between the promised land and the harsh reality, which she always recognizes in its full force of rejection, violence, fear, and waste, is presented directly and without compromise. This is just the way things are on Mango Street, but the narrator will not give up her dream of the promised house. The lesson she must learn is that the house she seeks is in reality her own person. She must overcome her rejection of who she is and find her self-esteem. She must be true to herself and thereby gain control of her identity. Her search for self-esteem and her true identity is the subtle, yet powerful, narrative thread that unites the text and achieves the breakthrough of self-understanding in the last entries.

We can trace this search through some of its many moments. The narrative development begins in the first entry, "The House": "I knew then I had to have a house. A real house. One I could point to. But this isn't it. The house on Mango Street isn't it. For the time being, Mama says. Temporary, says Papa. But I know how those things go" (9). The narrator goes on to describe the family circle, where she has warmth and love but is lonely and, most of all, estranged from the world outside. Her name, Esperanza, in English means "hope": "At school they say my name funny as if the syllables were made out of tin and hurt the roof of your mouth. But in Spanish my name is made out of a softer something, like silver" (13). Fear and hostility are the alienating forces she tries to understand. Why do people of other color fear her? And why should she fear others? That's the way it is. "All brown all around, we are safe" (29). Changes are coming over her; she is awakening to sexuality and to an adult world. She explores the question of her identity in "Four Skinny Trees": "They are the only ones who understand me. I am the only one who understands them" (71).

"A Smart Cookie" touches on one of the most sensitive areas of the text: the mother-daughter relationship. Her mother remains nostalgic not for what was, but for what might have been: "I could've been somebody, you know?" (83). Being somebody is full of unarticulated significance, but in its impact on Esperanza, it means primarily to be herself and not what others want her to be. Her mother tells her that she had brains, but that she was also self-conscious and ashamed that she did not look as good as other, more affluent girls. She quit school because she could not live looking at herself in the mirror of the other girls' presence. She states forthrightly: "Shame is a bad thing, you know. It keeps you down" (83). The syndrome is there; it is a closed circle. You are poor because you are an outsider without education, you try to get an education, but you can't take the contrastive evidence of poverty and "it keeps you down." The constant movement of the narrative takes up one aspect after another of the circumstances of the emerging subject that is Esperanza Cordero.

There is a subtle sequential order to the short sections. The text opens with the description of the house and its significance to the narrator, moves on to a delicate image of the family group, and then, with the third piece, "Boys and

Girls," begins the highly lyrical exposition of the narrator's world, punctuated with entries of introspection in the narrator's struggle with her identity. "My Name," "Chanclas," "Elenita, Cards, Palm Water," "Four Skinny Trees," "Bums in the Attic," "Beautiful and Cruel," "The Monkey Garden," "The Three Sisters," and "A House of My Own" are the most significant entries because they mark the narrative development of identity. The text ends with the anticipated departure from the house and the literary return to it through writing. Although each entry can be seen as a self-contained prose poem, there is the subtle narrative unity of the enunciating voice's search for herself as she observes and questions her world and its social, economic, and moral conventions.

Esperanza Cordero observes, questions, and slowly finds herself determined through her relationship to the others who inhabit her world. She is drawn to the women and girls as would-be role models; within her family, her mother and her younger sister Magdalena (Nenny) are characterized, but the most searching descriptions are of girls her own age or, as she says, a few years older.[4] The enunciating voice never breaks her verisimilar perspective. She speaks about what she sees and what she thinks. Her style is one of subtlety, understatement, and generosity. When she reflects on social hostility or the brutality of wife-beating, it is not with violence or rancour, but with a firm determination to describe and to escape the vicious cycle of abused women: Rosa Vargas is the mother "who is tired all the time from buttoning and bottling and babying, and who cries every day for the man who left without even leaving a dollar for bologna or a note explaining how come" (30). Marín is not allowed out and hopes to get a job downtown so that she "can meet someone in the subway who might marry and take you to live in a big house far away" (27). Then there is "Alicia, who inherited her mama's rolling pin and sleepiness" and whose father says that "a woman's place is sleeping so she can wake up early with the tortilla star" (32); and "Rafaela, who is still young but getting old from leaning out the window so much, gets locked indoors because her husband is afraid Rafaela will run away since she is too beautiful to look at" (76). "Minerva is only a little bit older than me but already she has two kids and a husband who left . . . she writes poems on little pieces of paper that she folds over and over and holds in her hands a long time" (80). And there is Sally, whose father hits her and "her mama rubs lard on all the places where it hurts. Then at school she'd say she fell. That's where all the blue places come from. That's why her skin is always scarred" (85).

The first person moves effortlessly from observer to lyrical introspection about her place in the world. The language is basic, idiomatic English with a touch of colloquial speech and a few Spanish words. The deceptively simple structure of sentences and paragraphs has a conceptual juxtaposition of action and reaction where the movement itself is the central topic. For example, "Those Who Don't," which consists of three short paragraphs, is about alienation and fear in a hostile society, but it is only fourteen lines in total. It begins with a direct statement about life as she sees it: "Those who don't know any better come into our neighborhood scared. They think we're dangerous. They think we will attack them with shiny knives. They are stupid people who are lost and got here by mistake" (29). The second paragraph, five lines long, begins with the "we" that is the implicit opposite of the "they" of the preceding paragraph. "But we aren't afraid. We know the guy . . . ." With the economy of a well-written sonnet, the third five-line paragraph brings the "they" and the "we" into an inverted encounter: "All brown all around, we are safe. But watch us drive into a neighborhood of another color and our knees go shakity-shake and our car windows get rolled up tight and our eyes look straight. Yeah. That is how it goes and goes" (29). The description has been that of a keen observer; the composition is that of a poet.

This is a structure that operates through a conceptual back-and-forth movement of images, like the action of the shuttle in the loom.[5] An image appears which moves the reader forward following the woof of the first-person through the warp of referential world, but as soon as the image takes shape, it is thrust back toward the enunciator. The process is repeated again and again, slowly weaving the tapestry of Esperanza's Mango Street. For example, in "Those Who Don't," the initial image is about the others, "Those who don't know any better," but it reaches culmination with the observation that "they think we're dangerous." The countermove is that "They are stupid people." The new thrust forward is the reassurance of familiarity with the ostensibly menacing scene that greeted the outsiders and led them to fear they would be attacked. But when the shuttle brings back the narrative thread, it presents the inversion. The "we" are the "they" in another neighborhood. The movement back and forth will go on, the narrator says, "That is how it goes and goes." The color of the warp is different in each community; the woof keeps them next to each other, but their ignorance and fear keeps them separate. The tapestry that is being woven by this constant imagistic back-and-forth movement of the narrator's perceptions and thoughts is not a plotted narrative, but rather a narrative of self-invention by the writer-speaker. The speaker and her language are mutually implicated in a single interdependent process of poetic self-invention.

The poetic text cannot operate if we separate the speaker from her language; they are the inseparable unity of personal identity. There is no utterance before enunciation. There is a fictional persona, Esperanza Cordero, who will speak, and there is the implicit continued use of idiomatic American English. But the enunciation that we read is at once the speaker and the spoken, which discloses the subject, her subjectivity, and ours. An inescapable part of this subject is what she is expected not to be: "Mexicans don't like their women strong" (12). "I wonder if she [my great-grandmother] made the best with what she got or was she sorry because she couldn't be all the things she wanted to be. Esperanza. I have inherited her name, but I don't want to inherit her place by the window" (12). This reading of the text, with close attention to how it operates, suggests a movement and a countermovement which I have described metaphorically as the movement of a loom weaving the presence of subjectivity. Subjectivity is always seen against the background of her community, Chicago's changing neighborhoods. This determinate background gives narrative continuation, or narrativity, to the narrator's thoughts. The narrative development of this text can be described as the elaboration of the speaker's subjectivity. The symbolic space she creates should not be abstracted from the writing, because the writing itself is the creation of her own space.[6] The structure begins as a frame for self-invention, and as the writing progresses, so does the subject. She is, in the most direct sense of the word, making herself in a space of her own.

There are numerous empirical and verisimilar truth claims about the way of life in the neighborhood.[7] All of these references form a well-knit web of specific truth claims about social reality. At the same time, there is another kind of reference—to the narrator's own sense of the world, her wonderment, and her search for answers about why things are the way they are for her and for those who are her family, friends, and neighbors: Minerva "comes over black and blue and asks what can she do? Minerva. I don't know which way she'll go. There is nothing *I* can do" (80); "Sally. What do you think about when you close your eyes like that? . . . Do you wish your feet would one day keep walking and take you far away from Mango Street, far away and maybe your feet would stop in front of a house, a nice one with flowers and big windows" (78). Esperanza meditates after her Aunt Lupe's death: "Maybe she was ashamed. Maybe she was embarrassed it took so many years. The kids who wanted to be kids instead of washing dishes and ironing their papa's shirts, and the husband who wanted a wife again. And then she died, my aunt who listened to my poems. And then we began to dream the dreams" (57). This quest for answers takes on an explicit tension because of the depth of the themes the narrator treats, but the manner in which she develops her search for answers is the fundamental dialectic of self-world. She describes what is around her, responds to people and places, but, most importantly, she reflects on a world she did not make, and cannot change, but must control or she will be destroyed. She is a young, dark-skinned girl of Mexican parentage, born in Chicago, speaking English and feeling alienated.

The use of these determinate features is of primary importance, for it is through the interplay between the lyrical introspection and the truth claims that the fusion of self (enunciating voice) and person (character) takes place. The power of the text lies precisely in the creation of this presence. It is this human presence that transcends the time, place, and condition of the composition to create a literary metaphor for a woman coming of age. Readers half-way around the world, who have never seen Chicago and have never experienced what it is to live with the fear expressed in "All brown all around, we are safe," can, nevertheless, understand what it is to be lonely and alienated and how difficult it is to come out free from an environment that enslaves.

The images evoked by the text all signal a subject, Esperanza Cordero, an adolescent Mexican American girl who wants to be a writer. As critical readers, we read in a manner that creates ourselves as recipients, our own self-invention as the sympathetic listeners of the tale, attentive to actualize the words into images clothed in the colors of our own experience. The subject that emerges from our reading is neither the author's nor ours; she is a unique construct of intersecting designs and paradigms, those of the author's structure of the text and those of the larger cultural context we share in part with the author. But this construct can be reconstructed only from its effects on us, its readers. Thus, the subject I am dealing with in these pages is a deliberate reconstruction from the effects of reading.

In order to draw out the subject of this text, I will comment on three of the numerous images which are part of this work. The imagery in this text functions on three levels in the manner of prose poems. The images are effective because they function at the level of form, of plot, and of symbolic significance. Each of these images serves, first, to establish the identity of the enunciating voice; this is primarily a poetic function of creating the lyric presence who experiences and speaks. But the images also have a narrative function as a part of the story line, which is the search for the promised house. And, finally, each image takes on symbolic proportions because it participates in the rich intertextuality of literature.

"Four Skinny Trees" presents the most iconic image in the entire text. The trees are personified in the image of the narrator: "Four skinny trees with skinny necks and pointy elbows like mine" (71). But the description is also markedly referential to the specific urban setting of the text: "Four who grew despite concrete" (71). At the primary level of the enunciating voice's identity, the image evokes a clear statement about belonging and not belonging to the place where they happen to have grown: "Four who do not belong here but are here" (71). The narrative is composed of four short paragraphs. The first, with lyrical rhythm, establishes reciprocity between "I" and "they," four skinny trees. The second completes the personification: "they" completely supplants "trees." The third paragraph introduces their function: "they teach"; and the fourth gives the lesson: "to reach and not forget to reach and to be and be." At the level of story, the trees serve as a talisman of survival in a hostile environment:

Let one forget his reason for being, they'd all droop like tulips in a glass, each with their arms around the other. Keep, keep, keep, trees say when I sleep. They teach. When I am too sad and too skinny to keep keeping, when I am a tiny thing against so many bricks, then it is I look at trees. When there is nothing left to look at on this street. Four who grew despite concrete. Four who reach and do not forget to reach. Four whose only reason is to be and be. (71)

Esperanza's survival amidst surroundings that are negative and a rejection of her sensibility is not a denial of where she is and who she is, but rather a continual fight to survive in spite of Mango Street as Esperanza from Mango Street. It is, however, at the symbolic level that the image of the trees attains its fullest significance. There is a secret to survival that the trees make manifest—an unconquerable will to fight without respite in order to survive in an urban setting: "Their strength is secret. They send ferocious roots beneath the ground. They group up and they grow down and grab the earth between their hairy toes and bite the sky with violent teeth and never quit their anger. This is how they keep" (71). I want to emphasize that the visual aspects of the textual imagery engage the reader in the visual figuration of vertical movement in trees. Is this a form of intertextuality? I think it more appropriate to say that the visual imagery is a woman's prose painting.

The highly lyrical presentation of the "Three Sisters" evokes the fairy godmothers of fairy-tale lore, each with a unique image and gift for the heroine. Their gift is the gift of self: "When you leave you must remember to come back for the others. A circle, understand? You will always be Esperanza. You will always be Mango Street. You can't erase what you know. You can't forget who you are" (98). This poem-piece is unlike any of the others in form because it combines the prose-poem quality of the rest of the book with the most extended dialogue sequence. The three sisters speak to Esperanza. The speaking voices are of crucial importance, for through their enunciation they become full participants in the story-telling evocation with Esperanza.

At the level of plot, the sisters serve as revelation. They are the narrative mediators that enter the story, at the crucial junctures, to assist the heroine in the trial that lies ahead. It is significant that they are from Mexico and appear to be related only to the moon. In preconquest Mexico the lunar goddesses, such as Tlazolteotl and Xochiquetzal, were the intermediaries for all women (Westheim, 105). They are sisters to each other and as women, sisters to Esperanza. One has laughter like tin, another has the eyes of a cat, and the third hands like porcelain. This image is above all a lyrical disclosure of revelation. Their entrance into the story is almost magical: "They came with the wind that blows in August, thin as a spider web and barely noticed" (96), for they came only to make the gift to Esperanza of her selfhood. At the symbolic level, the three sisters are linked with Clotho, Lachesis, and Atropos, the three fates. Catullus depicts them weaving their fine web of destiny: "Three sisters pealed their high prophetic song,/Song which no length of days shall prove untrue" (173).[8] The tradition of the sisters of fate runs deep in western literature from the most elevated lyric to the popular tale of marriage, birth, and the fate awaiting the hero or heroine. In Cisneros' text, the prophecy of the fates turns to the evocation of self-knowledge.

The last image I shall discuss is based on the number two, the full force of opposition between two houses, the one on Mango Street and the promised house, which is now the projection of the narrator. Although this image runs throughout the text, "The House on Mango Street," "Alicia," "A House of My Own," and "Mango Says Goodbye Sometimes" are the principal descriptions. The imagery of the house is in constant flux between a negative and a positive, between the house the narrator has and the one she would like to have: "I knew then I had to have a house. A real house. One I could point to. But this isn't it. The house on Mango Street isn't it" (9). On the level of the narrative voice's sense of belonging and identity, it is clear from the first entry that the house is much more than a place to live. It is a reflection, an extension, a personified world that is indistinguishable from the occupant. The oppositional pull and push continues throughout and reaches its climax in the last three entries. In "Alicia and I Talking on Edna's Steps," the pull and push is in the form of reported dialogue: "No, this isn't my house I say and shake my head as if shaking could undo the year I've lived here. I don't belong. I don't ever want to come from here . . . I never had a house, not even a photograph . . . only one I dream of" (99). Because the house has become an extension of the person, the rejection is vehement. She knows the person she is does not belong to the hostile, ugly world she lives in.

"A House of My Own" expands on the promised house of her dreams in subtle, yet evocative, intertextuality to Virginia Woolf's *A Room of One's Own*:[9] "Only a house quiet as snow, a space for myself to go, clean as paper before the poem" (100). The house is now a metaphor for the subject and, therefore, the personal space of her identity. The last entry resolves the oppositional tension by transforming it into writing, into the metaphor of going away from Mango Street in order to return.

At the level of the plot, the opposition of the house on Mango Street and a house of her own provides the narrative thread for the text. It is the movement implicit in the description of hostility and poverty and the belief in a better life that gives the story its inner cohesion and builds the consistency of the narrator's reflections. The fact that this conflict between alienation and the need to belong is common to persons of all cultures and across history gives the text its thematic link to world literature. There is a perfect circularity in the plot insofar as the text ends when the writing begins. The opening lines of the text are the closing. Esperanza has made her tension a tension creative of her subjectivity. The idea of creative tension is well known to us through the work of Gaston Bachelard's *The Poetics of Space* and *The Poetics of Reverie* as well as Paul Ricoeur's *The Rule of Metaphor*; however, we must be reminded that this idea was already implicit in Aristotle's discussion of representation as the tension between the object known to be represented and the means used to represent it. In my work, I follow the theory that the image is not the residue of an impression, not an imprint that fades with time; on the contrary, the image that is produced through speech gives us the speaking subject and the subject spoken of, entwined in a unity of expression. If we move from speech to the written text, the situation becomes richer with possibilities. The text makes the image possible, the reader makes it actual, and the image is something new in our language, an entity of reflection that was not there before; it is the poetic subjectivity in which we participate.

My commentary on these pages is reflective, aimed at participation and not at imposing closure on the text for other readers. As readers, regarding the self-invention of writing, we must respect the specificity of the self-invention, that is, a Chicana coming of age. In all patriarchal societies, but especially in Chicano culture, there is the imposition of the sign of gender which serves to silence women, to force them to particularize themselves through the indirect means of the way and style in which they serve others. This is the ideological meaning of "a daddy's house." By writing, this young woman has created herself as a total subject and not a gender role or a disembodied voice.

The symbolic level of the image of the house is the most basic expression of existence. Everything about the house on Mango Street repels the lyric narrator. This house is not hers and does not reflect her presence. The house of her dreams is first described in negative terms, by what it cannot be: "Not a flat. Not an apartment in back. Not a man's house. Not a daddy's" (100). This is followed by its attributes: "A house all my own. With my porch and my pillow, my pretty purple petunias. My books and my stories. My two shoes waiting beside the bed" (100). And it also excludes: "Nobody to shake a stick at. Nobody's garbage to pick up after" (100). The problem is that she belongs to the house on Mango Street, and to deny it would be at the expense of herself, of her identity. She belongs to a world that is not hers; it is an opposition that will not be resolved in a synthesis or a compromise. The metaphor of a place of her own draws upon the continuing tensional opposition. She learns not only to survive but also to win her freedom, and the text itself with its title and its search for the promised house is the creative tension of poetry. The semantic impertinence of belonging and not belonging creates the metaphorical meaning of identity as one who does not forget to reach and to reach and whose only reason is to be and be. The conclusion, "Mango Says Goodbye Sometimes," is lyrical and meditative: "Friends and neighbors will say, What happened to Esperanza? Where did she go with all those books and paper? Why did she march so far away? They will not know that I have gone away to come back. For the ones I left behind. For the ones who cannot out" (101–102).

The liberation of Esperanza through her writing draws from a rich tradition of a writer's self-creation. Reflection, in this tradition, is the movement toward the very core of being. Not only does the past become present through the act of writing, but also, of more consequence, the projection into the self's future is predicated on the self-knowledge of this existentialized consciousness. To remember, therefore, is not just to go back in time; it is the recovery of the past that makes the future. Esperanza remembers the time when her blind aunt listened to the poem she whispered in her ear, and she reflects on her aunt's response: "You must keep writing. It will keep you free, and I said yes, but at that time I didn't know what she meant" (56).

Sandra Cisneros' text is a fictional autobiography of Esperanza Cordero. This is a postmodern form of fiction, a stitching together of a series of lyrical pieces—"lazy poems," Cisneros calls them in "Do You Know Me?" (1987, 79)—into the narrativity of self-invention through writing. In her study on autobiography, Sidonie Smith establishes a theoretical position which is at once lucid and fully applicable to my endeavor in this study. Esperanza's position as a woman gives a particularity to the writing itself in four places: the fiction of memory, of self, of the reader, and of the narrativity itself. Her position of authority to interpret herself must be asserted by writing, but it must be done against the grain, for she lives in a patriarchal Mexican American culture, where stories about women silence and subjugate them, as in the case of her namesake, her great-grandmother. Finally, Esperanza's basis of authority—she knows what she has lived and felt—is vulnerable unless she asserts her presence in a specific everyday reality; in other words, it cannot slip into a day-dream escape route which would be an evasion, not a liberation; she must make her presence, the presence of a woman writing.[10]

Cisneros begins the end of her text with the affirmation of self-invention that displaces men's stories about women: "I like to tell stories. I am going to tell you a story about a girl who didn't want to belong" (101). By writing, Esperanza has not only gained control of her past, she has also created a present in which she can be free and belong at the same time. Her freedom is the fundamental freedom to be herself, and she cannot be herself if she is entrapped in patriarchal narrativity. Mango Street will always be part of this woman, but she has taken the strength of trees unto herself and has found the courage to be the house of her dreams, her own self-invention.

The public response from readers of *The House on Mango Street* has been predictably of three kinds: (1) reviews in the daily press, especially in the U.S. Southwest, where Cisneros' original publishers are located (Arte Público, Houston, Texas); (2) some academic commentators, especially those concerned with women's writing; and (3) the ethnic press. All three have clear ideological commitments which are the focal means of commentary. What was not predictable when the book appeared was that the public response was largely irrelevant to the success of the text. The success of this novel is based on a unique formal configuration that inserts the symbolic addressee—*las mujeres*—into the reading experience. Sandra Cisneros has written a novel with a symbolic reader who is her sister in opposition, but in order to address her she has had to develop an implied reading strategy for reader participation.

The author's implied reading strategy can be construed as an ideological calculation to attract some readers, to confront others, and perhaps to mark the author's place within the social group. Sandra Cisneros is writing this first novel in the explosive mid-1980s in the United States. She situates herself as author, as a woman, and as a member of one of the multiple ethnic minorities that strive for the dignity of difference in a multicultural world. In order to address this situated reading of *The House on Mango Street*, I have constructed an approach which begins with a review of reviews and ends with the basic issues of identity. My analysis has five parts: (1) a review of public response; (2) an analysis of Cisneros' symbolic reader, that is, *las mujeres*; (3) the strategy of implied reading and reader participation; (4) the intersection of symbolic reader and implied reading; and (5) the novel as a part of a poetics of cultural identity.

The published response to *The House on Mango Street* has followed traditional patterns. In the years 1984 and 1985, newspaper reviews appeared, for the most part brief impressions of the book, often hampered by the lack of literary context in which the writers were reporting. In 1986 and 1987, academic response began, stressing the significance of the generic innovation and, in general, introducing this new author through careful and measured description. In 1988 and 1989, there were interpretive essays probing into the feminist and cultural depth of the poetic discourse, and by the 1990s, the novel was treated within the context of scholarly books on culture and literature. In total, I shall review thirty publications, including nine by Sandra Cisneros herself.

In June 1984, Bonnie Britt wrote in the *Houston Chronicle* that Cisneros' stories express the reality of voiceless women, that the narrator is the embodiment of female possibility, a metaphor for a woman who takes charge of her own life. Jewelle Gomez wrote in *Hurricane Alice* in the summer of 1984 that Cisneros had produced a series of prose poems which explore the bifurcated world of Hispanic women today. Bryce Milligan, writing in the San Antonio *Express-News* in October 1984, remarked that *Mango Street* must be read as a real place where real people grow up and not some ethereal place of the imagination. José David Saldívar reviewed the book in *Melus* and commented that above all the prose evokes an extraordinarily beautiful and moving sense of identity of Esperanza Cordero, the narrator, and at the same time expresses feminist concerns through a powerful socially symbolic imagination. By far the worst review written to date is Cecilia Cota-Robles Suárez's brief commentary in *Lector*, which characterizes the novel as "a valuable, if not extraordinary, addition to Hispanic children's literature." This novel reminds the reviewer of *A Tree Grows in Brooklyn*; one cannot but ask whether the reviewer read the book.

The year 1985 added more reviews and, of special significance, two autobiographical essays by Cisneros in response to some of the questions about her novel and its purported autobiographical content. Roy Gomez wrote in *VíAztlan* (San Antonio) that this novel brings home the emerging consciousness of the modern Chicana and saw at the core of the novel a struggle to redefine her existence. In general, this reviewer was sensitive to the richness of Cisneros' text, but there are some unfortunate statements that were to become focal points of controversy. Roy Gómez writes: "Esperanza's dream of a spacious home is a metaphor for independence" (21). The emphasis on size brings in questions of affluence, the inner city/outer city, and so on, all of which are not the material of the novel. Esperanza never stresses the size of her house, but rather her identity with it. The other, even more, unfortunate statement opens the next paragraph: "Men, for Esperanza, represent the freedom denied women" (21). The unequivocal feminist political statement of the novel is wholly lost in the inaccurate use of the word "represent." Men have freedom; women do not; that is the point. If there is any representation of freedom in the novel, it is that of the three sisters, *las comadres*, who reveal to her that she can find freedom through her writing. Erlinda González-Berry and Tey Diana Rebolledo wrote a brief comparison of Cisneros' novel and Tomás Rivera's *. . . y no se lo tragó la tierra*. Noteworthy is their emphasis on what they consider Cisneros' use of myth in the development of her coming-of-age novel.

Of special significance for the public dialogue about this novel were two autobiographical essays presented and published by Cisneros. The first was published in the 1985 text edited by Wolfgang Binder, *Partial Autobiographies. Interviews with Twenty Chicano Poets*. I quote Cisneros: "I know I do not want to become so anonymous that I am American. I want to retain my distinctiveness and yet we are inheritors of our new speech, products of our educations" (73). The other essay is "My Wicked, Wicked Way: The Chicana Writer's Struggle with Good and Evil or las hijas de la mala vida" and was delivered at the Modern Language Association convention in Chicago in 1985.

A new array of reviews came out in 1986, some poor, some mediocre, and at least two quite revealing of the social pressures on Chicanos in the United States. David Medina quoted Nicolás Kanellos, the publisher of the book, who asserted that *The House on Mango Street* is not a feminist text; "it is a celebration of femininity and the maternal" (14); the political agenda of this statement is self-evident. Juan Rodríguez reported in the *Austin Chronicle* that Cisneros' novel expresses the traditional ideology of the American dream—a large house in the suburbs and being away from the dirt and dirty of the *barrio* is happiness. He hammers away that Esperanza seeks "to become more Anglicized," to lose her ethnic identity. This is a good example of a reviewer reading into the text the fears and anxieties that plague the reviewer at the expense of the text.[11] The social conditions depicted in the novel are deplorable to all who live there, but especially to the women; Esperanza would deny herself and Chicana women if she did not break out of the prison that the *barrio* imposes. Kimberley Snow commented in the Santa Barbara *News-Press* that *Mango Street* is an extraordinary work that reveals the profound wisdom of the emerging consciousness of a young girl coming of age in the *barrio*. Finally, also in 1986, the only review published in Mexico was the commentary written by Elena Urrutia in the feminist journal *fem.*; it is an incisive descriptive review.

In 1987 Cisneros published five articles which added considerably to the discussion of the ideological context of a Chicana feminist poet and novelist. An interview given to Beatriz Badikian added some insight into Cisneros' attention to the development of her craft as a writer, her concern with the rhythms of speech transferred to the written text. The same year the dean of Chicano critics, Luis Leal, wrote a review article which underscored the text's portrayal of Chicano life. Julián Olivares' interpretive essay of 1987 was published in the book *Chicano Creativity and Criticism*. This commentary draws extensively on Gaston Bachelard's *Poetics of Space* in examining Cisneros' text. Fundamentally, he sees the house as a metaphor for the house of fiction. This careful and insightful study, however, overlooks the essential factor that this is a woman's point of view written by a woman and dedicated to other women. This oversight is partially overcome by Yvonne Yarbro-Bejarano's powerful if too short comment in a review of current trends in Chicana literature. The co-editor of the volume, María Herrera-Sobek, added a brief but deeply perceptive commentary on Esperanza's loss of innocence in "The Red Clowns." Esperanza's pained and disillusioned protest is aimed "not only at Sally, the silent interlocutor, but at the community of women" (178); this is the narrative addressee or symbolic reader that hovers over the entire text.

Heiner Bus' 1988 essay on Chicano literature of memory marks a turning point in Cisneros criticism, moving as it does into the wide-open cross fire of North American multiculturalism and out of the more limited focus of ethnic writing as nostalgia and survival of identity.

By 1989, critics responding to *The House on Mango Street* no longer felt constrained to explain the *barrio* or the author's relation to it or what it means to be a Chicana writer. These later critics have now come to terms with the creative power of the text. Ellen McCracken's study, "Sandra Cisneros' *The House on Mango Street*: Community-Oriented Introspection and the Demystification of Patriarchal Violence," forcefully engages the ideological domination over the literary canon, gives a fine reading of the text, and concludes with a careful point-by-point rebuttal of the *macho*-Chicano attitude of Gutiérrez-Revuelta (1986). In her feminist critical analysis, she points out how Esperanza rejects sexual reification, and she brings out the strength and power of Cisneros' Esperanza as a person who attains her identity and individuality because of and through her community. Also from 1989 is Renato Rosaldo's book, *Culture and Truth*. Chapter 7, "Changing Chicano Narratives," dedicates five pages to *Mango Street*. Here there is a clear recognition of the changes in Chicano narratives that novels like this one have produced: "In trying new narrative forms, Cisneros has developed a fresh vision of self and society; she has opened an alternative cultural space, a heterogeneous world, within which her protagonists no longer act as 'unified subjects,' yet remain confident of their identities" (165–166).

In 1990 Marcienne Rocard's "The House Theme in Chicana Literature: A New Sense of Place" includes Cisneros' novel in what this critic sees as the Chicana movement of liberation through self-expression. Finally, Ramón Saldívar's six-page commentary in his book *Chicano Narrative* recognizes Esperanza's "A House of My Own" as a feminist plea for a site of poetic self-creation. He concludes: "Cisneros helps create an alternate space for the Chicana subject, one that is not subjected by the geometrical homogeneity of contemporary patriarchal culture" (186).

In all of this commentary, some academic critics have begun to examine the discursive textual relation between symbolic reader and the implied reading. The articles by McCracken and Yarbro-Bejarano are notable in that they recognize the powerful use of social paradigm and symbolism.

Cisneros' novel is dedicated to *las mujeres*; its focalizer is a preadolescent girl who is intrigued by the life that awaits her as a Mexican American woman in Chicago. The symbolic reader we shall construct is based on sociocultural factors which reflect the position of a reader who is outside the text, but is addressed by the text. Let us call this symbolic reader a vertical axis for the making of the text. The social entity brings together both the social structures and dialogical constructs of everyday life which come into the text as the sociohistorical conditions for the writing itself.

But Cisneros' novel is also an explicit composition. The author has designed, redesigned, written, and rewritten the discursive system of the text. Names, places, and situations have been organized into a specific structure. Emplotment has worked at every level of configuration as the writer has striven to give the right balance of determinate and indeterminate features. The preestablished paths of the symbolic reader resist the unique realization of the writer. Therefore the resistance to individuality has its own peculiar struggle on this horizontal axis of the implied reading plan. The writer seeks to convey a personal sense of truth to her readers; the more intimate, personal, and singular the writing becomes, the more difficult it will be to achieve the desired level of communication. The implied reading plan is therefore a concept, primarily a strategy, to bring about a degree of communication of the author's personal vision. It is at the intersection between sociohistoric factors and the emplotment of the text that we find a transformation of observable reality into a metaphorical truth that each reader must make for herself. The complexity of the elements in play—sociohistoric, ideological codes, internal textual codes, and the power of figurative realization of the reader—produce of necessity a polysemy of the fictional text.

Let us take up each of these axes of figuration in turn and then conclude with an assessment of the interaction which is the reading experience. The concept of Cisneros' symbolic reader is quite specifically Chicano women, their identity and their status in society. I want to emphasize that I am not dealing with the personal intentions of the woman Sandra Cisneros, but rather with her avowed symbolic reader and its sociohistorical context. This is a concept I have adopted from the semanalysis of Julia Kristeva (1975, 1980). In this first category of the sociohistoric subject chosen by the author, I am dealing with ungrammaticalized enunciation, the saying, thought, word, and gesture not yet formulated into a coherent structure, not yet a discourse, but that which is about to become a structure through the deliberate elaboration of discourse. When this happens, we will be dealing with composition or the implied reading plan. But let me return to the symbolic reader. This is the signifying process that actualizes experience in an apparently incoherent and fragmented way. Both the author and all of her readers share in this chaotic jumble of thoughts, fears, joys, and the memory of pain. The subject itself, Chicano women, plunges us into this storm of conflicting responses.

There are four semic categories which will help us establish the scope of the symbolic reader: space, time, others, and self (see Table 2). Each of these has a number of specific words and phrases that are used to bring the specific context into play. All of these signs have both determinate and indeterminate meanings which lead the reader into generalized areas of thought.

The implied reading plan is another axis: altogether this is a strategy for reader response that is part craft and part inspiration. It is the age-old plan of every writer to reach her readers. This plan of action brings to bear devices and techniques, as well as ideas and symbols; it is the reign of intertextuality as writers use the achievements of other writers.

These two states of enunciation, one social and not clearly articulated, the other literary and highly articulated, come together in the reading experience by which the signifying system is generated. The axis of the modeling system is a picture that must be woven, thread by thread, a tapestry of one year in the life of a young Chicana. The symbolic codes that operate do so within each of the forty-four narrative reflections to create self-contained images of alienation, poverty, wife-beating, and rejection which I have examined in the first part of this chapter. Most of the images are closed; only those of the narrator's introspection remain open. Each of the closed images adds another figure to the tapestry of the paradox of not belonging where you belong. They represent the lives and impoverished existence of the narrator's mother, her sister Nenny, and Cathy, Blanca, Alicia, Lucy, Rachael, Marín, Edna, Rosa Vargas, Elenita, Ruthie, Lois, Mamacita, Rafaela, Sally, and Minerva. The open-ended reflections are the narrator's search for an answer to the enigma: how can she be free of Mango Street and the house that is not hers and yet belong as she must to that house and that street? The open-ended entries come together only slowly as the tapestry takes shape, for each of the closed figures are also threads of the larger background figure which is the narrator herself. The final colors of the concluding entry complete the picture: "but what I remember most is Mango Street, sad red house, the house I belong but do not belong to" (101).

The temporal shifts in the last paragraphs (101–102) are the essential final threads in the woven picture. We move from past memory ("What I remember most of Mango Street"), to the present writing ("I put it down on paper and then the ghost does not ache so much"), to future projection ("One day I will say goodbye to Mango"), and then from the future time when neighbors will ask, "Why did she march so far away?" back to the historical present that has characterized the entire novel, and finally to the narrative present, which is the end that in fact is the beginning: "I have gone away to come back."

The implied reading plan weaves a portrait of Esperanza from the forty-four figures. The two streams of enunciation, one sociohistoric and the other a discursive strategy, come together in the reader's experience of making the text. The symbolic reader and the implied reading plan merge in our reading.

I have taken up the public response to Cisneros' novel as well as the dual intentionality of the text: first, the sociohistorical context, which I have called the symbolic reader, since these directions and ideologies are all quite deliberate choices of the author. And second, the implied reading plan, a term borrowed from Wolfgang Iser (1978) but enriched with Kristeva's theory to include not only the explicit design of the text but also the intertextual deployment of symbolic codes.

The reviews, with few exceptions, are an ideological response to the challenge of the creative power of the text. The critical studies of Cisneros' text that offer an interpretation of the reading experience without imposing closure on the text are few and far between, but they are growing in number and are most welcome as the dialogue on Esperanza Cordero grows. The most limited and useless responses are those that use the text in order to express the ideological posture of the commentator.

The reader response that is most valuable is neither the public review process nor the private solitary reading, but the intersubjective, communal readings wherein individuals read, create, and share this creation. The reading experience of Cisneros' novel is a disclosure of feminist clarity. The power of the feminist writer is not to be measured in negative terms of subversion, opposition, or rejection of patriarchy, although it does all of these. The power of writing is the creation of women's space independent of the feminine categories of life that women have been indoctrinated into accepting as duty. The highest duty of any person and, especially of every woman, is self-realization.

Postmodernity is a time of serious questioning of basic assumptions and truths which were purportedly self-sustaining. This reflexive inward turn has many sides to it, but one of the most pronounced is a crisis in faith and, subsequently, in identity. At the end of the tunnel of reflection, writers like Cisneros have come to the recognition that because they are always on the cultural mar-

Table Two   Semic Categories

SEMIC ONTOLOGICAL CATEGORIES		SIGN MEANING	DETERMINATE MEANINGS	INDETERMINATE DIRECTIONS
Space	House	Dwelling	Haven Prison	Belonging Alienation
	House on Mango St.	Owned by family	Safety Decrepit	Security Shame
	Dream house	Owned by Esperanza	Own space Not on Mango St.	Identity Alienation
	Neighbor-hood	Known part of city	Familiar Decrepit	Security Fearful to outsiders
	Mexico	Birthplace of parents, grandparents, etc.	Nostalgic Unknown	Identity problem Alien and familiar
Time	Past	Fragmentary remembrances	Before, only data, or rejected	Quest for identity
	Present	Narration	Consciousness	Rejection/ belonging Questing
	Future	Conclusion	Imaginative projection	Objective: belonging
Other	Mama, Papa Carlos, Nenny, Kiki Uncle Nacho Aunt Lola	Family	Security Loneliness	Alienation
	Landlord Nuns Owner of laundromat	Outsiders	Fear Rejection Unknown threat	Alienation

Table Two (*continued*)

SEMIC ONTOLOGICAL CATEGORIES		SIGN MEANING	DETERMINATE MEANINGS	INDETERMINATE DIRECTIONS
	Grandfather grandmother great-grandfather	Ancestors	Unknown	Search for identity
	Cathy, Joe Benny, Blanca Alicia, Lucy Rachael, Gil, Meme Ortiz, Louie, Marin, Louie's male cousin, Edna Davey, Baby, Eddie, Fat Boy, Rosa Vargas, Efren Vargas, Darius, Elenita, Geraldo, Ruthie, Earl, Tito, Sire, Lois, Mamacita, Rafaela, Sally, Minerva, three sisters	Neighbor-hood people	Men abusers Women abused	Threat Sisters
Self	We I Esperanza Girl Mexican Zeze the x Spanish girl Esperanza Cordero Esperanza from Mango St.	Family Speaker Name Gender Ethnicity Anonymity Persona Name Name and identity	Identity	Leave Come back

gins, they have come to learn to live on many levels, live many lives simultaneously. This multiplicity of selves means an intensification in the probe of identity. Poets in all periods live in language rather than merely use it, and from time to time they create constellations of words we call poems. Poetry transcends the subject to become a public place of the imagination. The power of language is such that these public places have no limitations; we can be in them and yet leave to return when we want to. When we are in Cisneros' narrative poems, for example, we find an epiphany of the self, first of the lyric voice, then of the countless others who could be in her place and, ultimately, of the reader herself. The age of faith ended with the renaissance, the age of reason ended with romantic subjectivity, and the modernist age of ideology has ended abruptly, leaving us with a lack of symbols, a dismissal of authority, and a generalized sense of absence. The replacement of new figures of authority for the old ones is futile. Cisneros' response is to create a public poetry, a song for others to sing with her. The electronic emergence of interactive media only whets the appetite for participation in that public space of the narrative poem. Cisneros' public space for the Chicana is a constellation of words that belongs to all who read it. The limits are not clear, the images are not detailed, and the indeterminacy of the narrative are all part of an invitation for the reader to make it her song and thereby reach into the identity of a woman on the margins.

Nine   *Like Water for Chocolate*

A Celebration of the Mexican Pre-Aesthetic

*C*omo agua para chocolate (1988; Like water for choco-
late), the first novel of the Mexican writer Laura Esquivel, is a postmodern celebration of being a woman, and, significantly, it is a celebration without repro-
bation. Esquivel has subsequently written the filmscript for the motion picture
which was released in 1992. Both novel and film have had, and continue to
have, extraordinary success in the Spanish-speaking world and also in English
and French.

The study of verbal and visual imagery must begin with the understanding
that both the novel and, to a lesser extent, the film, work as a parody of a genre.
The genre in question is the Mexican version of women's fiction published in
monthly installments together with recipes, home remedies, dressmaking patterns, short poems, moral exhortations, ideas on home decoration, and the cal-
endar of church observances. In brief, this genre is the nineteenth-century
forerunner of what is known throughout Europe and America as a woman's
magazine. Around 1850 these publications in Mexico were called "calendars for
young ladies." Since home and church were the private and public sites of all
educated young ladies, these publications represented the written counterpart
to women's socialization and, as such, they are documents that conserve and
transmit a Mexican female culture in which the social context and cultural
space are particularly for women by women.

It was in the 1850s that fiction began to take a prominent role. At first, these
installment novels were descriptions of places for family excursions, moralizing tales, or detailed narratives on cooking. By 1860 the installment novel grew
out of the monthly recipe or recommended excursion. More elaborate love
stories by women began to appear regularly by the 1880s. The genre was never

considered literature by the literary establishment because of its episodic plots, overt sentimentality, and highly stylized characterization. Nevertheless, by the turn of the century every literate woman in Mexico was or had been an avid reader of the genre. But what has been completely overlooked by the male-dominated literary culture of Mexico is that these novels were highly coded in an authentic women's language of inference and reference to the commonplaces of the kitchen and the home which were completely unknown by any man.[1]

Behind the purportedly simple episodic plots, there was an interhistory of life as it was lived with all of its multiple restrictions for women of this social class. The characterization followed the forms of life of these women rather than their unique individuality; thus the heroines were the survivors, those who were able to live out a full life in spite of the institution of marriage, which in theory, if not in practice, was a form of servitude-for-life in which a woman served father and brothers only to move on to husband and sons, whom she served together with her daughters and, of course, the women from the servant class. The women's fiction of this woman's world concentrated on one overwhelming fact of life: how to transcend the conditions of life and express oneself in love and in creativity.[2]

Cooking, sewing, embroidery, and decoration were the usual creative outlets for these women, and, of course, the conversation, storytelling, gossip, and advice which pervaded the daily life of the Mexican lady of the house.[3] Writing for other women was quite naturally an extension of this intrahistoric conversation and gossip. Therefore, if one has the social codes of these women, one can read these novels as a way of life in nineteenth-century Mexico. Laura Esquivel's recognition of this world and its language comes from her Mexican heritage of fiercely independent women who created a woman's culture within the social confinement of marriage.[4]

Like Water for Chocolate is a parody of nineteenth-century women's periodical fiction in the same way that *Don Quijote* is a parody of the genre known as the novels of chivalry. They were both expressions of popular culture that created a unique space for a segment of the population. I am using the term parody in the strict sense in which Ziva Ben Porat has defined it. I quote from her 1979 study: "[Parody is] a representation of a modeled reality, which is itself already a particular representation of an original reality. The parodic representations expose the model's conventions and lay bare its devices through the coexistence of the two codes in the same message" (247).

Obviously, for the parody to work at its highest level of dual representation, both the parody and the parodic model must be present in the reading experience. Esquivel creates the duality in several ways; first, the title of the novel, *Like Water for Chocolate*, is part of the linguistic code which translates as "water at the point of boiling," and is used as a simile in Mexico to describe any event or relationship that is so tense, hot, and extraordinary that it can only be compared to the scalding boiling water that is called for in the preparation of the most Mexican of all beverages dating from at least the thirteenth century: hot chocolate (Soustelle, 153–161). Second, the subtitle, *A Novel in Monthly Installments*, is taken directly from the model: a novel in monthly installments, with recipes, love stories, and home remedies. The title and subtitle therefore cover both the parody and the model. Third, the reader finds on opening the book, in place of an epigram, a traditional Mexican proverb: "To the table or to bed you must come when you are bid"; the woodcut that decorates the page is the typical nineteenth-century cooking stove. The fourth and most explicit dualistic technique is that Esquivel reproduces the format of her model.

Each chapter is prefaced by the title, the subtitle, the month, and the recipe of the month. The narration that follows consists of direct address on how to prepare the recipe of the month, interspersed with story telling about the loves and times of the narrator's grandaunt Tita. Each chapter ends with the information that the story will be continued and an announcement of what the next month's, that is, the next chapter's, recipe will be. These elements, taken from the model, are never mere embellishments. The recipes and their preparation, as well as the home remedies and their application, are an intrinsic part of the story. There is therefore an intricate symbiotic relationship between the novel and its model in the reading experience. Each is interacting with the other. The verbal imaging of the novel makes use of the elaborate signifying system of language as a dwelling place. The visual imagery that at first expands the narrative in the film soon exacts its own place as a nonlinguistic signifying system, drawing upon its own repertoire of referentiality and establishing a different model of the human subject than that elucidated by the verbal imagery alone.

The speaking subject or narrative voice in the novel is characterized, as Benveniste has shown, as a living presence by speaking. The narrative voice in this novel begins in the first person, speaking the conversational colloquial Mexican Spanish of a woman from Mexico's north, near the U.S. border. Like all Mexican speech, it is clearly marked with register and sociocultural indicators of the landowning middle class, mixing colloquial local usage with standard Spanish. The entry point is always the same, the direct address of a woman telling another woman how to prepare the recipe she is recommending. As one does the cooking, it is quite natural for the cook to liven the session by some story telling prompted by the previous preparation of the food. As she effortlessly moves from first-person culinary instructor to storyteller, she shifts to the third person and gradually appropriates a time and place and refigures a social world.

A verbal image emerges of the model Mexican rural middle class woman. She must be strong and far more clever than the men who supposedly protect her. She must be pious, observing all the religious requirements of a virtuous daughter, wife, and mother. She must exercise great care to keep her sentimental relations as private as possible and, most important of all, she must be in control of life in her house, which means essentially kitchen and bedroom, or food and sex. In this novel, there are four women who must respond to the model: the mother, Elena, and the three daughters, Rosaura, Gertrudis, and Josefita, known as Tita.

The ways of living within the limits of the model are demonstrated first by the mother, who thinks of herself as the embodiment of the model. She interprets the model in terms of control and domination of her entire household. She is represented through a filter of awe and fear; the ostensible source is Tita's diary-cookbook written beginning in 1910 when she was fifteen years old, but it is now transmitted by her grandniece, whose own experience of her mother colors her interpretation. Therefore, the verbal images that characterize Mamá Elena must be understood as those of her youngest daughter, who has been made into a personal servant from the time the little girl was able to work.

Mamá Elena is depicted as strong, self-reliant, and absolutely tyrannical with her daughters and servants, but especially so with Tita, who from birth has been designated as the one who will not marry because she must care for her mother until she dies. Mamá Elena believes in order—her order. Although she observes the strictures of church and society, she has secretly had an adulterous love affair with an African American, and her second daughter, Gertrudis, is the offspring of this relationship. This transgression of the norms of proper behavior remains hidden from public view, although there is gossip, but Tita discovers that Gertrudis is her half-sister only after her mother's death. The tyranny imposed on the three sisters is therefore the rigid self-designed model of a woman's life pitilessly enforced by Mamá Elena, and each of the three daughters responds in her own way to the model.

Rosaura never questions her mother's authority and follows her dictates submissively; after she is married, she becomes an insignificant imitation of her mother. She lacks the strength, skill, and determination of Mamá Elena and tries to compensate by appealing to the mother's model as absolute. She therefore tries to live the model invoking her mother's authority because she has none of her own. Gertrudis challenges her mother indirectly by expressing her emotions and passions in an open manner that is unbecoming of a lady. This physical directness leads her to adopt an androgynous life-style: she leaves her house and her mother's authority, escapes from the brothel she landed in, and becomes a general of the revolutionary army, taking a subordinate as her lover and, later, husband. When she returns to the family *hacienda*, she is dressed like a man, gives orders like a man, and is the dominant sexual partner. Tita, the youngest of the three, speaks out against her mother's arbitrary rule, but cannot escape until she temporarily loses her mind. Tita was able to survive her mother's harsh rule by expressing her love, joy, sadness, and anger through her cooking. Tita's emotions and passions are the impetus for expression and action, not through the normal means of communication, but through the food she prepares. She is therefore able to consummate her love with Pedro through the food she serves: "It was as if a strange alchemical process had dissolved her entire being in the rose petal sauce, in the tender flesh of the quails, in the wine, in every one of the meal's aromas. That was the way she entered Pedro's body, hot, voluptuous, perfumed, totally sensuous" (52). This clearly is much more than communication through food or a mere aphrodisiac; this is a form of sexual transubstantiation whereby the rose petal sauce and quail have been turned into the body of Tita.

Thus it is that the reader gets to know these women as persons but, above all, the reader gets involved with the embodied speaking subject from the past, Tita, represented by her grandniece, who transmits her story and her cooking. The reader receives verbal food for the imaginative refiguration of one woman's response to the model that was imposed on her by accident of birth. The body of these women is the place of living. It is the dwelling place of the human subject. The essential questions of health, illness, pregnancy, childbirth, and sexuality are tied very directly in this novel to the physical and emotional needs of the body. The preparation and eating of food is thus a symbolic representation of living, and Tita's cookbook bequeaths to Esperanza, and Esperanza's daughter, her grandniece, a woman's creation of space that is hers in a hostile world.

The novel is very cinematographic, reflecting Esquivel's roots in screenplay writing. There are many cinematographic touches in the novel, primarily the numerous cuts and fade-outs of the story in order to feature the cooking. The camera's visual language is intrusive and can engulf its subject in a visual language that is unique to the voyeur or can replace verbal referentiality by overwhelming the viewer. For example, the opening shot of the film, which fills the entire screen with an onion that is being sliced, plunges the viewer into food preparation in a way that no spoken word could parallel for its immediate effect. Similarly, the numerous close-up shots of food being prepared, served, and eaten heighten the dominance of the performance of cooking and eating as both sustenance and social ritual. These images and this emphasis on the joy, sensuality, and even, lust of eating the Mexican cuisine of Tita's kitchen can be compared with the scenes of the monks eating in Annaud's *The Name of the Rose*, or the raw meat displayed in the monastery's refectory, where the emphasis is on the denial of the flesh through mortification. On the other hand, Gabriel Axel's film *Babette's Feast* contains both poles of this opposition between gratification and mortification of the body. The minister's two daughters, who substitute religious practice for living and who eat as punishment for having a body, are suddenly exposed to the refinement of food as art, pleasure, and gratification. In the film *Como agua para chocolate*, directed by Alfonso Arau, the preparation of food is expressed visually and the consummation of eating is seen in the faces of the diners, but it must be also emphasized that there is a full spectrum of effects here ranging from ecstasy to nausea.

Perhaps the major difference between the novel and the film is that there is a visual intertext in the film that evokes the Cinderella fairy tale by using the ghostly appearance of the mother and making her death the result of the attack on the *hacienda* by the outlaws. In the novel, she does not die until long after the attack and lingers on in partial madness, convinced that Tita is trying to poison her. By cutting short her death to one sudden violent episode and having her face return to taunt Tita until Tita is able to renounce her heritage, the film makes Tita the Cinderella-like victim of personal abuse. In the novel, the rigidity of Mamá Elena is overwhelmingly sociocultural and not peculiar to Tita as victim.

The visual intertext of fairy-tale language creates an effective subtext in the film, bringing out the oppression of the protagonist and her magical transcendence. Instead of a fairy godmother, Tita has the voice of her Nacha, the family cook who raised her from infancy amidst the smells and sounds of the kitchen. Instead of a magical transformation of dress and carriage to go to the prince's ball, Tita is able to make love through the food she prepares; she is also able to induce sadness and acute physical discomfort. She is, therefore, able to keep Pedro from having sexual relations with his wife Rosaura by making certain that she is fat, has foul breath, and is given to breaking wind in the most nauseating manner. The first ghostly appearance of Mamá Elena comes one hour into the film; she has the upper hand since she threatens to curse the child Tita is presumably carrying. The final confrontation between Tita and the ghost is ten minutes after the first. Tita defeats the ghost by telling her that she knows that Gertrudis is illegitimate, that she hates her for everything she has never been to her.

The film's visual language is able to evoke images of provocation, contempt, and abuse that were not in the novel. For example, the film shows Tita carrying out her Cinderella-like duties. The film also shows that Tita is the only one permitted to assist Mamá Elena in her bath and her dressing. The despotic abuse of Tita by Mamá Elena is clearly borrowing visual images of the cruel stepmother. The magical intermediary is not a beautiful woman in a ball dress, but the wrinkled old woman, the cook Nacha, who has given Tita the love Mamá Elena has denied her. Nacha's voice and face guide Tita. It is Nacha who tells her to use the roses Pedro gave her for the preparation of quail in rose petal sauce, and it is Nacha who prepares the bedroom for the final consummation of love between Tita and Pedro at the end of the film.

Tita's magical powers are all related to food, with the exception of the kilometer-long bedspread she knits in her long nights of insomnia. Tita's cooking controls the pattern of living of those in her household because the food she prepares becomes an extension of herself. The culmination of this process of food as art and communication is food as communion. The transubstantiation of Tita's quail in rose petal sauce becoming her body is at once a part of the Roman Catholic doctrine of the communion wafer becoming the body and blood of Christ, but, on a deeper level, it is the psychological reality of all women who have nursed an infant. When the baby Roberto loses his wet nurse, Tita is able to take the infant and nurse him in spite of the fact that she has not given birth. Her breasts are filled with milk not because she would have wanted to be the mother of the child, but because the child needed to eat and she is the provider of food.

The viewer of the film must develop her expressive capacity as she broadens her affective experience. Mexican women seeing the film, and to some extent Latin American women in general, relive their family history, and this is so not only because of the strong and open cultural links between Latin American women in this century, which both the novel and film draw on, but also and perhaps primarily because of the skillful use of the parodic model. The intertext of women's magazines and the loves, trials, and tribulations featured in the stories they published is used by Esquivel as a discursive code that transcends whatever the regional differences may be. The social registers, the forms of address, and the language of the female domain are somewhat lost in translation because as in cooking, the substitution of ingredients changes the taste. The representation of women in this novel and film touches on that deepest reservoir of meaning which is the human body as described, seen, and, on the deeper level, understood as the origin of identity.

Women from other cultures and other languages can develop an empathetic relationship with Tita, her cooking, her love, and her life. Men of any culture, but especially Mexican men and Latin American men, have the greatest deficiency in experiencing this film and therefore have the most to learn. They must gain access to some fragment of the expressive code of visual and verbal images that are the intrahistoric codes of their mothers, wives, and daughters. If they cannot gain access to the expressive system, they will not have access to the affective experience of these lives. The imagery of nourishing the body in both the novel and the film provides us with the means for articulating the experiences of cooking, eating, making love, and giving birth in previously unsuspected ways, and thus allows the male intruder a peek into reality.

It is in the play between the intertextual referentiality and the narrative story that Esquivel builds a narrative world that is at once fiction and nonfiction. The indeterminate factor in this novel is not a specific unnarrated gap but rather the future of the narrator, who has been told so often that she has a strong resemblance to her grandaunt that she has grown to identify with this woman who died before the narrator was born. She believes that her grandaunt lives in her through the cookbook that she has left and that is, of course, the frame of the novel itself. The feminist recuperation of artistic creativity within the confinement of the house and, especially, the kitchen and the bedroom, is not presented by Esquivel in an ideological argument,[5] but rather by means of an intertextual palimpsest which is the hallmark of postmodern art.

Ten   Conclusion

There Must Be Another Way

$\mathbf{M}$y conclusion to this book has two parts: censure and celebration. In these pages I want to summarize the blight of four hundred years of sexism and yet, also, to celebrate the creative imagination as the power we have to endow our world with new forms of living.

A quantifying approach to the status of women in Mexico today involves our objectifying life. This neutralization of experience is attained by the use of statistical evidence of the key indicators of society: education, employment, communication, and the rule of law. In all of these categories, the present status of women is one of inequality. Only comparisons to the past give us a glimmer of hope, with the notable exception of criminality, and specifically the statistical evidence for an unprecedented increase in violence against women. I want to review this situation in conjunction with public discourse by and about women in Mexico.

All legal codes legislate against violence specifically directed against women; rape and wife murder are the extreme forms. The established means of the social and civil order in most communities of the world are woefully inadequate to deal with the rising wave of violence against women, and Mexico is no exception (see Chapter 7, note 19). I am concerned with such forms of violence here because I believe that there are links between violence against women and discourse in the social structure itself.

One of the ironic aspects of social violence is that certain forms of violence are linked to the rise of political power which purportedly aims to protect the population from individual acts of violence. From the moment we first realize the link between the language of rape and the discourse of the political structure, we begin to realize that this violation of women is not a question of individually deranged sexual psychopaths, but of a form of violence tied to the exercise of power in the social structure itself. My aim is to question the discourse of social organization in relation to the discourse of violence in general and violence against women in particular.

If we begin with some rather basic notions, I think we can at least make some progress in defining the problem. The only just basis for power being invested in the state is that it is the power of the collective will of the people which governs. This state, bound by political design and history, can only make just decisions through the collective will of the population. Historically, most Latin American states cannot be readily counted as just societies because the collective will of the people has rarely been acknowledged. This simple, although important, first step comes out in favor of some form of liberal democracy, but it also hides the inner reality that even if there were to be the application of the collective will of the people in the formation of the state, not all members of the community would be able to speak with the same authority. There are a number of exclusions from expressing a political will, exclusions made on the basis of competence to judge the issue; exclusions of those elements of the population who are too young, or too infirm, or foreign, or incompetent. In Mexico, some women and some native communities would also be excluded. I refer to those women and to those non-Spanish-speaking communities which have been by-passed by the political process.

Injustice is political violence against the person, and when political violence is directed against an identifiable sector of the population, it becomes the institutionalization of violence. In my view there is an effective link between rape and the political disenfranchisement of women. Political discrimination against women is a calculated and selective use of authority whose objective is to keep power in the hands of those who have it.[1] Why has gender been a universal form of division in social systems as distant and different as India, Iran, and Mexico?

Throughout human history, resorting to violence appears as a basic problem for all persons who seek to establish a community of consent of the governed. Violence is always the interruption and negation of dialogue. When the violent exercise of power by the state or by the individual speaks, it is a means of self-justification. If the self-justification ever allows discussion, then dialogue can suspend violence, but as long as the other voice remains silent, violence will be the only way to maintain control.

When language is used to silence the other voice, it is the language of violence. Dialogue must prevail if there is to be an end to violence. It is the task of the feminist sociocritic to unmask the language of violence and to promote dialogue as the fundamental human negation of violence.

An individual may resort to violence for a number of very different hidden psychological reasons, such as frustration or a psychological predisposition for self-destruction. When the state resorts to violence, it is a calculated act to retain control, and violence has other names like "protection" or "justification."

The everyday language of Mexico, in the spoken language as well as the written, is permeated by violence. Whenever there is a reference to gender, the violence comes forth in the continual obstinacy of men who hold on to the notion that women are property and not persons. Violence in speech arises when the speaker believes that only a particular kind of speech is valid, his or her own. Nonviolence in critical language begins with the respect for the plurality and diversity of human minds and languages. It is important to recognize diversity in the types of dialogue and to accept the rightful place of each *without* abandoning the language and belief system one holds, but being prepared to grow and change. If one is to have a dialogue one must listen as well as speak.

It is for these reasons that I believe that literature as the expression and continuation of the identity of a community is a major area of work for women and that to write feminist literary sociocriticism in the third world is a political act of liberation.

Mexican literature today, as in the past, explores a wide spectrum of human relations. The notable change is that today, in contrast to the writing at mid-century, the voice of women writers is heard alongside that of their male counterparts. The differences among today's writers can be drawn on the basis of a number of factors, but gender is not one. One can find both men and women on the same side of any social or cultural issue. The public discourse of Mexico is also changing, although at a much slower pace than the social status of women. In this case, social discourse is lagging behind the reality of the workplace. But in both areas, there is a long way to go before there is social equality. The discourse of *machismo* has been eliminated from polite speech, but it is very much in evidence in the private register of men speaking to men. The reporting of violent crimes against women is at an all-time high and has become a prime factor in the growing rejection of *machista* discourse. Not only are a large number of cases of family violence now being reported that were before hidden, but also there is an awareness that women have a voice that, if not equal to men, can no longer be ignored. The female subject who speaks is therefore a subject with expressive power.

There is no question in my mind that the self is constituted through exchange in language, and since every speaker and every writer has a lesser or greater stake in the collective discourse of the community, our participation in society is part of a formative process where we develop through language use, and the language of the community changes through our use. Of course, if one is not heard, it is impossible to speak of meaningful participation. The new-found voice of women in Mexican society will not be wasted. As discourse changes, so does society, and the more society changes, the more will the social institutions of social order change. The last to change will be the legal codes and the courts, but they also change and adapt.

An important aspect of the postmodern revolution has been that in questioning authority, traditionally marginalized sectors of society have risen to the challenge and have added support to the acceleration of the demise of the male white institutionalized authority.[2] In English all over the world, from Sri Lanka to the southern United States, nonwhite writers have in almost singular voice called for the end of colonialism.[3] Women writers in English, French, German, Japanese, Portuguese, and Spanish are being published at an unprecedented pace, breaking with the male monopoly of letters.[4] They use irony to implicate and subvert, they draw on parody to challenge the authority of the text itself, and, most significant of all, they remind us that works of literature are the work, the composition, design, organization, selection, and effort of an individual that becomes part of the community's discourse and that, consequently, this human construct which in the past was indeed often a man-made construct for the perpetuation of a self-serving world of exploitation is now a means to curtail it.

There should be no mistake about this state of affairs. There is no going back except in the escapism of nostalgia. The intertextual linkage of the wider world with the world of the text does not move the reader or the community to homogenization. The reverse is the case. Postmodern art in all its manifestations is always pointing out difference, differences within any grouping, differences made visible by positioning of the singular in relation to the others.

In the contemporary postmodern novel there are numerous examples of direct and indirect intertextuality; there is nevertheless the always effective breaking of the illusion of the novel's own self-contained limits by the intertwining of discourses. It is in the work of writers like Laura Esquivel, Carmen Boullosa, and Afro-American writers like Alice Walker and Toni Morrison that we find ironic intertextuality used to such powerful ends, both ideological and aesthetic, as subversion of the old rules of the game of life and a rewriting of the new rules. These writers exploit intertextuality; they set up and then challenge male traditions in art.

Postmodernity is both an artistic and cultural phenomenon and an intellectual and philosophical climate. If we can call the middle ages the age of faith or the eighteenth century the age of reason, we should refer to the second half of the twentieth century as the age of questioning. Most of the major thinkers of our time have contributed in a direct or indirect manner to postmodernism.

Philosophers like Heidegger, Gadamer, Ricoeur, Habermas, Derrida, and Wittgenstein are now woven into the tapestry of our disbelief. This is not the place to examine the philosophy of postmodernism, but I do want to stress that one of the fundamental concepts in this discussion is a philosophy of language that begins with Heidegger's idea that we do not merely communicate through language; we *live* in language.

Perhaps the most influential linguist of this half-century was Emile Benveniste of the Collège de France, who in many respects laid out the groundwork for the victory of postmodern thinking over the stubborn rear guard of logical positivism. Benveniste examined the full consequences of speaking to another in a natural language, and he did so not in the analytical terms of structural linguistics but in the probe and argument method of the philosopher. In 1971 he wrote that the self-identification consequence of speaking is the basis of subjectivity which is the "capacity of the speaker to posit himself as subject" (English translation 1977, 224). Subjectivity is thereby established as a fundamental property of language; once again I quote from Benveniste: "It is in and through language that man constitutes himself as a subject, because language alone establishes the concept of ego in reality, in its reality" (224). Benveniste's ideas do not, however, lead to a mythification of language but rather to an unparalleled inquiry into discourse as the means of making meanings, making the self, and, of course, making the world for the entire community of speakers. No one is more explicit on this issue than Paul Ricoeur, who writes that meaning is not to be found in words or in semiotic systems; rather, it is the result of words in sentences, that is, discourse, and therefore the proper level of inquiry is semantics ("The Hermeneutical Function of Distanciation," 133).

We thus have a volatile situation, what our scientist friends would call a critical stage, which is the intersection of a theory that probes and questions all assumptions, rejects all norms, and does not replace them; it pursues open-ended debate and features an artistic practice that uses irony and parody, that moves freely in an intertextual discourse of dialectic narrativity. The artistic break with modernism runs much deeper than a mere rejection of one kind of order for another; it is the full embrace of nonlinear modes of order and the invitation to examine one's own sense of order.

I do not wish to paint the whole scene with the same colors of revolution, for there are many ways of breaking down the established order and offering the reader the chance to think for herself as self and as other. At this time I cannot go into the numerous, powerful, postmodern novels written by women that have contributed to a liberating discourse which helps in the continuing battle against the previously dominant discourse.

I want to conclude this book on the identity of Mexican women with three observations on their representation in postmodernism: (1) this is not a protest movement; rather, it is a celebration of the space of one's own which may have been hidden from view in the past but is now open to all; (2) at the center of postmodernism is the vesting of creative authority in the reader, and this makes intertextuality a means of providing an interpretive context (in the case of Esquivel, it was our grandmother's kitchen and bedroom); (3) there is a growing maturity of feminist criticism today that has transcended the limitations of an anti-*macho* program, and the challenge today is to celebrate women's creativity in the full domain of the human adventure from the so-called decorative arts to the fine arts and science. This most current direction is being called postfeminism.

Some practical-minded readers may question my concentration on literature and, more specifically, on the emphasis I give fictional characters in a book purportedly about female identity. I owe a response to this apparently reasonable objection. But, first, I must remind these readers of some of the definitions I have given throughout this book. A fictional character consists of a determinate and an indeterminate side. On the determinate side there are those distinctive traits provided by description, speech, and comportment which permit us to recognize the same textual entity again whether or not it is named. On the indeterminate side, we have to contend with the fact that all description is incomplete and demands some degree of reader enhancement, and all speech and behavior is interpreted by the reader whether or not other narrative voices do so in the text. Thus fictional characters have both an empirical base and an interpretive function. The range of interpretations which can be produced by the same database is immense but not limitless, since all reading takes place at a given time, in a given place, and by readers with specific historicities.

It can be argued that feminist critics tend to give a disproportionate emphasis to female fictional characters as representative of a way of existing, one which is linked to the critic's own finite perspective affecting the world of things, ideas, values, and persons. Undoubtedly this is a view most nonfeminist critics hold. However, if the feminist critic is good, the commentary will be insightful; if not, it can be trite; there is no critical license just because one is a feminist. But it should be clear that without claiming to have a superior vantage point, my objective in this book is different. I am after a more general level of character interpretation that can be shown to be related to the problematic of female identity in society, specifically that of Mexico today. The characters I have examined in this book—ranging from Harriet, la Garduña, Moon Face to Susana San Juan, Sor Juana's lyric alter ego, Castellanos' unnamed feminist, Hernández' María Antonia, Puga's young narrator, Poniatowska's Jesusa and Mariana, Pacheco's girls and women, Cisneros' insightful Esperanza, and Esquivel's Tita—are all part of my world. They are all acquired identifications of one reader's configuration, but these fictional others have entered and belong to my sense of community. They do not belong to me, nor are they exclusively part of my world, for I share them with tens of thousands who have also responded to the demands of their truth claims.

In writing this book, I have reintroduced the narrative unfolding of these characters into the larger, always unfinished narrative unfolding of the identity of Mexican women. Both the fictional characters in their stories and the lives of Mexican women must be set back within the temporal movement of narration in order to be understood and discussed. My work here has been to relate the fictional characters to the women of Mexico, each within their narrative and yet both in a symbiotic relationship to the other.

If we probe into individual human life, we discover that our knowledge about ourselves and those we consider our others is primarily based on stories, narratives, sometimes dramas—but always stories. The stories we receive all impose plots and sometimes heroes and villains. But the real story, what Unamuno called the *intrahistoria* of a woman or a man or the history of a people, is not a story in which preexistent goals are triumphantly celebrated or failures mourned, although individual human lives are full of celebration and mourning. In the interior story of life, there is no constant external grinding force even if, from time to time, one should take refuge in such a notion; nor is there an unfailing interior light of inspiration to direct one's actions in spite of the fact that we so desperately seek it. Instead, to see one's life, or the life of one's community, as an ongoing tale with no knowable beginning save birth and no end in sight except death is to see life as a process of self-transcendence. The source of such a narrative may be a narrative of self-reflection, but, more often than not, the source is the life of a writer who can look back on the past and rewrite it because she has found a way to know the past which those living in the past never knew. And she has thereby invented herself, found a self to be which her precursors never knew was possible. Sor Juana Inés de la Cruz was such a woman, and, closer to our time, Rosario Castellanos was another. We recognize that we need a proliferation of such writers in order to reinvent the Mexican woman. We look into our grandmother's wardrobe mirror and we recognize that it is a concave mirror that we must shatter. This is the challenge and the motivation that stands behind this book.

Notes

Introduction

1. According to Benveniste, it is in and through language that the individual constitutes herself as subject, because language alone establishes what we know as reality, which is the reality of living in the everyday world of action (*Problems of General Linguistics*, esp. chapters 6 and 15).

2. The general proposition held by Jürgen Habermas, that ideological forces distort and impede communication in the community of speakers, takes on extreme dimensions when a woman speaks in a sexist environment. In Mexico the most notable victory over sexist ideology has been the work of women journalists like Elena Poniatowska and Cristina Pacheco. These women have withstood sexist prejudice and have gained for themselves preeminent respect as serious commentators on society. They are still the notable exceptions, but they have also become the role models for a younger generation of newspaper women like Guadalupe Loaeza, Josefina Estrada, Lucía Alvarez Henríquez, and Clara Guadalupe García.

3. After five hundred years of exploitation, the native peoples of Mexico have survived in their oral culture and are today one of the ethnic minorities in the world that are demanding basic social justice. The native peoples of Mexico comprise 15 percent of the total population, with an additional 10 percent that move in and out of the ethnic communities and the mainstream of Mexican society. This total group of 25 percent of the population lives at the lowest levels of subsistence. Their culture is a mixture of native traditions and languages with the Mexican mainstream and the Spanish language; their literature is almost entirely in the oral tradition. In their new militancy, the native groups have articulated demands for ethnic pluralism in national policy, bilingual education, legal recognition of native languages, local self-government, and legislative representation in the national government (see Bonfil, 107). The January 1, 1994, armed uprising in the state of Chiapas called world attention to the plight of one of the most

exploited sectors of Mexico. Although Chiapas is one of the richest states of Mexico in natural resources, the feudal system of estate ownership has kept the majority of the native population in abject poverty. In most villages the living conditions are among the poorest of the third world. Some statistics are in order: 69 percent of the women of Chiapas have never gone to school; only 20 percent of women attend regularly. Only 12 percent have official employment. The average birth rate is the highest in Mexico. Native women between the ages of sixteen and forty have an average of five children. The working hours of these women average sixteen to eighteen hours a day. Chiapas has the highest rate of infant mortality in Mexico, and more women die in childbirth than anywhere else in Mexico. Only the attention of the international media stopped the killing of the Zapatista rebels. The union of estate owners, the church, and the political authorities has not been threatened by the uprising. The demands of the Zapatistas are nothing more than the human rights the United Nations charter states as the basic rights of all peoples (see Casas, Laura Castellanos, and Steinsleger).

4. Paul Ricoeur's assessment of ideology is central to my argument: "What characterizes ideology is that it cannot be treated as a particular case of misunderstanding, amenable to interpretive methods which would dissolve it into a higher understanding. Ideology is first of all a distortion engendered at the same level where work, power and discourse are intertwined. Moreover, ideology is a distortion stemming from violence and repression" ("Ethics and Culture. Habermas and Gadamer in Dialogue," 1974, 255–256). Ricoeur moves here from a commentary on Habermas' critique of Gadamer to a central proposition of his own philosophy, out of which I have developed my theory of feminist sociocriticism. Ricoeur writes: "My thesis here is that the interest in emancipation would be empty and anaemic unless it received a concrete content from our practical interest in communication" (286).

5. Silvia Bovenschen, in a ground-breaking study of feminist art, calls the female outlets for creativity, when confined to the ghetto of home and kitchen, the realm of the pre-aesthetic. Also see Showalter, "Piecing and Writing," who compares the feminine art form of the quilt to literary form. In regard to Frida Kahlo, see Claudia Schaefer-Rodríguez (1992, esp. 3–36).

6. During the three hundred years of colonial history, the majority of Mexican women were kept nonliterate. And the scant few, mostly of European ancestry, who did learn to write were denied a public voice (see Appendix 1, Women's Education in Mexico).

7. Since the 1982 and 1994 devaluations of the peso, the price of books has gone beyond the reach of all sectors but the affluent upper middle class. For example, the daily newspaper costs the equivalent of U.S. $.52; a magazine costs from U.S. $2 to U.S. $5, and an average book costs U.S. $15. The basic monthly wage for a university assistant professor is $240.

8. Most commentaries on Iser's reader reception theory have overlooked his initial pragmatic statement about the implied reader: "Norms are social regulations, and when they are transposed into the novel they are automatically deprived of their pragmatic nature. They are set in a new context which changes their function, insofar as they no

longer act as social regulations but as the subject of a discussion which, more often than not, ends in a questioning rather than a confirmation of their validity" (1974, xii).

Chapter One

1. The early years of women's studies in the United States is well documented in *Female Studies* (1970–1975); its diversity and geographic distribution are found in Tamar Berkowitz et al.'s *Who's Who and Where in Women's Studies*; for an analysis of this rapid growth see DuBois et al.'s *Feminist Scholarship*. Stimpson gives a succinct review of the first twelve years (1986, 4). Some pertinent sources for feminist studies in the United States are *Women's Studies Abstracts, Feminist Studies, Women's Studies Quarterly, Signs,* and *Frontiers*. For bibliographies in this area, see Ballou, Humm, Loeb, and Watson. In twentieth-century Mexico feminists have fought for women's rights in an organized way since the first congress of feminists, held in Mérida, Yucatán, in 1916. There was, however, no printed forum until the establishment of *fem.* in 1976. One of the editors of *fem.*, Elena Urrutia, founded the interdisciplinary program on women's studies (PIEM) in the prestigious graduate school of the Colegio de México in 1983. The PIEM has published most of the scholarly work done in Mexico on women and feminism (see Benería and Roldán, Domenella and Pasternac, González Montes, López González et al., Massolo, Oliveira, Ramos Escandón, Salles and McPhail, Tarrés, Urrutia). In 1990 a rigorous feminist intellectual biannual journal, *debate feminista*, was begun. The Center for Women's Studies was established in 1984 at the National University of Mexico's Faculty of Psychology. Their primary area of research has been on psychological perspectives on sex and gender, violence, and harassment. Women's studies courses are also offered by the Faculties of Political and Social Sciences and Philosophy and Letters (see Bustos Romero, 1989; Carreras). In 1994 the first graduate program on women's studies was started at Mexico City's Universidad Autónoma Metropolitana in the Division of Political Sciences. A recent addition is a center for women's studies in Guadalajara. For a review of the last twenty-five years (1970–1995) of the women's movement in Mexico, see *debate feminista* 6.12 (October 1995).

2. Germaine Greer's lead article in the *Tulsa Studies in Women's Literature*, first issue, Spring 1982, is one of the best assessments of the forces of production of the early canon.

3. See the inaugural editorial by anthropologist Marta Lamas, *debate feminista* 1.1 (1990): 1–5: "*debate feminista* is without a doubt committed to the political process in Mexico but we are also concerned with maintaining an international perspective . . . In Mexico the various sides of the feminist movement have become trapped, in the best of cases, in denunciation of social and economic injustice and, in the worst, in the 'womanist' discourse" (2).

4. I am well aware that the emerging feminist canon of the sixties and early seventies has been questioned for some time by a new generation of feminist critics, but the tendency still remains amongst many to mimic, although in an inverted hierarchy, the

paradigm of thinking in terms of domination and orthodoxy of patriarchal education. Millet's, Ellmann's, and Rogers' works featured shock tactics that had a political function at the time of publication. One of the most balanced studies of Latin American women's writing is Debra Castillo's *Talking Back*. Her long chapter, "Writing in the Margins: Rosario Castellanos and María Luisa Puga," is unique among feminist Hispanists because of her understanding of the multicultural makeup of Mexico. Castillo writes: "Marginalized peoples are excluded from the great conversation that makes up national discourse; their voices and their very being are erased as an unpleasantly dissonant background" (1992, 234). In the book *Women and Change in Latin America*, edited by Nash and Safa, the articles are concerned with social, economic, and political issues, but not with the images and discourse about women. My argument in this book is that feminist literary sociocriticism in Latin America functions as a critique of ideology without which an assessment of society is incomplete.

5. For U.S. feminists who disclaim speaking for all women see, for example, Stimpson (1986), and Weed (xxv). In *Woman and the Demon*, Auerbach takes a strong position: "I am suggesting that we need a freer context for understanding the complex life of woman in culture, one which welcomes any society's capacious avenues of power, as well as excoriating its particular conventions of oppression" (2).

6. See, for example, Elu de Leñero, *La mujer en América Latina* (Women in Latin America), and specifically Hilda Araujo Camacho's study (21 ff.); and the landmark publication *Slaves of Slaves: The Challenge of Latin American Women*, written by the Latin American and Caribbean Women's Collective in 1977. Also see Barbieri's excellent review of the cultural consequences of the mass media (1975, 58–62); García Calderón's chapter "La mujer como símbolo de la mercancía. La revista femenina en los ochenta" (Women as symbol of commodity. Women's magazines of the eighties) 141–162; and Bustos Romero (1992).

7. Nash and Safa write in their introduction to *Sex and Class*: "In the change from a domestic mode of production, in which women shared the tasks of production, to a capitalist mode, the differential spheres of male and female activity have led to increased inequality, reflected in the attendant ideology" (xi). With regard to the historical dimensions of the female stereotype, Arrom writes: "In the rare instances when women are mentioned at all [in histories of Mexico] they are portrayed as passive, powerless beings, absorbed in familial duties, confined to the home, and totally subordinated to men" (1). The ideological propagation of the female stereotype is not only a reflection on the past; it is also the blueprint for the future.

8. This aspect of Latin America, and specifically Mexican ideology, is examined in my study of a short story by Carlos Fuentes (Chapter 3).

9. Although the Mexican civil code of 1884, which followed the Napoleonic code and Roman civil law in denying all civil rights to married women, has been completely revised, it has left a popular legacy of married women as mere agents of their husband's authority. In practice, the only married women who are empowered by the civil code are those who have wealthy and powerful fathers, brothers, and so on. A married

woman by herself is virtually powerless before a judicial system that fails to recognize her without qualification as a political person (see Aresti et al; Galindo; Lugo; Ruiz Harrel; Valdemoro). Arrom traces the roots of women's legal incapacity in Mexico from the conquest to 1857 and concludes that repeatedly the justification for the legal provisions consolidating the male's supremacy in all matters was his superior corporal strength (57). One of the best assessments of the inequality of women in Latin America, and in Mexico particularly, is CEPAL's *Mujeres en América Latina: Aportes para una discusión* (Women in Latin America: Contributions for a discussion), edited by Marshall Wolfe and published in Mexico for the Economic Commission for Latin America (1975). In the article by Jorge Graciarena, a lucid exposition of the magnitude of female exploitation (26–45, esp. 39 ff.), he locates the major impediments to progress in the institutionalized ideology of *machismo*, which is directly linked to the economic exploitation of third world economies by multinational corporations. Women today constitute the most victimized sector of the third world (see Arizpe, 1989, 26).

10. Statistical examples of the church's role in maintaining the status quo of women's condition can be seen in Elu de Leñero (1969) and in Portugal's *Mujeres e iglesia* (1989; Women and church, 5–7). For women's leadership and participation in the violent Catholic uprising against the anticlerical government (1925–1929), in which almost twenty thousand women took part, see Barbara Miller.

11. The lack of documentation on violence against women is decried by researchers such as Barbieri (1989); but we should note that in a society that accepts and even sanctions violence against women, such as routine beatings for real or imagined transgressions, the condemnation of rape is not shared by the authorities. Police routinely treat the victim like the criminal, and judges make a mockery of redress even when the accused is found guilty. For example, a judge fined an accused rapist 300 pesos (U.S. $1.50) for the victim's torn blouse as the full payment for his crime (Aresti et al., 30). In 1990 Barbieri reported that there has been an apparent change in official policy on violence against women; the government approved reforms to the penal code on these matters.

12. See "Dress and Adornment" by Irmgard W. Johnson, which documents the endless variety of geometric designs with free improvisation on certain traditional rules and techniques in embroidery, needlework, and weaving.

13. For studies on this phenomenon, see Nash and Safa (1980), esp. Jorge Gissi Bustos (34–35, 39–40). The political scientist Evelyn Stevens discusses Latin American social stereotypes against the background of generalized social stereotypes. Although her study lacks in-depth empirical data, she does offer a valuable historical perspective (see 90 ff.).

14. I know that my selection is incomplete and that there are many subtle distinctions that I have not been able to consider, but I think that even if my choice of literary authors and works appears to be limited, it will nevertheless provide new points of departure for others to continue the inquiry. I am well aware of the rapid growth in the number of women writers in all areas of literature (see Steele 14–15, 154–156). Although it is not my task here to review the field, I would like to mention those whose work I

have read and would have treated in a historical overview of the participation of women in Mexican literature from 1975 to the present (see Appendix 2, Other Leading Contemporary Women Writers of Mexico).

15. Kate Millet's *Sexual Politics* has been one of the main focal points of feminist debate since it was published in 1970, and as such has been highly influential in developing a direct engagement with patriarchal ideology. Feminist criticism has matured as feminists have developed a rich, thorough, and wide array of critical positions ranging from psychoanalysis and deconstructive methods to hermeneutics and sociocriticism (e.g., Nancy Miller, Moi, Showalter, and Stimpson).

16. The critical study of truth claims as the foundation of literary world-making has been examined by Mario J. Valdés in his *World-making* (1992).

17. The theater "La Capilla" (The chapel) was founded in 1953 by Salvador Novo. It ran into financial difficulties, as all small theaters have. One of the recent (1992) solutions was to open a cabaret style theater in an adjoining space, thereby supporting this home of experimental theater and performance. One of the central dramatists in this venture has been Jesusa Rodríguez, whose pieces are often performed here (see Cynthia Steele's commentary).

18. I often use the first-person plural in these closing comments rather than the first-person singular, as in the earlier pages where I was developing my theoretical framework of feminist sociocriticism. The *we* is an acknowledgment that I have greatly benefited from the work of my colleagues in *fem.* and the women's studies group of the Colegio de México and its coordinator, Elena Urrutia, one of the leading feminists in Latin America. I also wish to acknowledge common cause with the Paris group "Collectif de femmes d'Amérique Latine et de la Caraïbe" (Collective of Latin American and Caribbean Women).

19. In this respect important works of nineteenth-century literature by Mexican women have been recovered by the workshop group on Mexican women's writing of the Interdisciplinary Program of Women's Studies of the Colegio de México. The relatively limited number of texts brought out by this team of scholars gives further evidence for the need for much more intense research into both the pre-aesthetic arts and nonfiction prose such as local history and confessional writing by women during the centuries of imposed silence (see *Las voces olvidadas. Antología crítica de narradoras mexicanas nacidas en el siglo XIX*, edited by Ana Rosa Domenella and Nora Pasternac. (Forgotten voices. Critical anthology of Mexican narrators born in the nineteenth century). In my fourth chapter I shall make the argument that Juana Inés de la Cruz is indicative of the social repression suffered by women as artists and philosophers, and her experience highlights the need for a reexamination of women's creative and intellectual expression. One such volume is *Feminist Perspectives on Sor Juana Inés de la Cruz*, edited by Stephanie Merrim.

20. See the special issue "Presencia y ausencia de la mujer en las letras hispánicas" (Presence and absence of women in Hispanic letters) which I edited in 1990 for *Revista Canadiense de Estudios Hispánicos*.

Chapter Two

1. Juan Rulfo was born in the state of Jalisco in 1918 and died in Mexico City in 1986. He began publishing short stories in 1945. Rulfo is the author of four books: *El llano en llamas* (1953; The burning plain and other stories); *Pedro Páramo* (1955; English trans. 1959); *El gallo de oro y otros textos para cine* (1980; The gold rooster and other texts for the cinema); *Donde quedó nuestra historia. Hipótesis sobre Historia regional* (1984; Where our History remained. Hypothesis about regional History). His work, especially *Pedro Páramo*, has been translated into all the major languages of the world and has become significant in the development of Latin American postmodernism. In this chapter I am citing from the English translation by Lysander Kemp, but I have corrected translation errors; for example, p. 98 of the Spanish text reads "tocar mis senos"; p. 74 of the English translation reads "touched my forehead."

2. Studies on *Pedro Páramo* fall generally into five critical categories: (1) historical and thematic studies (see Blanco Aguinaga, González Boixó, Pupo-Walker, Rodríguez Luis, Ruffinelli, Sacoto Salamea); (2) archetype and mythical studies (Alvarez, Befumo Boschi, Canfield, de la Colina, Ortega, and Peralta); (3) narratological studies, especially following Genette (Bastos and Molloy, Befumo Boschi, González Boixó, Jiménez de Báez, Pimentel); (4) semiotic studies following Greimas or Barthes (Ezquerro, Portal); and (5) linguistic studies (Gutiérrez Marrone). For extensive bibliographies on *Pedro Páramo*, see González Boixó (1983) and the special Juan Rulfo issue of *Cuadernos hispanoamericanos*, also prepared by González Boixó, as well as Luis Leal's book.

3. A number of critics have focused on Susana San Juan, with varied insight; one of the first was José de la Colina, who can be considered a prime example of a western canonic appropriation of this character. A more balanced view is that of Luis Ortega Galindo, but still, invariably, only looking at Susana through the perspective of the male, to whom she is the object of desire, or of the male reader, who sees Susana as his object of desire (see Sacoto Salamea).

4. This is the late stage of the Mexican revolution (1910–1929), which was predominantly fought in the north and northwest of Mexico from 1926 to 1929. The states of Jalisco, Colima, Guanajuato, Michoacán, and Durango were affected most. The Cristero campaign was fought against the revolutionary government in Mexico City because of its separation of church and state and its general anticlerical stance; see Díaz and Rodríguez and Francis Patrick Dooley.

5. Although the contemporary Mexican state has changed dramatically from the quasi-feudal system of power of the *cacique* at the turn of the century, the legacy of arbitrary self-interest has been transferred to the Mexican government and the pyramid of power it has institutionalized through the ruling political party. For a lucid description of both the *cacique* and the contemporary heir to the *cacique*—the local political appointee of the government—see González Casanova, 32–36 and 67–69. The all-pervasive malaise of Mexican government corruption should not be taken as an indication that the Mexican people are passive victims. Besides the sporadic armed uprisings

against the PRI and the local enforcers, it should be noted that there are grass roots civic groups such as "adopt a Mexican politician," which concentrate on local politicians in an effort to examine how they become enriched by plundering the public purse. Nor does the daily press have any shortage of journalistic courage; new reform-minded independent newspapers like *Reforma* in Mexico City keep springing up, much to the chagrin of the government. But the news agencies and the all-powerful Televisa network are de facto propaganda agencies for the government, with no political voice of their own. In the recent spate of scandals, even the hardened veterans of Televisa were shaken by the extent of the public media's complicity and involvement in corrupt politics; see the 1996 book by the *Miami Herald*'s Andres Oppenheimer.

6. Ricoeur (1992) has outlined a philosophical hermeneutics of the self which encompasses a dialectic of selfhood and otherness (16–23).

7. For the finest archaeological study of this symbolism in Teotihuacan, see Laurette Séjourné.

8. One of the finest critics to examine this novel is Carlos Blanco Aguinaga, who points out that Susana's presence in Pedro's life makes him the only character with an intimate life as well as a public one. I agree with Blanco Aguinaga, but would also point out that Susana has the same two sides; however, these are further complicated by her implicit history of sexual abuse by her father and objectification by Pedro.

9. Miguel León-Portilla demonstrates with extensive documentation that the dominant social structure of preconquest Mexico was a theocracy which depended for its economic survival on a powerful work ethic and a basic cooperative economic infrastructure (see 134–145). The conquest brought about the complete breakdown of the pre-Hispanic social structure, and in the ensuing chaos, there developed a hybrid of the Spanish *cacique* and the pre-Hispanic *Tlamatine* (wise elder); as the older traditions receded into the distant past, however, the prime characteristic came to be the ruthless exercise of power.

10. Laurette Séjourné (178) explains the role of the goddess Chantico as the primary symbol of burning water, which is congruent with agricultural goddesses from other cultures.

11. Befumo Boschi: "Florencio, quien no sabemos si existió" (Florencio, who we do not really know existed, 146); Ezquerro: "une passion devorante pour Florencio, personnage enigmatique, qui semble inventé par la folie amoureuse de Susana" (a devouring passion for Florencio, enigmatic character, who seems invented by Susana's mad love, 109); González Boixo: "Las ensoñaciones de Susana sobre Florencio que terminan aquí, plantean la duda al lector de si responden a un hecho real o son fantasías, dado su alto nivel de idealización"(Susana's dreams of Florencio, which end here, raise the reader's doubt as to whether they are based on reality or are fantasies, given their high level of idealization, 184).

12. See p. 82 for Bartolomé's statement to Susana: "You're a widow, but I told him that you're still living with your husband, or that at least you act that way." And Pedro's monologue to Susana: "But I learned from the messenger that you had married, and then that you were a widow" (80).

Chapter Three

1. Carlos Fuentes, *Burnt Water*. All quotations followed by page number are drawn from the 1980 English translation, which includes a number of stories published earlier than the quartet of the Mexican edition; the translation is by Margaret Sayers Peden. The Spanish text "El día de las madres" is one of four narratives in *Agua quemada* (1981).

2. *Feminophobia* is my term. I have turned to it because it has elegance of simplicity and it is, at the same time, deeply significant. Feminophobia is an acute state of sexual alienation in which the male-dominated social group assigns specific personae to the female and steadfastly refuses to consider women as individuals. The cause of this social psychotic state is fear of the female's difference, of the female body, of her sexual organs, and, at the anxiety level, fear of the threat of castration which the psychotic state perceives as the remaking of the male into a female-like object. My topic is "masculine domination of life accompanied by extreme sexual polarization," to use Carolyn G. Heilbrun's apt phrase. Her *Toward a Recognition of Androgyny* remains a source of inspiration. I would also like to acknowledge Paul Ricoeur's philosophical study, "Violence and Language."

3. There are numerous thematic studies of stereotypes of women. An influential book that is well researched is Sandra M. Gilbert and Susan Gubar's *The Madwoman in the Attic*; see esp. 20–27 for a discussion of female character as an angel who is redemptive because she is cast in the image of the Virgin Mary. Of primary significance to my topic is Cynthia Griffin Wolff's article "A Mirror for Men: Stereotypes of Women in Literature." I would only point out that there is a basic difference between unconscious stereotyping in the narrative focalization and ironic stereotyping in the fictional narrator's point of view. Wolff deals with the former and I am working with the latter.

4. Octavio Paz's commentary on the Virgin of Guadalupe, written in 1950, is still one of the most influential studies we have: "It is no secret to anyone that Mexican Catholicism is centered about the Virgin of Guadalupe. In the first place, she is an Indian Virgin; the scene of her appearance to the Indian Juan Diego was a hill that formerly contained a sanctuary dedicated to Tonantzin, 'Our Mother,' the Aztec goddess of fertility. . . . The defeat of these (masculine) gods—which is what the Conquest meant to the Indian world, because it was the end of a cosmic cycle and the inauguration of a new divine kingdom—caused the faithful to return to the ancient feminine deities. The phenomenon of a return to the maternal womb, so well known to the psychologist, is without doubt one of the determining causes of the swift popularity of the cult of the Virgin." See also *The Labyrinth of Solitude*, 84–85. My own contribution to the Guadalupana phenomenon traces its development from colonial syncretism to national symbol in Mexico and ethnic symbol of identity in the United States' Chicano communities. One of the most significant recent examples of the symbolic viability of the Virgin of Guadalupe among the Chicano communities is *The Goddess of the Americas/La Diosa de las Américas*, edited by Ana Castillo (1996).

5. Octavio Paz gives a succinct view of the Mexican version of the saint–sinner syn-

drome of female characterization in society: "In a world made in man's image, woman is only a reflection of masculine will and desire. When passive, she becomes a goddess, a beloved one, a being who embodies the ancient, stable elements of the universe: the earth, motherhood, virginity. When active, she is always function and means, a receptacle and a channel. Womanhood, unlike manhood, is never an end in itself" (35–36). Another more recent commentator on the role of women in Mexico is Carlos Monsiváis. In "Sexismo en la literatura mexicana" (Sexism in Mexican literature), he writes: "By nature and definition, Mexican culture is a sexist culture. In an elementary way it rests on the conviction that, having women as inferior beings, what follows is to exploit them. . . . Her initial capital is her passivity, her marriage is her goal and realization; her adultery is expulsion from paradise; her promiscuity her extermination. In a ritual manner, she represents two extremes of a theology of consumption: she is the fallen woman or the personification of grace" (104, 114; my translation).

6. Fuentes writes in the "Author's Note," dated in Mexico, February 1985: "This book was begun in a train between Chihuahua and Zacatecas in 1964 and finished in Tepoztlan, Morelos in 1984" (my translation; Spanish version, 189). *The Old Gringo* was translated by Margaret Sayers Peden and Carlos Fuentes and published in 1985. In 1988 the Argentinean Luis Puenzo, known for his prize-winning "The Official Story," directed the movie *Old Gringo*. The principal actors are Jane Fonda in the role of Harriet Winslow, Gregory Peck as Ambrose Bierce/the old gringo, and Jimmy Smits as Tomás Arroyo. The script is by Aida Bortnik and Luis Puenzo. The production is by Luis Bonfligio and Fonda Films for Columbia Pictures. The differences between Carlos Fuentes' text and the filmscript are enormous. The celluloid Harriet is a feminine stereotype which nullifies and distorts women's reality as human beings; time after time she appears on the screen with wide-open eyes and mouth—a cardboard character, all superficiality with no depth. The dialogical tension between the social person and the individual is nonexistent. Fuentes' Harriet embodies a complex human reality which represents not only the encounter of two cultures and two different social classes and sexes but, of greater importance, also a woman with her own particular perspectives on reality. The Woman with the Moon Face has been reduced to a character who hardly speaks in the film; her exceptional monologue is not included. On the other hand, La Garduña is well presented. Paradoxically, the novel displays more cinematographic technique in the characterization as well as in the discursive montage, the changes of fade-in, fade-out, and close-up than does the film, which has all the cliches of a romance illustrated with photos.

7. The Mexican revolution erupted in 1910; the country celebrates its anniversary on the twentieth of November. Mexico lived through ten years of armed turmoil in which its leaders frequently changed: Madero, Carranza, Huerta, Zapata, Villa, Obregón. Civil peace was restored with the 1917 constitution, and with the 1920 Obregón presidency, a political system began which still rules the country. What began as a means to end the Porfirio Díaz dictatorship became a total revolutionary movement which changed Mexican society, economy, and identity. In 1913, Madero was betrayed and assassinated; there were several U.S. interventions (the port of Veracruz was seized

in 1914). Pancho Villa assembled his Northern Division with thousands of men and by December 1914, he was in power in Chihuahua. The seventy-one-year-old writer Ambrose Bierce crossed the border and went deeply into Chihuahua looking for Villa, who had begun to be a legend; to the cry of "Viva Villa," peasants revolted from places as distant as Yucatán. All the historical facts in the novel are accurate. Even the Mirandas recall the powerful Terrazas of Chihuahua. In the "Author's Note," Fuentes writes: "In 1913, the North American writer Ambrose Bierce . . . entered Mexico in November and nothing else was known of him. The rest is fiction" (my translation; Spanish version, 426). See Jonathan Tittler's study on the author's note.

8. For critical commentary on these aspects of Fuentes' work, see Becky Boling, and, especially, Donna Bassin, "Woman's Image of Inner Space" (200). Also see the study by Mexican commentator Carlos Monsiváis, "Sexismo en la literatura mexicana" (Sexism in Mexican literature). I quote a key paragraph: "How many things is sexism? It is an ideology, that relies on the needs and values of the dominant group and is patterned by what the members of this group admire in themselves and find convenient in their subordinates: aggression, intelligence, power and efficiency in men; passivity, ignorance, docility, virtue and inefficiency in women. It is a psychology which seeks to be a passport for the patriarchal ideology and minimizes—through social beliefs, ideology and tradition—any egalitarian possibility of the feminine ego. It is a class phenomenon, a sociological fact, an economic and educational matter, a theory of power, a biological supposition, an anthropological structure which conquers myths and religion. Sexism meets its most successful political form in patriarchy and its most evident institution in the family" (1975, 102; my translation).

9. In this novel Fuentes mainly uses an omniscient, third-person narrative voice, but it is through the dialogical process of the focalizer/focalized aspect of the character-narrator, Harriet Winslow, that the diegetic space is developed. There is a creative tension of the dialogical imagination in the characterization of Harriet, as Cherie Meacham has acknowledged. This tension emerges between the character in her public speech of repressed gringa and the intimate language of her desires. The creative force of this tension is what Bakhtin has accepted as the principal means of leading a literary character to successful realization in the readings by multiple and unknown readers. Bakhtin describes this tensional aspect of language thus: "Such is the fleeting language of a day, of an epoch, a social group, a genre, a school and so forth. It is possible to give a concrete and detailed analysis of any utterance, once having exposed it as a contradiction-ridden, tension-filled unity of two embattled tendencies in the life of language. The authentic environment of an utterance, the environment in which it lives and takes shape, is dialogized heteroglossia, *anonymous and social as language, but simultaneously concrete, filled with specific content and accented as an individual utterance*" (1981, 272; my emphasis). Harriet Winslow's dialogue and monologue constitute a tensional language which every reader appropriates, a subversive language revealing a feminine intimacy in search of liberation from the patriarchy of native country or foreign land.

10. One of the distinguishing features of this novel is the characterization of the Woman with the Moon Face in her dual role as social symbol and confessional inter-

locutor. What Bakhtin writes about Dostoevsky can well be applied to La Luna's characterization: "His heroes' most important confessional self-utterances are permeated with an intense sensitivity toward the anticipated words of others about them, and with others' reactions to their own words about themselves. Not only the tone and style but also the internal semantic structure of these self-utterances are defined by an anticipation of another person's words" (1984, 205). Besides Fuentes' technique, one must bear in mind the ideological force in the denunciation of religion and patriarchy in the form of confidences between women. Rita Felski comments on this situation of feminist revelation: "Feminist confession thus seeks to affirm a female experience which has often been repressed and rendered invisible by speaking about it" (112). Chapter 18 is a conversation between Harriet and the Woman with the Moon Face. The fact that La Luna does not write this confession, even though she is one of the few *hacienda* characters who is literate, is in itself symptomatic of her condition between revelation and rebellion. Felski writes: "The act of writing promises power and control, endowing subjective experience with authority and meaning" (112). None of the women of *The Old Gringo* writes.

11. Chapter 18 in the novel's English version is 19 in the Spanish version.

12. Obviously, the differences between a carnival's ambient and a revolution are great, but in spite of the differences between the comic and parodic spirit and the destruction and annihilation of any trace of the past regime, the two social phenomena have in common the creation of a period of liberation from social restrictions governing daily life. The parody of carnival has implicit within it the destructive force of the revolution, and the revolution carries within its impetus the regenerative force of the carnival. Bakhtin identifies four characteristics of carnival which also apply, with certain adjustments, to the revolution: (1) In carnival everybody participates in one way or another. Carnival has no actors and spectators; everybody lives it. (2) Carnival establishes new kinds of interrelations between individuals. (3) Carnival brings together the most disparate in a normal regime—the high and low; the powerful and the insignificant; wisdom and stupidity. (4) Carnival subverts the established order and profanes it (1984, 122–123). This view of the deepest social implications of carnival clearly shows that all the distinctive characteristics are equally applicable to the revolution. Carnival's mask is not the thief's mask; it is the licence to reveal and not to hide. Traditionally, makeup has been part of disguise, and thus it has the same inverse possibilities as the mask.

13. The symbolic use of mirrors and looking into them and in the eyes of the other is subtly developed in this novel. Tomás Arroyo's gaze objectifies Harriet as an object of desire, but his gaze in the ballroom's mirrors paralyses him and attracts him toward a labyrinth of infinite reduplication. On the other hand, Harriet refuses to look in the mirrors and only looks at herself in Tomás' eyes. In her strong stare of confrontation, she looks at herself as he sees her and stares back at his stare. See Debra Castillo (1989), who emphasizes Harriet's seduction by Tomás, looking at being looked at in the mirrors. I agree with the seduction scene as far as Castillo develops it, but there is more; most significantly, the failure of Harriet's intention to seduce Tomás.

14. The antifeminist posture by the church and clergy is not simply the idiosyncrasy of this particular, celibate institution in a society deeply based on sexism; the Catholic religion and the theology which institutionalizes it are the historical product as well as the bulwark of women's subordinate social status. Doubtless, the version of the trinity stated by the Woman with the Moon Face represents an unsophisticated explanation, a figurative exposition by a rustic mind without the elegance of official Thomism. However, the monologue reveals not only the reality of popular religion but also, with complete innocence—from La Luna's standpoint, since from Fuentes' it is a piece of cunning—reveals that religion's theological pillars are misogynist; see especially Thomas Aquinas' *Summa contra gentiles*, book 3, which deals with ethical matters, and book 4, which discusses the mystery of the trinity. In the third book, the mental and physical superiority of man over woman is taken as starting point to establish the moral code buttressing the subjugation of women for procreation within monogamous matrimony or devoted to the contemplation of God, observing a rigorous celibacy. Thus it is understandable that a rational argument is used to elaborate a social code that better protects the community's interests. Every woman has to be controlled from birth to death because her body is the source of the sin of concupiscence (lustfulness). It is the father's duty to protect his daughters' virtue (read virginity) until he delivers them to their husbands in the holy sacrament of matrimony or to the religious community where they will be distanced from the world. In the fourth book, Thomas condemns the Greek church for not accepting Rome's teaching regarding the Holy Spirit. The son was conceived in the virgin by the Holy Spirit, but not through carnal union. Nor is the son carnal, in Aquinas' account, which would be an absurdity amounting to saying that he is son of himself, since Christ, God the Father, and the Holy Spirit are one. The contradiction between a carnal pregnancy, a natural birth from the mother's womb, and a spiritual insemination is a mystery of faith. La Luna's version transforms the mystery through magic and myth in which the gods frequently change their nature.

15. The technique used by Fuentes in chapter 18 has explicit antecedents in João Guimarães Rosa's *Grande Sertão: Veredas*; see the recent study by Luiz Fernando Valente, in which the critic explores the relationship of replacement that the reader assumes due to the silent listener.

16. Rof Carballo's work is a constant search for the cultural constructs of Spaniards through a psychoanalysis of that society. His sources are varied and rich in philosophical depth. Among those which concern this study, I note especially the *Introduction to a Science of Mythology* by C. G. Jung and C. Kerenyi and *Unterwegs zur Sprache* by Martin Heidegger, which Rof Carballo aptly quotes.

17. My study on this work by Carlos Fuentes has a limited purpose, which is to examine the institutionalized sexism of Mexico and the function of literature to propagate the ideology or to subvert it. Fuentes stands out among contemporary authors as one of the most subversive of patriarchy. Only the essayist Carlos Monsiváis has expressed these social truths with comparable clarity; for example, writing about the Mexican man's attitude: "'I am Mexican: therefore it is fitting for me to be irresponsible, suicidal, a failure in carrying out my obligations, *macho* up to the multiplication of my women,

as courageous as my vocation of impunity.' At a very high price this nationalism abolishes feminine participation, exchanges solidarity for complicity, deifies paternalism" (1987, 210). Fuentes' novel has the power of subversive refiguration in his readers' world.

18. The concept of the reader's refiguration is the foundation of my literary criticism and is based on Paul Ricoeur's work; see *Time and Narrative*, vol. 1, 71, where he writes: "[refiguration] marks the intersection of the world of the text and the world of the hearer or reader; the intersection, therefore, of the world configured by the poem and the world wherein real action occurs and unfolds its specific temporality."

Chapter Four

1. Although Alfonso Méndez Plancarte notes that uncertainty surrounds November 12, 1651 as the date of birth of Sor Juana, the date given by Fray Diego Calleja, and he suspects 1648 as the true date, he concludes that until there is more proof, 1651 will probably be observed (lii–liii). Octavio Paz makes the correction based on evidence that she was baptized on December 2, 1648 (1988, 65).

2. Paz suggests the latter hypothesis. His reasons are as follows: (1) The Archbishop of Mexico is on record as hating women and, with special fury, Sor Juana. Paz quotes from Francisco Sosa: "In the history of the Mexican church, the archbishop's aversion toward women was so extreme that it could be classified as mania" (409). His biographer, José de Lezamis, reports that the archbishop suffered almost constantly from the temptation of lust, especially after he became archbishop and came to Mexico City. Paz sums up: "His charity was despotism, his humility pride and his chastity a mental debauch" (409). (2) Antonio de Vieyra's sermon of 1650 (two years after Sor Juana was born) was constantly cited by the archbishop as theological thought of the highest order. This was a sufficient incentive for Sor Juana to study the sermon in detail and to expose it to a most severe critique in her intellectual salon. Thus an attack on Vieyra's sermon was an attack on the archbishop. (3) She put it in writing after being assured protection by the Bishop of Puebla. (4) When Fernández de Santa Cruz published her critique and extolled its intellectual qualities but chided Sor Juana for her lack of piety, he was helping to attack his arch-rival the Archbishop of Mexico, and yet he protected himself by his invocation of ascetic piety. By stressing her lack of religiosity he exonerated himself from the reaction that was sure to come. Paz sees Sor Juana as a naive ally. It is quite clear that neither Sor Juana nor Fernández de Santa Cruz realized the severity of the archbishop's revenge; Sor Juana had been assured of Fernández de Santa Cruz's support, but when confronted with the archbishop's fury, the bishop left her to face the attack alone.

3. The introduction and critical commentary make this remarkable text available to scholars in the English-speaking world. The annotations to the text are the finest published to date.

4. Sor Juana criticism offers us a unique case study of the historical context of the reception accorded a woman's writing. In Appendix 3, Sor Juana Criticism, I review only a select cross section of hundreds of critical materials that highlight the poet's reception before and after the impact of the feminist movement. Compare, for example, Castro Leal's (1944) praise of Sor Juana as "the ornament of the seventeenth century" (vii) with Electa Arenal's 1994 assessment: "Sor Juana's intellectually and literarily active life challenged the social, cultural, and religious mores that kept women physically and mentally confined" (vii).

5. I am following the edition of Méndez Plancarte in the *Obras completas*, vol. 1; the translation is mine. I have consulted the translation by Alan S. Trueblood.

6. Octavio Paz's article of 1950 (included in *Las peras del olmo* [Pears of the elm tree]) is, as he says, a distant forerunner of the major book on Sor Juana. What is most noteworthy is that Paz is deeply concerned with the possibility of misunderstanding a period which, in so many respects, was far more distant than three hundred years. The crisis of New Spain as a censured and silenced land, burdened by a distant and closed-minded bureaucracy of both church and state, was reflected in every aspect of the attack on Sor Juana, which lasted four years, from 1690 to her death in 1695. Paz insists that it is not possible to understand the case of Sor Juana unless one understands the crisis of New Spain in those years. The article of 1950 states the case; the book of 1982 proves it.

7. I am following the Spanish text of "Piedra de sol" in the Weinberger edition; the translation is mine. I have consulted Weinberger's translation.

8. The Cartesian aspects of Sor Juana's philosophy have been treated many times before, if not specifically in the terms of my argument, certainly in the general understanding of Cartesian rationalism. I cite only the articles that develop the argument: Abreu Gómez's (1948) prologue, although flawed in exposition because of his many prejudices, does make the first case for Sor Juana's Cartesian thought. It was followed a few years later by Anita Arroyo (1952), and Electa Arenal (1983, 147–183).

9. Two books have given us a fresh insight into Sor Juana's philosophy in relation to Thomistic philosophy; see Montross and Tavard.

10. At long last there has been sufficient historical work done on Sor Juana so that it is possible to separate her theological arguments and even her religious beliefs from the church politics of the late seventeenth century. The duplicity of don Manuel Fernández de Santa Cruz, which led to her downfall, can only be grasped within the context of the politics of the church in Mexico. In fact, the accusation of betrayal and deceit is so flagrant that one is taken aback that he was not denounced centuries ago for what he did to a talent far superior to any he had ever known. It is therefore also important to be aware of criticism as late as 1971. For a contrast in ideological presentations, see Flynn's treatment of Sor Juana's downfall in what he calls "the incident of the letters" (17–24) and Paz's part VI (1988, 389–470). Flynn is determined to save the name of a good Catholic nun in spite of herself; Paz is equally determined to right what he considers to be a profound wrong and a shameful cover-up (488).

Chapter Five

1. The point I am making is not that authors like Carlos Fuentes, for example, have not created complex and significant female characters, as indeed he has in *La región más transparente* (Where the air is clear) and *Aura*. My argument is that they have not created female centers of consciousness. Aura, for example, the youthful reincarnation of an older woman, is distinguished as a male object of desire. Fuentes comes much closer to creating a female center of consciousness with the Woman with the Moon Face in *The Old Gringo* (see Chapter 3 of this book), but even there the narrative voice counterpart to the character's speaking voice is absent and does not contribute to building the center of consciousness. The theoretical background to this issue is taken from Mikhail Bakhtin's "Discourse in the Novel," in *The Dialogic Imagination*: "A speaking person's discourse in the novel is not merely transmitted or reproduced; it is, precisely, artistically represented and thus—in contrast to drama—it is represented by means of authorial discourse. The speaking person in the novel is always, to one degree or another, an ideologue, and his words are always ideologemes. A particular language in a novel is always a particular way of viewing the world, one that strives for a social significance. It is precisely as ideologemes that discourse becomes the object of representation in the novel" (333).

2. It is important to note that before the decade of the 1950s, a woman writer in Mexico normally wrote on a limited set of "feminine" topics such as family life, maternity, and education. See Elizabeth Rosa Horan.

3. For a wider perspective on the topic of women's writing, see Marting's *Women Writers of Spanish America*, which lists a total of only twelve women writers in nineteenth-century Mexico, none in the eighteenth century, and only Sor Juana and two others before that.

4. Rosario Castellanos' interest in women's place in Mexico started as early as her student days, when she chose the subject for her master's thesis: "Sobre cultura femenina" (1950; On feminine culture), a particularly grim assessment of women's contribution to culture. Throughout her life, she kept probing into the subject of women's voices and silences, presence and absence, freedom and oppression. The more she became aware of other cultures, the more she returned to her own with a passion to promote change in the name of the millions of women's minds that had been wasted. References are from the English translation.

5. The lecture's title is "Woman's Contribution to Culture. Self-Denial Is a Mad Virtue." The date was February 15, 1971, at the Mexican Museum of Anthropology. Mexico's president was among the very large audience. See Elena Urrutia (1988).

6. Prostitution as a social phenomenon has been treated through numerous approaches. Sartre and others have written that sexual desire itself is the desire to possess, to gain recognition of one's own freedom at the expense of the other. By degrading her or him, one reduces her or him to an object. This view opens up the topic to its fullest significance, which is the treatment of the other exclusively as a sexual object rather than as a complex relationship wherein numerous and sometimes conflicting attitudes

mix. The basic point that appears in Rosario Castellanos' work is that a *macho* attitude helps block out all aspects of the other but one, her sex; therefore, the prostitute is to be used and discarded as soon as possible so that there is no chance to find out that she is more than an object for the satisfaction of sexual desire. See Jagger and Sartre (396–405).

7. Article 34 of the 1857 Mexican constitution unequivocally uses Spanish masculine gendered language to describe a Mexican. In 1917 the Constitutional Congress denied the petition of women's right to vote or be elected to public positions. From 1917 to the 1930s, there were sporadic attempts to obtain political rights. In 1935 women's organizations got together more than fifty thousand women in the "Front for Women's Rights." In 1937 the right to vote came close when President Cárdenas promised (a women's hunger strike was being staged in front of his house) to initiate in congress a reform to article 34 to read "Mexican citizens are all those men and women." Nevertheless, it was not convenient for the PRI, the party in power, to have women exercising their rights at the next election, so it was not until February 1947 that women were allowed to participate in *municipal* elections, and October 1953 when women finally had full voting rights; 1958 was the first federal election in which Mexican women voted. The amendment to article 34 reads: "citizens are the men and women." For more details see Enriqueta Tuñón; also Francesca Miller (68–144).

8. Bachofen (1815–1887) was the noted Swiss anthropologist whose major work, *Das Mutterrecht* (1861; Myth, religion, and mother right,) questions the prevailing patriarchal theory of social evolution. Having found what he discerned to be evidence of matrilineal descent in ancient Greece and in areas of Africa and America, he developed a three-stage theory of social evolution. In the beginning promiscuity prevailed; then order was established by matriarchy, and, eventually, men gained power and patriarchy was permanently established. The serious flaws in his theory are that he confused matrilineal descent with matriarchy. In western culture no society in which women were predominant has been found, with the exception of religious groups.

9. Luisa Josefina Hernández holds that women are not oppressed in Mexico any more than men, and that the many social problems of Mexico are not gender related, but primarily political, with a highly privileged upper class, an exploitative small middle class, and a massive lower class in which the impoverished and disenfranchised of the vast majority of Mexicans live. See Grace W. Bearce, Michèle Muncy, and Kirsten Nigro. What she and other antifeminist women in Mexico do not realize is that the exploitation and abuse of the poor by the rich is reproduced in scale at all levels of this society, as individuals at every peg down seek to have someone lower, whom they can dominate, and it is in this situation of exploitation that women of all social classes are scapegoats on whom the frustrated male can vent his rage. See Chapter 1 of this book for documentation.

10. María Luisa Puga's writing has begun to receive critical attention. Although she is not mentioned in Marting's *Spanish American Women Writers*, her work has been treated in Jean Franco's *Plotting Women*. She published her first novel in 1978: *Las posibilidades del odio* (The possibilities of hatred); followed by *Inmóvil sol secreto* (1979;

Secret and immobile sun), *Cuando el aire es azul* (1980; When the air is blue), *Accidentes* (1981; Accidents), *Pánico o peligro* (1983; Panic or danger), *Intentos* (1987; Intents), *La forma del silencio* (1987; The form of silence), *Antonia* (1989), *Las razones del lago* (1991; The lake's reasons), and *La ceremonia de iniciación* (1994; Initiation ceremony). She states in an interview for Gustavo Sainz's collection *Jaula de palabras* (Cage of words) that she is an intuitive rather than a systematic writer. Her narrative technique has developed into an effective means of expression for her highly metaphoric view of reality.

Chapter Six

1. For over thirty years the term "testimonial literature" has been used to designate a cross-over genre between fiction and direct reporting from the subjects' own testimony. In recent years, however, it has come to be associated primarily with a symbiotic narration wherein the subject's story is organized and structured by a professional writer, usually an anthropologist or a journalist. My use of the term aims at a more controlled usage: whatever narrative techniques are used and irrespective of the writer's instruments and sources, the essential characteristic in my usage is that the narrative voice of the testimonial persona and the organizing writer together produce a narration that bears witness to concrete historical events and people. The narrating persona is the direct source who informs and reports, but it is the writer who organizes sequentiality and creates focalization. The most important studies on Latin American testimonial literature to date are the following: John Beverly, Margarita Fernández Olmos, David William Foster, Jean Franco, René Jara and Hernán Vidal, Elzbieta Sklodowska, and Doris Sommer.

2. The fundamental difference between biography and testimonial literature is that the emplotment of biography is entirely that of the biographer, who intersperses letters, diary entries, and other writings of the subject in order to personalize the event being described, while in the case of testimonial literature the narrative thread follows the direction of the subjects' story-telling idiom. For a good example of well-researched biography to compare in terms of narrative emplotment, see Doris Meyer.

3. Moema Viezzer is a Brazilian social worker and teacher. She has worked primarily in community projects in the northeast of Brazil. Domitila Barrios de Chungara is the wife of a Bolivian miner and mother of seven children. She was among the few working class women to take part in the International Forum on the Status of Women, organized by the United Nations in Mexico City in 1975.

4. Elizabeth Burgos-Debray is a Latin American social scientist. She studied clinical psychology at Paris VII and ethnology at the Ecole de Hautes Etudes. Rigoberta Menchú is a Maya Quiché woman from the highlands of Guatemala. She was twenty-three years old when her testimony was taken by Burgos-Debray; she had only learned Spanish three years before. Menchú was awarded the Nobel Peace Prize in 1992 in recognition of her work in support of all native peoples.

5. Hebe de Bonafini, a working class wife and mother from the outskirts of Buenos

Aires, was transformed into a protest leader by the abduction and murder of her two sons and daughter-in-law by the military dictatorship of Argentina in the 1970s. Her story was tape-recorded over a month and a half in 1985 by Matilde Sánchez, who sought Hebe out after she had become the protest leader of the Mothers of Plaza de Mayo. Sánchez, a middle class Argentinean, works as a journalist for the Buenos Aires daily newspaper *Clarín*.

6. Poniatowska has also written the text for various books of photographs by Mexican women photographers. One of these is *Juchitán de las mujeres* (1989; *Juchitán, a town of women*). This is a book of photographs by Graciela Iturbide and commentary by Poniatowska that features the dominant women of the extraordinary village of Juchitán in the isthmus of Tehuantepec in the Mexican state of Oaxaca. This Zapotec community (150,000 population) is well known in Mexico because of the strength, independence, and uninhibited sexuality of its women.

7. Poniatowska, her sister, and her mother moved to Mexico City after the fall of France in 1940. French was spoken at home and English at the Mexican English school she attended. Spanish was learned as a second language at school and as a first language with the family's servants. In 1954 she began to work as an interviewer for the daily newspaper *Excelsior*. At first her interviews were with writers, artists, and composers, but soon she added politicians. After a few months she moved to *Novedades* and added to her interviews of celebrities testimonies of the daily life of ordinary people. Her colleagues honored her with the Mexican National Journalism Prize in 1978. Her first work of fiction, *Lilus Kikus*, was published in 1954. In 1961 she published a book of selected interviews, *Palabras cruzadas* (Crossed words) and in 1963 *Todo empezo en domingo* (It all began on Sunday), which consists of testimonial chronicles on how lower class Mexicans spend Sundays. Not even the author could have anticipated the effect that this first testimonial book was to have; Poniatowska gave a voice to the working classes of Mexico City. She has published three works of testimonial collage: *La noche de Tlatelolco* (1971; *Massacre in Mexico* 1975), *Fuerte es el silencio* (1980; Silence is strong), and most recently *Nada, nadie* (1988; Nothing, nobody) to the unanimous acclaim of critics and public. With the Spanish publication of *Massacre in Mexico*, Poniatowska demonstrated her social commitment and courage by making public the most piercing denunciation of the government's violence against opposition. Her other testimonial works are *Hasta no verte, Jesús mío* (1969; Until we meet again), and *Gaby Brimmer* (1979; coauthored with the cerebral palsy protagonist). Her epistolary novel *Querido Diego, te abraza Quiela* (1976; *Dear Diego*) met with great success. She has also published two volumes of short stories, *Los cuentos de Lilus Kikus* (1967; The stories of Lilus Kikus), and *De noche vienes* (1985; You come by night) and several books of interviews. Her last novel, *Tinísima* (1992), is based on the life of Tina Modotti, photographer and militant communist who led a tempestuous existence during the first half of the twentieth century. Her last book, *Luz y luna, las lunitas* (1994; Light and moon, little moons), includes two reprinted newspaper articles of 1978 and 1987 in which she outlines her relationship with Jesusa and reflects on the entire process of the writing of *Hasta no verte, Jesús mío*.

8. The first book-length study on the work of Elena Poniatowska was published re-

cently (1994); Beth Jorgensen gives major emphasis to *Hasta no verte, Jesús mío* and *La noche de Tlatelolco.*

9. Juan Rulfo, of all Mexican writers, has had the keenest sense of the lower class idiom. See, for example, his short story "Paso del norte" in the collection *El llano en llamas* (The burning plain).

10. See María Elena de Valdés, "Paraliterature as a Sociocultural Index of Mexico."

11. There are three exceptions to this generalization. The first is José Joaquín Fernández de Lizardi (1776–1827), the outstanding nineteenth-century advocate of Mexican independence. When freedom of the press was suspended in Mexico in 1815, he turned from the political essay to prose fiction. His most important novel, often called the first novel of Latin America, is the picaresque novel *El periquillo sarniento* (1815; The mangy parakeet). The language and customs of the lower classes are the background for this and his other novels. His ideals of social reform are given a forum here. Of some interest to us is *La Quijotita* (1818; The little Quijote and her cousin), which focuses on the education of women in Mexico and the severe limitations imposed by the clergy. The second novelist of the lower classes is Guillermo Prieto (1818–1897); his *Memorias de mis tiempos, 1828–1853* (1906; Memoirs) were forerunners of the present-day chronicles of daily life in Mexico City. Also of some interest is *Los San Lunes de Fidel* (1923; Fidel's holy Mondays), which collects a number of his journalistic short stories of the trials and troubles of the poor in the city. The third is Angel de Campo, (pseud. Micrós; 1868–1908), who wrote short stories in the manner of Zola with detailed descriptions of the living conditions, but with much more involvement with the plight of the characters than is to be found in the French novelist.

12. See Dorrit Cohn for a discussion of the movement in first-person narration from narrative proper to monologue: "paths leading from the *narrating* self to the autonomous monologue. The present tense in these texts was always a 'true' tense; it referred to a temporal moment of its utterance" (198).

13. The surname of the French priest is particularly significant; it sounds French, but in German it is the name of the devil.

14. The notion of free love as an expression of love of God is an ancient belief which became widespread in the thirteenth century in a number of lay communities formed in Italy. In origin they were radical groups within the Franciscan monastic movement, but as they developed into self-contained communes, the Franciscans tried to disassociate themselves. These communities are generally known as the *fratecelli*. The proliferation of these communities and the political influence of the papacy greatly contributed to the rapid decline of the power of the Franciscan order by the end of the thirteenth century. See Henry Dwight Sedgewick, esp. chapters 2, 5–7, and 25.

Chapter Seven

1. I am indebted to Paul Ricoeur's essay *Le discours de l'action* (The discourse of action). His basic idea is that the world as we know it is the configuration each of us makes

through the medium of narrativity, which we receive in our exposure to language from infancy on and which we learn to use as a form of the necessary projection of rational action. This argument has become the starting point for my theory of feminist socio-criticism.

2. As noted in the previous chapter, the term "testimonial literature" has been commonly used at least since 1968 to refer to fictionalized reporting of the events and lives of concrete individuals. Ricardo Pozas, a Mexican anthropologist, transcribed the life story of a Tzotzil, *Juan Pérez Jolote*, into Spanish in 1948. The U.S. anthropologist Oscar Lewis used a tape recorder and a keen sense of narrative structure to write his *Children of Sánchez* and *Five Families*, and Elena Poniatowska used the journalistic interview as the basis for her fictionalized version of Jesusa Palancares in *Hasta no verte, Jesús mío* (Until we meet again). As I indicated in the previous chapter, I want to give the term more rigor and specificity. Whatever narrative techniques are used, and irrespective of the writer's instruments and sources, the essential characteristic that establishes testimonial literature is that the narrative voice and the implied author bear witness to concrete events and people. This means quite specifically that the narrative voice is the presence that informs and reports but does not dramatize his or her point of view and thereby does not engage in direct or indirect commentary on the incidents that have been presented. Of course, this type of observer narrative voice has been used by many novelists, but with relative freedom to break out of the perspective and deliberate at the end of the story and with the added flexibility of being able to mix concrete individuals whose lives are part of the world of action with fictional entities. Mexican women's writing has given a new vigor to testimonial literature. Since 1975 there has been a steady increase in the number of women publishing short stories on a weekly basis in the newspapers of Mexico City.

Prominent among these writers are Guadalupe Loaeza (1946–) and Josefina Estrada (1957–), whose work, like Pacheco's, also originated in the daily newspapers of Mexico City.

3. Cristina Pacheco (née Romo) was born in San Felipe, a small town in the state of Guanajuato; the family migrated to Mexico City, where she did all her schooling. Her life's vocation has always been writing. She began with the book section in the daily newspapers *Novedades* and *Popular*; this first assignment was followed by imaginary interviews signed with the masculine pseudonym Juan Angel Real and published in *Sucesos para todos*. She considers this early phase of her work to be of great importance for her career (see Samanes Cadillo). She directed three women's magazines (*La familia, La mujer de hoy*, and *Crinolina*). Since 1976 she has published interviews in the weekly *Siempre!*, and in 1977 she started to publish three stories per week in the daily newspaper *El Día*. But from 1986 on, every Sunday her numerous readers turn to the back page of *La Jornada*, where her weekly collaboration "Mar de historias" (Sea of stories) is printed. This remarkable woman has also hosted a weekly television program for fifteen years, "Aquí nos tocó vivir" (Here is where it was determined for us to live). She combines interviews and investigative reporting and concentrates on the poor of Mexico City. She also has a radio spot every day. In 1996 she was voted Woman of the Year.

4. All translations of Pacheco's work are my own. Paul Ricoeur comments that the concept of identity, be it of a nation or of an individual, is formed, strengthened, and developed by the oral or written stories which are part of our world consciousness; see "The Human Experience of Time and Narrative" (115).

5. To my knowledge, besides myself, the critics who have examined Pacheco's work are Schaefer-Rodríguez (1991), Steele (13–14), and Espinosa Rugarcía et al.

6. One must be aware that both French criticism of the last century and contemporary Mexican criticism denounce such writing on "aesthetic grounds." Zola's work was said to be "unsubtle and crude, oversimplified and melodramatic, psychologically rudimentary and improbable . . . If this were all, *Germinal* would be a mere political pamphlet containing all the half-truths, exaggerations and oversimplifications familiar in any work of propaganda. It would not be a work of art. A work of art must have some fundamental human truth; it must not merely make a number of puppets dance to a political tune" (*Germinal* 5, 13). These comments are by L. W. Tancock, summarizing criticism in Paris at the end of the century. Pacheco's work is not propaganda; it is part of the aesthetic perspective which we know from medieval literature to the present as a didactic aesthetic.

7. Theoretically I want to insist on the inappropriateness of applying critical methods derived from the study of European canonical literature to this hybrid genre. Documentary literature functions through a syllogistic structure, not a poetic one; the character who is a social symbol is not presented as a psychological extension of its author, and, above all, these stories present a temporality which must always be now. Literary theory which pretends to offer a master key for all writing is only one more universalizing fantasy. Literary theory, as scientific theory, acquires its legitimacy upon answering the problems which have been identified as operative in the inquiry.

8. Social symbol must be understood as a motivated sign, that is, a sign with an obvious intentionality to represent a general circumstance through and by a character or particular incident. Intrahistorical or *intrahistórico* is a concept first developed by Miguel de Unamuno in *En torno al casticismo* (Regarding casticismo) and has also been given historiographic validity by the eminent French historian Fernand Braudel; see *The Structures of Everyday Life*. In this chapter, I call attention to the intrahistorical domain as the field of action for the social symbol.

9. Due to Pacheco's determination to appropriate the daily incidents of the massive impoverished sector of Mexican society (more than 40 percent of Mexico City), the commentaries on demographic conditions and the data offered about the city in the capital's daily newspapers have been the principal sources for this chapter. Work by researchers in the fields of sociology, anthropology, and demography offer a wider perspective but one that is not contrary to the information offered daily by the newspapers. Pacheco's sources are clearly journalistic, but validation at the level of literary criticism must include both newspaper reportage and social scientific research.

10. See Bárcena, especially p. 8, on the lack of nutrition for Mexican children. Also see Guillermo; I quote from p. 26: "Half of the Mexican population is poor and fifteen million people are extremely poor. The latter can only meet half of their most basic sur-

vival needs" (According to García Medrano, *La Jornada*, April 18, 1989, the total population that year was just over eighty million). See Lustig, from the Colegio de México, who has studied this problem in depth. Also, Gutiérrez y Gutiérrez: "In Mexico only 17.2 percent of the population eats adequately, about 30 percent consumes a survival diet and the 50 percent left has badly balanced meals" (104).

11. See Bárcena. It must be taken into account that 40 percent of the Mexican laborers work for less than the official minimum salary (Lustig, 1988). It is estimated that half a million families in Mexico City live in the most extreme poverty without hope of ever getting out (*La Jornada*, August 22, 1990). Also see "Mentally Deficient in Mexico," which states that there are four million persons who are mentally deficient due to malnutrition (*El Universal*, June 19, 1989). It is important to add that according to Juan Carlos Rodríguez, chief of information of the Mexican Center for the Rights of Childhood, it is calculated that there are around one million street children in Mexico City and an extra-official figure of mortality of 170 children for each thousand born in the city (see Muñoz Valle). But the fundamental figure on nourishment for Mexican children is that which indicates that during the six-year period from 1982 to 1988, a million Mexican children died of malnutrition (see *La Jornada*, April 30, 1989).

12. Since 1962 Suárez del Real has warned that dependence on corn as the basic food staple is the biological tragedy under which the Mexican poor live. Also see Flores.

13. The May 30, 1989 newspaper *El Universal* reported that 880,000 elementary school children abandon their studies each year in Mexico. The census data for 1970 (last reliable figures available) showed that of the population group over 25 years, 37 percent had no education, 17.8 percent had attended one to two years, 21.7 percent had from three to five years, and only 13 percent had completed grammar school; also see Mina.

14. Arizpe (1985) concludes in her study on peasants and migration that "in the case of the families of peasants of no means . . . it usually is the case that the majority of first-born daughters tend to migrate [to Mexico City] at a very early age . . . it is very probable that this is a deliberate strategy to send off the first-born daughters either to obtain an income they can send back home, even if partially, or to permit the family to save on their keep" (115).

15. The repetition of situations and incidents in Pacheco's stories has been dictated by the daily reality of Mexico City. See the following sources to verify the relation between Pacheco's "repetitions" and the crudity of life in Mexico City: "Children Workers in Mexico Without Any Labor Protection" (*La Jornada*, June 14, 1989), and Elena Poniatowska's long prologue to *Se necesita muchacha* (Servant wanted), by Ana Gutiérrez (7–86). A 1989 study by Mary Goldsmith Connelly outlines the general tendencies of domestic service in Mexico.

16. See Hernández Tellez. Aguirre and Camposortega studied the degree of error in infants' death indexes obtained from vital statistics and concluded that "the underestimates of infant mortality appraisals make the condition of this phenomenon appear in a much more favorable light than it actually is" (464). Mina's long study starts with this explanation: "It is known that in Mexico, the necessary information to obtain reli-

able estimates of the early age 'mortality' phenomenon, particularly in the first year of life, is notoriously insufficient, in reference to quantity and quality" (85). García y Garma reports that "infant deaths represent . . . 8.9 percent or 89 per thousand" (295).

17. The newspaper *El Universal*, April 30, 1988, reported that 90 percent of parents who abuse their children are alcoholic.

18. The newspaper *El Universal*, May 30, 1989, reported that 400,000 children annually are born to minor-age mothers.

19. For data on the continuing struggle against violence directed against women, see "1986: A Review of the National Information Related to Women. Women and Violence," *fem.*, 50 (Feb. 1987), 4–5; Barranco and Rodríguez. The newspaper *El Universal*, July 25, 1989, reported that there were 1,200 reports of sexual aggression against minor girls during 1988; but it should be noted that only 5 to 10 percent of sexual aggression against women is reported and reaches a judicial verdict (see *La Jornada*, January 29, 1990); *El Nacional*, March 11, 1991, reported that in the state of Mexico during the previous year there were 85,000 rapes, and that of this figure, only 5 percent were reported. On November 26, 1996 the Mexican government ratified the October 1996 Belem (Brazil) International Convention Condemning Violence Against Women. It was further reported that violence against women in Mexico has increased at an alarming rate of growth. From 1990 to 1996 more than half a million cases of physical aggression have been reported, and yet this staggering number does not begin to reflect a true picture, since a vast number of victims do not report attacks. In Mexico City the incidence of rape has also reached crisis proportions; from January to October 1996, 9,500 cases of rape were reported, and 60 percent of these cases involved the rape of girls under thirteen years of age (Saldierna and Zendjas).

20. The topic of *machismo* in Mexican life was explored forty years ago by Octavio Paz in his *Labyrinth of Solitude*; more recently by Carlos Monsiváis (1981, 103–126), and for a sociological assessment see Barbieri (1984).

21. These basic concepts of the individual in society have been derived from the work of philosophers like Paul Ricoeur ("The Model of the Text") and Jürgen Habermas, and their development of the concept of society as a community of language users. This post-Heideggerian and post-Wittgensteinian revision of the subject-object dualism proposes a cultural process of participation through language in a community of human interests wherein the individual must respond to her own confrontation between the established ethical norms and her sense of identity.

Chapter Eight

1. Cisneros was National Endowment for the Arts Fellow in 1982 for poetry and in 1988 for narrative. Her book of narratives, *Woman Hollering Creek and Other Stories*, was published by Random House in 1991. *The House on Mango Street* was published in 1984 with a publication grant from the National Endowment for the Arts. The book was written from 1977 to 1982, and is now in its fourth printing, which is the second revised

edition (1988). In an interview I had with Cisneros on December 30, 1988 in New Or-leans, she informed me that the publishers had made some overcorrections in the first edition of *The House on Mango Street*; she was not able to revise the edition until the fourth printing in 1988. It was reissued in 1991 by Vintage. She has also published three books of poetry: *Bad Boys* (1980), *My Wicked, Wicked Ways* (1987) and *Loose Woman* (1994).

2. I am primarily concerned in my criticism with the question of identity and gen-der in Mexico and its extension into the United States with Chicana writing. In addition to Kristeva's book *Desire in Language*, I have made use throughout the present study of the article "The System and the Speaking Subject."

3. Dorrit Cohn has given us an analysis of the kinds of narrating voices we find in *The House on Mango Street* in what she terms "diary and continuity."

4. Marín, from Puerto Rico, is featured in "Louie, His Cousin and His Other Cousin" and "Marín"; Alicia in "Alicia Who Sees Mice"; Rafaela in "Rafaela Who Drinks Coconut and Papaya Juice on Tuesdays"; and, most important of all, Sally in "Sally," "What Sally Said," "Red Clowns," and "Linoleum Roses." The older women are treated with a soft-spoken sympathy through imagery: Rosa Vargas in "There Was an Old Woman She Had So Many Children She Didn't Know What to Do," Ruthie in "Edna's Ruthie," the neighbor Mamacita in "No Speak English," and her own mother in "A Smart Cookie."

5. I use the metaphor of the loom not only because of its usefulness in describing the movement of the discourse but also quite consciously because this is a woman's writing and it privileges the gradual emergence of a woman's poetic space rather than a plot. If my study were to concentrate on the topoi of women's discourse, the metaphor of the quilt would have been more appropriate. But whether loom or quilt, there is the unmistakable design of imagistic narrativity in place of emplotment. I am indebted to the work of Showalter (1986), and through her I have gained much greater insight into the recovery of women's art in the article by Lucy Lippard.

6. I find it essential to repeat that the critical strategy that effaces the female signa-ture of a text is nothing less than the continuation of a patriarchal tradition of appro-priation of the female's work through the destruction of her signature. Cisneros has cre-ated a female voice who writes with strength in a social context where doing so is an act of transgression, and she writes "A las mujeres" (To the women), as the dedication so poignantly states.

7. I had occasion to have a second interview with Cisneros in Tijuana, Mexico, on May 12, 1989, at which time I asked her about the specific references to streets and es-tablishments in Chicago. She said that Mango Street itself is a fictional composite of streets and places. The references to other streets like Loomis, businesses, the church, and so on, are referentially specific to Chicago in the sixties.

8. The Spanish Latin poet Catullus in his "The Marriage of Peleus and Thetes" de-scribes the wedding gift of the three sisters, the Fates, all dressed in white, spinning their prophecy. Cisneros' allusion to the spider web gives the three sisters not only the gift of prophecy but also an emblem of the weaver of tales as "the organizers and custodians of

folklore and stories" (Showalter, 1986, 233). The prophecy of Cisneros' three sisters is the gift of her identity.

9. An essential point to my argument is to emphasize the importance of an open text in writing by women. Virginia Woolf's characters after *Jacob's Room* are created for the reader to develop by inference, and her essays, especially *A Room of One's Own*, are for the reader to collaborate in a dialogical relationship with the writer. The metaphor of a room of one's own is the highly charged space that comes to be through freedom to engage her other as equal in discussion—a right, not a privilege, traditionally denied to women.

10. In Sidonie Smith's discussion of Maxine Hong Kingston's *The Woman Warrior*, she touches the raw nerve of *The House on Mango Street*. Both texts, we have discovered through Smith, share in the complex act of writing about writing an autobiography, but in Cisneros' text, this is a fictional persona writing about writing her liberation. Cisneros' text, like that of Kingston, comes from the double marginalization of being female and a member of an ethnic minority in the United States. Both force the issue of difference in terms of the community's narratives of selfhood.

11. Julián Olivares responded to the review of *Mango Street* by Juan Rodríguez and commented on the latter's ideological critique "that Esperanza chooses to leave Mango St., chooses to move away from the social/cultural base to become more 'Anglicized,' more individualistic; that she chooses to move from the real to the fantasy plane of the world as the only means of accepting and surviving the limited and limiting social conditions of her barrio becomes problematic to the more serious reader." Olivares disagreed: "Esperanza transcends her condition, finding another house which is the space of literature. Yet what she writes about—third-floor flats, and fear of rats, and drunk husbands sending rocks through windows, anything as far from the poetic as possible—reinforces her solidarity with the people, the women, of Mango Street" (169).

Chapter Nine

1. Mexican cookbooks in the nineteenth century were often handwritten, hand-sewn books which were passed on from one generation of women to the next. I am fortunate to have inherited such a book. The recipes and home remedies are all presented through a running narrative together with short stories prompted by the recipe in question. In the United States, Irma S. Rombauer's first edition of the *Joy of Cooking* (1931) follows the same tradition. Unfortunately her daughter, Marion Becker, has not chosen to continue the narrative tradition. Susan J. Lombardi has written an important critical analysis of the genre in English as a significant mode of gendered discourse.

2. The U.S. feminist critic Elaine Showalter recognized in 1977 that the cultural situatedness of women must be the starting point for any aesthetic consideration of their work. She writes: "Women have generally been regarded as 'sociological chameleons,' taking on the class, lifestyle, and culture of their male relatives. It can, however, be argued that women themselves have constituted a subculture within the framework of a

larger society and have been unified by values, conventions, experiences, and behaviors impinging on each individual" (1982, 11).

3. Judy Chicago's efforts to raise the aesthetic awareness of women to their work for the home has been revolutionary. Laura Esquivel's novel is written as a Mexican recognition of this woman's art form. Chicago writes: "A dinner party where family traditions are passed down like the carefully preserved tablecloth made by a beloved grandmother. A dinner party where women provide an environment of comfort, an elegant setting, and a nourishing and aesthetically pleasing meal. A dinner party where women put the guests at ease and facilitate communication between them. A dinner party, a traditional female act requiring both generosity and personal sacrifice" (8–21).

4. There have been numerous reviews of the novel and the film around the world. Each reviewer finds points of comparison to the local culture and, to varying degrees, expresses fascination or dismay at what he or she calls the magical realism of the novel and film. Of course, magical realism is a category invented by critics who are not from Latin America. The dimensions of the real in Latin America are very much a part of the oral tradition and the hybrid creation of extreme variability. The best review from Latin America of the novel/film that I have read is that published by Ramos Escandón.

5. A 1994 study of the film by Gastón Lillo offers an interesting neo-marxist interpretation. Although the generalizations he makes about Mexico's unique configuration of social class structure and race relations are valid and obvious demographic factors, he ignores three basic facts about the film which almost completely mitigate his negative views: (1) the screenplay is an adaptation of a novel and uses filmic narrative techniques to present a life story rather than an epic of the Mexican revolution; (2) the novel is a parody of nineteenth-century women's writing which carries with it a strong sense of recovery of women's space; and (3) the way of life along the Mexican–United States border from the 1850s to the narrative time of 1895–1934 was a period of constant border crossing and thousands of continuing intimate ties not only within families that had been arbitrarily separated by the border, but also between Mexicans and Anglo newcomers. It is only during post–World War II United States–Mexico relations that the border has become a barrier.

Chapter Ten

1. One recent example of the violation of human rights in Mexico was the gang rape on June 4, 1994, of three Tzeltal women in Chiapas by thirty officers and soldiers of the Mexican army. This attack was not committed in time of war, but was rather a deliberate attempt to intimidate the native support for the Zapatista insurgents (reported in a special issue on violence against women, *fem.* 18.138 [1994]: 13). When the Mexican government had not responded to the legal procedures of laying charges, the women's groups and their lawyers decided to take the case to international tribunals concerned with the violation of human rights (*fem.* 18.139 [1994]: 21).

2. Postmodern literature in general rejects the claim of direct social representation

that dominated for so long. In French, Spanish, and English literatures from the seventeenth century on, the mimetic dominated to such an extent that we could excuse Georg Lukacs for finding art and mimesis as synonymous. In postmodern literature, in contrast, the writing is an exploration of the unseen, the testing of authority and of the accepted, and, finally, the cultivation of the creative metaphor as a paradigm for creativity coming out of conflict. The idea that the literary work of art could disclose or reveal the deeper meaning of life that was in some sense already there in the human condition has been all but destroyed in the postmodern.

3. English-language literatures have responded in the postcolonialist attack on the discourse of the class structure of British colonial institutions in the Indian subcontinent, North America, the West Indies, and South Africa. The number of great postcolonial writers in English is growing and includes Michael Ondaatje, Derek Wolcott, Salman Rushdie, Toni Morrison, and Alice Walker.

4. In 1991 Margaret Higonnet and I organized a workshop at the International Comparative Literature Association congress in Tokyo on women writers around the world. The proceedings were published in December 1993 with the title *New Visions of Creation*. It bears witness to the worldwide breakthrough in the publication of women writers today.

Appendix   **Women's Education in Mexico**
One

The statistics for women's education in colonial Mexico give ample evidence of the denial of education to all but the most privileged women. The first school for women, a religious boarding school run by nuns, opened in 1753, a lay school opened in 1757 and a third in 1767. In 1790 only 450 girls received the rudiments of education out of a population of 130,000 women. The legacy of such denial of education to women in spite of government statements to the contrary, continues (Arrom, 16). In 1970, 35.2 percent of Mexican women had no exposure to education; 26.4 percent had minimal exposure from one to three years. Another 28.9 percent had four to six years (primary school is six years in Mexico). The figures drop dramatically for attendance at the secondary school level. Only 8.4 percent had secondary schooling, and only 1.2 percent of the female population of Mexico received any university education (see CEPAL's *Estudios e Informes de la CEPAL, 1983* [Studies and reports of the CEPAL]).

Reliable statistics on education during the recent period of extreme fiscal constraint (1982–1988, presidency of De la Madrid; 1988–1994, presidency of Salinas de Gortari) have not been made available. No official or unofficial statistics on the percentage of the population who have attended school over these twelve years have been issued. What we do have are statistics on what percentage of the school population girls and women make up. In 1965–1966, 47.7 percent of primary school children were female, while in 1988–1989, the percentage had risen marginally to 48.6 percent. The most notable change was the percentage of the university population who were female; in 1965–1966 women accounted for only 17 percent but in 1988–1989 they made up 38.6 percent. But it remains clear that only one out of every five university graduates is a woman (Tarrés, 40–41).

These statistics when translated into practical terms mean that in 1970, at the height of Mexico's industrial and economic expansion, 90.5 percent of all Mexican women had 0–6 years of schooling. (The minimal literacy statistics given by the census for 1970 identify 33 percent of the female population as illiterate.) The literate workforce of Mexican women was drawn largely from the 8.4 percent who attended secondary school. The meagre 1.2 percent who went beyond secondary and preparatory school includes the affluent classes who have had access to education abroad.

What could be more indicative of the denial of access to education to women than the added statistical information that only 4.03 percent of those girls who attended secondary and preparatory school passed (see Filgueira), and that only .43 percent, less than one-half of 1 percent, of women who went to university passed their first year. The magnitude of the challenge of attempting to generate a liberalizing force among Mexican women is so great that it makes all first world feminist generalizations irrelevant.

Thus it is that the oral narrativity of the marginalized majority of women in New Spain has been passed on in the substratum of "old wives tales," ghost stories which merge with the lives of saints, legends, and the general popular folklore which so enriches Mexican culture today. In this respect the popular, uncultivated *Cancionero* and the collections of legends are to a large extent the heritage of women.

Women in New Spain who were literate quite naturally wrote not for publication, but for themselves and other women in the minor genres of correspondence narrating family history, memorials such as family records, inventories with commentary, and diaries. In her 1989 book, *Plotting Women*, Jean Franco describes the analogy made by the clergy of New Spain between the silver mines and the nuns who were ordered by their confessors to write down their experiences; both must be mined and made productive. Although these women were reluctant writers, they were once again writing as witnesses to experience rather than as creators of texts. These modes of writing are closely linked to the mainstream of oral narrativity, in which women's culture subsisted after the conquest and eventually flourished in isolation. Although these forms of writing are often scorned because of their utilitarian purpose or their lack of elegance, I would counter with claims for the significance of their wit, inventiveness, and the writers' sheer will to survive as members of a community. It is important to distinguish between vocational training and learning. Almost all women in colonial Mexico received some form of vocational and religious training in keeping with their social class and the work that they were expected to perform. Learning was generally denied on the basis of ingrained biases purporting women's intellectual inferiority and the incompatibility of study with future responsibilities as wife and mother. These basic facts will help to understand why Juana Inés de la Cruz was such an extraordinary exception, and why the only surviving colonial texts written by women other than her tend to be didactic pleas for the right of women to education, or the usual religious tracts on moral duties.

Appendix   **Other Leading Contemporary Women**
Two   **Writers of Mexico**

The compiler of a survey of contemporary writers must outline the basis on which the selection was made, for there is always a selection. I want to offer the reader a brief review of other contemporary women writers of Mexico whom I would have included in a historical study. Although my list covers most of the important women writers in Mexico, it is not intended to be exhaustive or canonical. The writers I treat in this book and those I take up in this appendix have all in one way or another participated in the debate on the description and the remaking of the Mexican woman. In chronological order of birth they are Elena Garro (1920–), Inés Arredondo (1928–1989), Margo Glantz (1930–), María Luisa Mendoza (1931–), Angelina Muñiz (1936–), Guadalupe Loaeza (1946–), Silvia Molina (1946–), Angeles Mastretta (1949–), Carmen Boullosa (1954–), Ethel Krause (1954–), and Josefina Estrada (1957–). Collectively, they represent two generations of women, and they have shared the experience of the women's movement, the economic and social crisis of Mexico in the 1990s, and, in general, this age of radical skepticism.

The work of Elena Garro (1920–) covers plays, novels, and short stories. Her writing is, in turns, transgressive and subversive; that is, when she is breaking barriers of literary convention, she is undermining the basic assumptions of a mimetic narrative discourse through parody and irony. *Testimonios sobre Mariana* (Testimony about Mariana) is Garro's most markedly feminist work. The central issue is the representation of a woman. This portrayal emerges from the inner assumptions of representation, but also from the perspective of the implicit referentiality in such a description, and finally from a vantage point that would deny validity to any mimetic representation of another. This highly conflictive idea of representation is indicative of the present era, when Mexican women writers must try to find the real person among the ruins of the destruction of the patriarchal representation of womanhood. Garro has collected twelve dramatic works under the title *Un hogar sólido* (A stable home). Her novels include the critically acclaimed *Los recuerdos del porvenir* (Recollections of things to come), *Reencuentro de personajes* (Reunion of characters), and *La casa junto al río* (The house next to the river). Her collections of shorter narratives include *Andamos huyendo Lola* (We are fleeing Lola) and *La semana de colores* (The week of colors). She has also written a screenplay and an autobiographical narrative, *Memorias, España 1937* (Memoirs, Spain 1937).

Andamos huyendo Lola. Mexico City: J. Mortiz, 1980.
La casa junto al río. Mexico City: Grijalbo, 1982.
Un hogar sólido. Xalapa: Universidad Veracruzana, 1983.
Memorias, España 1937. Mexico City: Siglo XXI, 1992.
Los recuerdos del porvenir. Mexico City: J. Mortiz, 1963.
Reencuentro de personajes. Mexico City: Grijalbo, 1982.
La semana de colores. Mexico City: Grijalbo, 1987.
Testimonios sobre Mariana. Mexico City: Grijalbo, 1981.

The reputation of Inés Arredondo (1928–1989) as a writer rests primarily on her short stories, "La señal" (The sign) and "Rio subterráneo" (Underground river). Her only novel is *Los espejos* (The mirrors). Arredondo's writing is a dialectic reflection on life which often led her to probe the liminal situations of impending death and insanity. In this respect, she is representative of the post–World War II concern with existential authenticity. Her short stories deal with simple facets of lived lives, but there is throughout an insistence on openness with regard to her female characters. The narrators hint, suggest, but never attempt to give us the whole, for the whole can never be known, but must be surmised. Her stories have no sense of an ending, but rather are always beginnings—beginnings of intuition and feelings of the truth of being alive in a world one did not choose, one in which subversion is survival. Her complete works were published in 1988.

Los espejos. Mexico City: J. Mortiz, 1988.
Obras completas. Mexico City: Siglo XXI, 1988.

Margo Glantz (1930–), prolific essayist, critic, and academic, has published an autobiographical novel, *Las genealogías* (The family tree), and two collections of short stories, *Doscientas ballenas azules* (Two hundred blue whales) and *Síndrome de naufragios* (Shipwreck syndrome). She is an erudite, intellectual creator of stories in the spirit of Borges. Her short story prose style is lyrical and extraordinarily rich in detail and indeterminate suggestion. She has published eleven academic works and eight works of fiction.

Margo Glantz's writing is above all an intertextual palimpsest of direct references and allusions to the hundreds of authors who inhabit her prose, but in all of this weaving in and out of texts and authors' lives, there is the undeniable reality of the writer at the center of this web, spinning it and ultimately catching her readers.

Apariciones. Mexico City: Alfaguara, 1986.
Borrones y borradores. Ensayos de literatura colonial. Mexico City: UNAM-Equilibrista, 1992.
De la amorosa inclinación a enredarse en cabellos. Mexico City: Océano, 1984.
El día de tu boda. Mexico City: Martín Casillas Editores, 1982.
Doscientas ballenas azules y cuatro caballos. Mexico City: UNAM, 1980.
Erosiones. Toluca: Universidad del Estado de México, 1985.
Esguince de cintura. Ensayos sobre narrativa mexicana del siglo XX. Mexico City: Conaculta, 1994.
The Family Tree. London: Serpent's Tail, 1991.
Las genealogías. Mexico City: Secretaría de Educación Pública, 1981.
Huérfanos y bandidos: Los bandidos de Río Frío. Mexico City: Cuadernos de Malinalco, 1995.
Intervención y pretexto. Mexico City: UNAM, 1980.
La lengua en la mano. Mexico City: Premiá, 1984.
Las mil y una calorías. Novela dietética. Mexico City: Premiá, 1978.
No pronunciarás. Mexico City: Premiá, 1980.
Repeticiones. Ensayos sobre literatura mexicana. Xalapa: Universidad Veracruzana, 1980.
Síndrome de naufragios. Mexico City: J. Mortiz, 1984.
Sor Juana Inés de la Cruz. ¿Hagiografía o autobiografía? Mexico City: Grijalbo, 1995.
Sor Juana Inés de la Cruz. Saberes y placeres. Mexico City: Instituto Mexiquense de Cultura, 1996.

María Luisa Mendoza (1931–) is one of the most versatile members of this group. She has published two books of drama criticism, six books of essays taken from her journalism, and a biography. Her fiction includes three novels—*Con El, conmigo, con nosotros tres* (With Him, with me, with us three), *De ausencia* (Of absence), and *El perro de la escribana* (The public notary's dog)—

and two volumes of short stories—*Ojos de papel volando* (Eyes of flying paper) and *El día del mar* (The day of the sea).

Con El, conmigo, con nosotros tres. Mexico City: J. Mortiz, 1971.
De ausencia. Mexico City: J. Mortiz, 1974.
Las cosas. Mexico City: J. Mortiz, 1976.
El día del mar. Mexico City: J. Mortiz, 1985.
Dos palabras dos. Crónica de un informe. Mexico City: n.p., 1972.
La O por lo redondo. Mexico City: Grijalbo, 1971.
Oiga usted! Mexico City: Editorial Samo, 1973.
Ojos de papel volando. Mexico City: J. Mortiz, 1985.
El perro de la escribana. Mexico City: J. Mortiz, 1982.
Trompo a la uña. Villahermosa: Gobierno del Estado de Tabasco, 1989.

Angelina Muñiz (1936–) is a university professor in the National University of Mexico. She has the same classical education as Margo Glantz, with the notable difference that Muñiz draws her fictional women from classical antiquity in order to express what is to her the essential question of who has control over a woman's body. She has written two books of poetry, *Vilano en viento* (Seed in the wind) and *El ojo de la creación* (The eye of creation). Her love poetry has a creative tension of great power. Among her novels are *Morada interior* (Interior dwelling), *Tierra adentro* (Inland), *La guerra del unicornio* (The war of the unicorn), *Huerto cerrado, huerto sellado* (Enclosed garden), and *De magias y prodigios* (Of magic and marvels). *La lengua florida* (Flowering language) is a scholarly commentary and anthology of Sephardic poetry.

De magias y prodigios. Mexico City: Fondo de Cultura Económica, 1988.
Dulcinea encantada. Mexico City: J. Mortiz, 1992.
Enclosed Garden. Pittsburgh, Pa.: Latin American Literary Review Press, 1988.
La guerra del unicornio. Mexico City: Artífice Ediciones, 1983.
Huerto cerrado, huerto sellado. Mexico City: Océano, 1985.
La lengua florida. Mexico City: UNAM-Fondo de Cultura Económica, 1989.
El libro de Miriam y primicias. Mexico City: UNAM, 1991.
La memoria del aire. Mexico City: UNAM, 1995.
Morada interior. Mexico City: J. Mortiz, 1972.
El ojo de la creación. Mexico City: UNAM, 1992.
Serpientes y escaleras. Mexico City: UNAM, 1991.
Tierra adentro. Mexico City: J. Mortiz, 1977.
Vilano en viento. Mexico City: Océano, 1983.

Guadalupe Loaeza (1946–), like Elena Poniatowska and Cristina Pacheco, has written extensively for newspapers. Collections of her chronicles include *Las niñas bien* (Affluent girls), *Las reinas de Polanco* (The queens of Polanco), *Primero las damas* (Ladies first), *Los grillos y otras grillas* (Crickets and other cliques), and *Compro, luego existo* (I buy, thus I exist). As a whole, her work can be taken as a counterpart to the chronicles of Cristina Pacheco, who deals almost exclusively with the poor of Mexico; Loaeza's prose has a rich ironic strain which undermines the protective isolation of Mexico's affluent women.

Compro, luego existo. Mexico City: Instituto Nacional del Consumidor, 1992.
Los grillos y otras grillas. Mexico City: Cal y Arena: 1991.
Las niñas bien. Mexico City: Océano, 1987.
Primero las damas. Mexico City: Cal y Arena, 1990.
Las reinas de Polanco. Mexico City: Cal y Arena, 1988.

Silvia Molina (1946–) is part of a generation of Mexican women writers who have worked primarily through journalism and the public media. Her first novel, *La mañana debe seguir gris* (The morning should stay gray), won the highly regarded literary prize Xavier Villaurrutia in 1977. She has published three more novels—*Dicen que me case yo* (They say I should get married), *La familia vino del norte* (The family came from the north), and *Imagen de Héctor* (Image of Hector)—as well as four books of short stories, and, most recently, children's literature. The most distinctive feature of her novels and stories is that her characters are developed within the psychological turbulence of finding self-esteem as women in Mexico's turbulent society. Molina's novels are deeply involved with her own personal search for identity.

Ascensión Tun. Oaxaca: Corunda, 1981.
Dicen que me case yo. Mexico City: Cal y Arena, 1989.
La familia vino del norte. Mexico City: Océano, 1987.
Imagen de Héctor. Mexico City: Cal y Arena, 1990.
Un hombre cerca. Mexico City: Cal y Arena, 1992.
Lides de estaño. Mexico City, n.p., 1984.
La mañana debe seguir gris. Mexico City: J. Mortiz, 1977.

Angeles Mastretta (1949–) published her first novel, *Arráncame la vida* (Mexican bolero), in 1985. It was an immensely popular novel, going through fourteen printings in the first eighteen months, and it has since been translated into twelve languages. A novel about postrevolutionary Mexico, it is narrated from the point of view of a woman, the wife of one of the new strongmen who have emerged from the conflict. Part of the success of this novel has been Mastretta's ability to build a woman's sense of time and place into the subgenre of the Mexican revolution, which had previously emphasized the male point of view exclusively. Her novel *Mal de amores* (1996; Lovesick) was awarded the prestigious Rómulo Gallegos 1997 prize; she is the first woman to be recognized with this honor. With this second novel Angeles Mastretta continues her development of women in Mexico's recent past as centers of consciousness, as subversive of the social codes and fiercely independent. She has published two books of short narratives—*Mujeres de ojos grandes* (Women with big eyes), which continues the development of the female point of view, and *Puerto libre* (Free port). The latter is a hybrid genre of stories, aphorisms, and vignettes which has the thematic unity of female space. It is part of a literary narrative mode that has been used with virtuosity by a number of women, including Cristina Peri Rossi, who wrote *Indicios pánicos* (Traces of panic).

Arráncame la vida. Mexico City: Océano, 1985.
Mal de amores. Mexico City: Alfaguara, 1996.
Mujeres de ojos grandes. Mexico City: Cal y Arena, 1990.
Puerto libre. Mexico City: Cal y Arena, 1993.

Carmen Boullosa (1954–) is one of the most active writers of Mexican literature today. In less than a decade she has published a collection of her dramatic texts, *Teatro herético* (Heretical theater), two volumes of collected poetry, *La salvaja* (The savage woman) and *Soledumbre* (Weight of solitude), and several novels: *Mejor desaparece* (Better disappear), *Antes* (Before; winner of the Villaurrutia prize), *Son vacas, somos puercos* (They are cows, we are pigs), *Llanto* (Lament), and *La Milagrosa* (The miraculous). Her work can be characterized as postmodern experimentation with shifting diegesis in a ludic creative metaphoric expansion. Boullosa's novels are quite demanding on readers. The narrative voices do not describe, depict, or develop the characters and events that are enunciated. The narrative voices thrust the reader into a process of making the fictional subject; that is, there is no presumed complete fictional character who is to be described in order to be known. The character does not exist before she is made by the reader, who must follow the hints and suggestions given in the text.

Antes. Mexico City: Vuelta, 1989.
Duerme. Madrid: Santillana, 1994.

Llanto. Mexico City: Era, 1992.

El médico de los piratas: Bucaernos y filibusteros en el Caribe. Madrid: Ediciones Siruela, 1992.

Mejor desaparece. Mexico City: Océano, 1987.

La milagrosa. Mexico City: Era, 1993.

La salvaja. Mexico City: Fondo de Cultura Económica, 1989.

Soledumbre. Mexico City: Universidad Autonóma Metropolitana, 1992.

Son vacas, somos puercos. Mexico City: Era, 1991.

Teatro herético. Puebla: Universidad Autónoma de Puebla, 1987.

Ethel Krause (1954–) has published almost continuously since 1982, when her first two books of short stories came out, *Niñas* (Girls) and *Intermedio para mujeres* (Intermission for women). Both books deal with problems and issues of women's lives in Mexico City in mimetic narratives with idiomatic language appropriate to class and age. She has published several collection of poems, *Poemas de mar y amor* (Poems of sea and love), *Para cantar* (To sing), *Fuego y juegos* (Fire and games), *Canciones de amor antiguo* (Songs of ancient love), and *He venido a buscarte* (I have come to look for you). Krause's novels are *Donde las cosas vuelan* (Where things fly) and *Infinita* (Infinite). She has also published a collection of short stories, *El lunes te amaré* (I will love you Monday), and a play, *Nona*.

Ethel Krause's poetry has enjoyed much more critical acclaim than her narratives; in part this may be due to her simple prose style, which concentrates on the disillusionment of women brought up to believe in the sentimental fantasy of marriage and the family unit in a world of deception, abuse, and loneliness. This narrative world is that of a Mexican middle class woman's senseless pursuit of happiness, bound up in a fraudulent pact of deceit and dishonesty; the outlook is bleak indeed. The myth of romantic love dies slowly, and in Krause's characters, the search for self-love is given as the way to go beyond living a lie.

Canciones de amor antiguo. Mexico City: J. Mortiz, 1988.

Donde las cosas vuelan. Mexico City: Océano, 1985.

Fuego y juegos. Mexico City: Océano, 1985.

He venido a buscarte. Mexico City: J. Mortiz, 1989.

Infinita. Mexico City: J. Mortiz, 1992.

Intermedio para mujeres. Mexico City: Océano, 1982.

El lunes te amaré. Mexico City: Océano, 1987.

Mujeres en Nueva York. Mexico City: Grijalbo, 1993.

Niñas. Mexico City: Océano, 1982.

Nona María. Mexico City: Océano, 1987.

Para cantar. Mexico City: Océano, 1984.
Poemas de mar y amor. Mexico City: n.p., 1982.

Josefina Estrada (1957–) is a new voice in Mexican literature. She has published two volumes of short stories, *Malagato* and *Para morir iguales* (To die as equals), and a novel, *Desde que Dios amanece* (Since God awakens). As is the case with most of the new writers, she began writing for the daily newspapers of Mexico City. Her writing is direct, evocative; her subject matter is the contemporary woman in Mexico City. Josefina Estrada's writing can be characterized as an expressionist description of physical pain and the psychology of suffering.

Desde que Dios amanece. Mexico City: J. Mortiz, 1995.
Malagato. Mexico City: Plaza and Valdés, 1990.
Para morir iguales. Mexico City: Planeta, 1991.

Appendix
Three

Sor Juana Criticism

Sor Juana criticism offers us a revealing case study on the impact of feminist theory and practice on the research done on a major author. In this review of criticism I will take 1975 as a convenient dividing line between critical works written before and after the feminist movement looked at Sor Juana. I know of sixteen books and another fifteen articles in journals, all published before 1975, which are still part of the corpus of Sor Juana criticism. In alphabetical order the authors are: Ermilio Abreu Gómez; Anita Arroyo; Antonio Castro Leal; Ezequiel Chávez; Génaro Fernández MacGregor; Gerard Flynn; Jesús Juan Garcés; Natalicio González; Julio Jiménez Rueda; Alfonso Junco; Alfonso Méndez Plancarte; Marcelino Menéndez y Pelayo; Amado Nervo; Ludwig Pfandl; Elías L. Rivers; and Elizabeth Wallace. Although Sor Juana has been treated by most Mexican literary historians over the years, this list demonstrates a growing interest in Spain and the first English-language study of her life and work. Antonio Castro Leal, Alfonso Méndez Plancarte, Marcelino Menéndez y Pelayo, Amado Nervo, and Elías Rivers are primarily interested in the historical accuracy of her biography and in some close reading of the poetry; among the others, one of the most influential is the introductory study of Abreu Gómez, who carefully argues that Sor Juana was a Cartesian philosopher and not a religious thinker. Ludwig Pfandl's book, on the other hand, attempts to interpret Sor Juana in Freudian terms of suppressed sexuality. Both Anita Arroyo and Elizabeth Wallace consider her choice of the convent as a rational choice, and not a religious one—the only real option for a young woman in seventeenth-century Mexico who wanted to pursue her studies. In retrospect, it seems extraordinary to us in the 1990s that such a logical and historically valid hypothesis should have been so difficult for so many male critics. Gerard Flynn, for example, is in constant consternation trying to reconcile Sor Juana to the holy mother church. Although a good part of the historical data was available during this period, the sense of Sor Juana's times was only touched upon briefly if at all.

Two articles of significance were also published in this period. The first, by Octavio Paz, was dated Paris 1950 and written for the Argentine journal *Sur* (1951). In 1951, there were a number of commemorative studies in honor of what was thought to have been the 300th anniversary of Sor Juana's birth. Paz later included this essay in his book, *Las peras del olmo* (1957; Pears of the elm tree). Not only is this article important as the first attempt to contextualize Sor Juana historically as a woman writer, but also it was the beginning of what became Paz's major book on her: *Sor Juana or The Traps of Faith* (1982; English translation 1988). Paz's short article in 1951 was a much-needed corrective on the sexist notions of a woman's place in the world of letters that prevailed at the time. In this respect, see Irving A. Leonard, whose sympathetic treatment of Sor Juana ironically reinforces notions of male intellectual superiority. The other article of lasting impact was by the distinguished philosopher José Gaos, who argues convincingly for consideration of Sor Juana as a philosophical poet.

The body of Sor Juana criticism after 1975 is impressive, not only because of its scope and the standards of scholarship that have established this body of work as mainstream scholarship of the first order, but also because gender issues are articulated. The list that follows is only a partial survey of a very active field of research. Electa Arenal's 1983 long article is one of the most notable in Sor Juana studies today; for the first time we have been given a rigorous historical study of convent life as a unique cultural space for women to escape the worst abuses of misogyny. This well-written and thoroughly researched study is a necessary starting point for all future work on Sor Juana. Emilie Bergmann (1990) takes full advantage of the historical and sociological background provided by Arenal, Paz, and others in order to raise the important issues of reader reception and specifically feminist reader reception. Jean Franco's (1989) informed incisive commentary on Sor Juana is a general overview on the writer and her time. The scholarly depth of the analysis of Sor Juana and seventeenth-century humanism is without equal in the book of Marie-Cécile Bénassy-Berling (1982). The publication in 1991 of Stephanie Merrim's edition of essays on Sor Juana is a milestone for Sor Juana studies in English-speaking North America. This edition brings together some of the most valuable essays of the past, with an important selection of new essays by the editor and others. The outstanding essays that are reprinted are Dorothy Schons's 1925 biographical contribution, Asunción Lavrin's 1983 study on the social symbol of the perfect nun in the religious literature of colonial Mexico, and what is perhaps one of the most influential articles of contemporary Sor Juana criticism, Josefina Ludmer's 1984 essay. The Mexican critic Margo Glantz (1995) has reprinted and expanded her previous work on Sor Juana; collectively it is an important addition. The single most significant book published on Sor Juana is the landmark 1982 *Sor Juana* . . . by Paz (English translation 1988). Whatever differences or disagreements feminists may have with Paz, there is no question that his historical contextualization of Sor Juana and her writing has changed the direction of research, and its subsequent 1988 translation into English has added a new and highly receptive readership to her writing. Herrera Zapién has written a balanced extensive commentary, "La Sor Juana de Octavio Paz" (Octavio Paz's Sor Juana) in his 1984 book; also of note is the review article by the noted Sor Juana scholar Georgina Sabat de Rivers, which appeared in *Modern Language Notes* in 1985. Her contribution to the discussion is her insistence on the portrayal of Sor Juana as a complex, brilliant woman whose intimate contradictions defy facile explanation. Finally, I would like to close this bird's eye view of sorjuanista criticism, citing two important interpretations of Sor Juana's major work *Primero sueño (Dream)*: Georgina Sabat de Rivers' 1976 book and Andrés Sánchez Robayna's 1990 commentary.

This review of Sor Juana criticism has of necessity concentrated on the critical works that have given us new directions. I have not attempted to include all the numerous excellent essays and monographs on Sor Juana, but this economy should not be taken as either a lack of interest or appreciation, it is an economy dictated by the topic at hand: Sor Juana's intellectual place between Descartes and Paz. See Tarsicio Herrera Zapién's informed commentary on current Sor Juana criticism, "Prólogo sobre el sorjuanismo actual" (9–18).

Works Cited

Abreu Gómez, Ermilo. *Poesías de Juana Inés de la Cruz.* 2d ed. Mexico City: Botas, 1948.

Aguirre M., Alejandro, and Sergio Camposortega. "Evaluación de la información básica sobre mortalidad infantil en México." *Demografía y Economía* 14.4 (1980): 447–466.

Alvarez, Nicolás Emilio. *Análisis arquetípico, mítico y simbológico de Pedro Páramo.* Miami: Ediciones Universal, 1983.

Araujo Camacho, Hilda. "Criterios y líneas de investigación en la problemática de la mujer." *La mujer en América Latina.* Ed. María del Carmen Elu de Leñero. 2 vols. Mexico City: SepSetentas, 1975. 1: 11–24.

Arenal, Electa. "The Convent as Catalyst for Autonomy: Two Hispanic Nuns of the Seventeenth Century." *Women in Hispanic Literature: Icons and Fallen Idols.* Ed. Beth Miller. Berkeley: University of California Press, 1983. 147–183.

———. "Where Woman Is Creator of the Wor(l)d. Or, Sor Juana's Discourses on Method." *Feminist Perspectives on Sor Juana Inés de la Cruz.* Ed. Stephanie Merrim. Detroit: Wayne State University Press, 1991. 124–141.

Aresti, Lore et al. "La violación, delito contra la libertad." *fem.* 32 (1984): 29–31.

Arizpe, Lourdes. *Campesinado y migración.* Mexico City: Secretaría de Educación Pública, 1985.

———. *La mujer en el desarrollo de México y de América Latina.* Mexico City: UNAM, 1989.

Arrom, Silvia Marina. *The Women of Mexico City, 1790–1857.* Stanford, Calif.: Stanford University Press, 1985.

Arroyo, Anita. *Razón y pasión de Sor Juana.* Mexico City: Porrúa, 1952.

Astelarra, Judith. "La violencia doméstica." *fem.* 37 (1984–1985): 7–9.

Auerbach, Nina. *Woman and the Demon. The Life of a Victorian Myth.* Cambridge, Mass.: Harvard University Press, 1982.

Babette's Feast. Dir. Gabriel Axel. Denmark, 1987.

Bachelard, Gaston. *The Poetics of Reverie.* Trans. Daniel Russell. New York: Orion Press, 1969.

————. *The Poetics of Space.* Trans. María Jolas. New York: Orion Press, 1964.

Bachofen, J. J. *Myth, Religion and Mother Right. Selected Writings of J. J. Bachofen.* Trans. Ralph Manheim. Princeton, N.J.: Princeton University Press, 1967.

Badinter, Elizabeth. *XY, on Masculine Identity.* Trans. Lydia Davis. New York: Columbia University Press, 1995.

Bakhtin, Mikhail M. *The Dialogic Imagination.* Ed. Michael Holquist. Trans. Caryl Emerson and Michael Holquist. Austin: University of Texas Press, 1981.

————. *Problems of Dostoevsky's Poetics.* Ed. and trans. Caryl Emerson. Minneapolis: University of Minnesota Press, 1984.

Ballou, Patricia K. *Women. A Bibliography of Bibliographies.* Boston: G. K. Hall, 1986.

Barbieri, Teresita de. "Algunas consideraciones en torno a la prevención de la violación." *fem.* 77 (1989): 22–23.

————. "La condición de la mujer en América Latina: Su participación social; antecedentes y situación actual." *Mujeres en América Latina.* Ed. Marshall Wolfe. Mexico City: CEPAL; Fondo de Cultura Económica, 1975. 46–87.

————. *Mujeres y vida cotidiana.* Mexico City: Sep/80, 1984.

————. with Gabriela Cano. "Ni tanto ni tan poco: Las reformas penales relativas a la violencia sexual." *debate feminista* 1.2 (1990): 345–356.

Bárcena, Andrea. "Los días de los niños: Un registro de la infamia." *fem.* 11.52 (Apr. 1987): 7–9.

Barranco L., Isabel, and Rosa Ma. Rodríguez M. "Miscélanea mi Luchita. Cifras, datos en torno a la violencia." *fem.* 12.71 (Nov. 1988): 37–38.

Barrios de Chungara, Domitila, with Moema Viezzer. *Let Me Speak! Testimony of Domitila, a Woman of the Bolivian Mines.* Trans. Victoria Ortiz. New York: Monthly Review Press, 1978.

Bassin, Donna. "Woman's Image of Inner Space: Data Towards Expanded Interpretive Categories." *International Review of Psychoanalysis* 9 (1983): 191–203.

Bastos, María Luisa, and Sylvia Molloy. "El personaje de Susana San Juan: Clave de enunciación y de enunciados en *Pedro Páramo.*" *Hispamérica* 7.20 (1978): 3–24.

Bearce, Grace W. "Interview with Luisa Josefina Hernández." *Hispania* 64.2 (1981): 301–302.

Becker, Marion Rombauer, and Irma S. Rombauer. *The Joy of Cooking.* New York: Bobbs, 1963.

Befumo Boschi, Liliana. "La mujer en *Pedro Páramo.*" *La mujer: Símbolo del mundo nuevo.* Ed. Vicente Cicchitti et al. Buenos Aires: Fernando García Cambeiro, 1976. 137–155.

Bénassy-Berling, Marie-Cecile. *Humanisme et religion chez Sor Juana Inés de la Cruz. La femme et la culture au XVIIe siècle.* Paris: Editions Hispaniques, 1982.

Benería, Lourdes, and Martha Roldán. *Las encrucijadas de clase y género.* Mexico City: El Colegio de México/FCE/Economía Latinoamericana, 1992.

Ben-Porat, Ziva. "Method in *Mad*ness: Notes on the Structure of Parody, Based on *MAD* TV Satires." *Poetics Today* 1 (1979): 245–272.

Benveniste, Emil. *Problems of General Linguistics.* Trans. Mary Elizabeth Meek. Coral Gables, Fla.: University of Miami Press, 1977.

Bergmann, Emilie. "Sor Juana Inés de la Cruz: Dreaming in a Double Voice." *Women, Culture and Politics in Latin America. Seminar on Feminism and Culture in Latin America.* Ed. Bergmann et al. Berkeley: University of California Press, 1990. 151–172.

Berkowitz, Tamar, Jean Mange, and Jane Williamson. *Who's Who and Where in Women's Studies.* Old Westbury, N.Y.: The Feminist Press, 1974.

Bernal, Francisca. "En tres palabras . . . Derechos del niño." *fem.* 13.83 (Nov. 1989): 40.

Beverly, John. *Del Lazarillo al Sandinismo: Estudios sobre la función ideológica de la literatura española e hispanoamericana.* Minneapolis: Institute for the Study of Ideologies and Literature, 1987.

Blanco Aguinaga, Carlos. "Realidad y estilo de Juan Rulfo." *La narrativa de Juan Rulfo. Interpretaciones críticas.* Ed. Joseph Sommers. Mexico City: Sep-Setentas, 1974. 88–116.

Boling, Becky. "Parricide and Revolution: Fuentes's 'El día de las madres' and *Gringo viejo.*" *Hispanófila* 95 (1989): 73–81.

Bonafini, Hebe de, with Matilde Sánchez. *Historias de vida: Hebe de Bonafini.* Buenos Aires: Fraterna/del Nuevo Extremo, 1985.

Bonfil, Guillermo. "Los pueblos indígenas: viejos problemas, nuevas demandas." *México hoy.* Ed. Pablo González Casanova and Enrique Florescano. Mexico City: Siglo XXI, 1980. 97–107.

Bovenschen, Silvia. "Is There a Feminine Aesthetic?" *Feminist Aesthetics.* Ed. Gisela Ecker. London: The Women's Press, 1985. 23–50.

Braudel, Fernand. *The Structures of Everyday Life.* Trans. Sian Reynolds. London: Collins, 1981.

Britt, Bonnie. "In Literature, Writer Sandra Cisneros Sees Power." *Houston Chronicle,* June 24, 1984: Section 8, 5.

Bus, Heiner. "Chicano Literature of Memory: Sandra Cisneros, *The House on Mango Street* (1984) and Gary Soto, *Living Up the Street. Narrative Recollections* (1985)." *Minority Literature in North America. Contemporary Perspectives.* Ed. Wolfgang Karrer and Hartmut Lutz. International Symposium at the University of Osnabrück, 1988. 159–172.

Bustos Romero, Olga L. "Los estudios sobre la mujer (y de género) en la UNAM: investigaciones y tesis." *Estudios de género y feminismo.* Ed. P. Bedolla et al. Vol. 1. Mexico City: Fontamara-UNAM, 1989. 123–147.

———. "Socialización, papeles (roles) de género e imagen de la mujer en los medios masivos: ¿Quiénes perciben los estereotipos difundidos?" *La investigación sobre la mujer: Informes en sus primeras versiones.* Ed. Vania Salles and Elsie McPhail. Mexico City: El Colegio de México, 1988.

———. "Visiones y percepciones de mujeres y hombres como receptoras(es) de telenovelas." *La voluntad de ser. Mujeres en los noventa.* Ed. María Luisa Tarrés. Mexico City: El Colegio de México, 1992. 113–135.

Cancionero folklórico de México. Ed. Margit Frenk. 5 vols. Mexico City: El Colegio de México, 1975–1985.

Canfield, Martha L. "Dos enfoques de *Pedro Páramo.*" *Revista Iberoamericana* 55.148–149 (1989): 965–988.

Carreras, Mercedes. *La docencia universitaria sobre la población femenina. Posibilidades y obstáculos.* Mexico City: UNAM, 1989.

Casas, Yoloxochitl, and Laura Castellanos. "Causas de la marginación de las mujeres chiapanecas." *fem.* 134 (1994): 16.

Castellanos, Laura. "Desesperadas, las artesanas indígenas chiapanecas. Un centenar teme agresiones militares." *fem.* 134 (1994): 17.

Castellanos, Rosario. *Balún Canán.* Mexico City: Fondo de Cultura Económica, 1957.

———. *El eterno femenino.* Mexico City: Fondo de Cultura Económica, 1975.

———. "The Eternal Feminine." Trans. Diane E. Marting and Betty Tyree Osiek. *A Rosario Castellanos Reader.* Trans. Maureen Ahern et al. Austin: University of Texas Press, 1988. 273–367.

———. "Language as an Instrument of Domination." Trans. Maureen Ahern. *A Rosario Castellanos Reader.* Trans. Maureen Ahern et al. Austin: University of Texas Press, 1988. 250–253.

———. *Oficio de tinieblas.* Mexico City: J. Mortiz, 1962.

———. "Self-Sacrifice Is a Mad Virtue." Trans. Laura Carp Solomon. *A Rosario Castellanos Reader.* Trans. Maureen Ahern et al. Austin: University of Texas Press, 1988. 259–263.

———. "Sobre cultura femenina." *debate feminista* 3.6 (Sept. 1992): 260–286.

Castillo, Ana, ed. *Goddess of the Americas. La Diosa de las Américas. Writings on the Virgin of Guadalupe.* New York: Riverhead Books, 1996.

Castillo, Debra. *Talking Back: Toward a Latin American Feminist Literary Criticism.* Ithaca, N.Y.: Cornell University Press, 1992.

———. "Tongue in the Ear: Fuentes' *Gringo viejo.*" *Revista Canadiense de Estudios Hispánicos* 14.1 (Fall 1989): 35–50.

Castro Leal, Antonio. *Poesía, teatro y prosa. Sor Juana Inés de la Cruz.* 4th ed. Mexico City: Porrúa, 1971.

Catullus. *The Poems of Catullus.* Ed. William A. Aiken. New York: Dutton, 1960. 164–176.

CEPAL (Estudios e informes de la Comisión Económica para América Latina). *Five Studies on the Situation of Women in Latin America.* Santiago, Chile: United Nations, 1983.

Chávez, Ezequiel. *Ensayo de psicología de Sor Juana Inés de la Cruz.* Barcelona: Araluce, 1931.

Chicago, Judy. *Embroidering Our Heritage.* Garden City, N.J.: Doubleday, 1980.

Cisneros, Sandra. "Do You Know Me? I Wrote *The House on Mango Street.*" *The Americas Review* 15.1 (Spring 1987): 77–79.

————. "From a Writer's Notebook. Ghosts and Voices: Writing from Obsession." *The Americas Review* 15.1 (Spring 1987): 69–73.

————. *The House on Mango Street.* Houston: Arte Público, 1984. 2d ed., rev., 1988.

————. *La casa en Mango Street.* Trans. Elena Poniatowska. New York: Vintage Español, 1994.

————. "Living as a Writer: Choice and Circumstance." *Feminist Writers Guild* 10.1 (Feb. 1987): 8–9.

————. "My Wicked Wicked Ways: The Chicana Writer's Struggle with Good and Evil or Las hijas de la mala vida." Paper delivered at the Modern Language Association Convention, Chicago 1985 and at Yale University, Spring 1986.

————. "Notes to a Young(er) Writer." *The Americas Review* 15.1 (Spring 1987): 74–76.

————. "Only Daughter." Paper read at "Writing Lives: Women as Writers." Third Latin American Book Fair. City College of New York, May 5, 1989.

————. "Sandra Cisneros. Chicago, Illinois, January 28, 1982." *Partial Autobiographies. Interviews with Twenty Chicano Poets.* Ed. Wolfgang Binder. Erlanger, Germany: Palm and Enke, 1985. 54–74.

————. *Woman Hollering Creek and Other Stories.* New York: Random House, 1991.

————. "Writing Out of Necessity." Interview with Beatriz Badikian. *Feminist Writers Guild* 10.1 (Feb. 1987): 1, 6–8.

Cohn, Dorrit. *Transparent Minds. Narrative Models for Presenting Consciousness in Fiction.* Princeton, N.J.: Princeton University Press, 1978.

Colina, José de la. "Susana San Juan (El mito femenino en *Pedro Páramo*)." *La narrativa de Juan Rulfo. Interpretaciones críticas.* Ed. Joseph Sommers. Mexico City: SepSetentas, 1974. 60–66.

Connelly, Mary Goldsmith. "Uniformes, escobas y lavaderos: El proceso productivo del servicio doméstico." *Trabajo, poder y sexualidad.* Comp. Orlandina de Oliveira. Mexico City: El Colegio de México, 1989. 103–132.

Cota-Robles Suárez, Cecilia. "*The House on Mango Street.*" *Lector,* n.d.

debate feminista. Mexico City, 1990–.

Cruz, Juana Inés de la. *Answer to Sor Filotea de la Cruz. The Answer/La Respuesta.* Ed. and trans. Electa Arenal and Amanda Powell. New York: The Feminist Press, 1994.

————. *Obras completas de Sor Juana Inés de la Cruz. I. Lírica personal.* Mexico City: Fondo de Cultura Económica, 1951.

Descartes, René. *Philosophical Letters.* Trans. and ed. Anthony Kenny. Oxford: Clarendon Press, 1970.

Díaz, José, and Román Rodríguez. *El movimiento cristero. Sociedad y conflicto en Altos de Jalisco.* Mexico City: Nueva Imagen, 1979.

Domenella, Ana Rosa, and Nora Pasternac, eds. *Las voces olvidadas: Antología crítica de narradoras mexicanas nacidas en el siglo XIX.* Mexico City: El Colegio de México, 1991.

Donovan, Josephine, ed. *Feminist Literary Criticism. Explorations in Theory.* 2d ed. Lexington: University Press of Kentucky, 1989.

Dooley, Francis Patrick. *Los cristeros, Calles y el catolicismo mexicano.* Trans. María

Emilia Martínez Negrete Deffis. Mexico City: SepSetentas, 1976. (The cristeros, Calles, and Mexican catholicism. Thesis. University of Maryland, 1972).

Dubois, Ellen Carol et al. *Feminist Scholarship. Kindling the Groves of Academe*. Urbana: University of Illinois Press, 1985.

Ellman, Mary. *Thinking About Women*. New York: Harcourt, Brace, Jovanovich, 1968.

Eltit, Diamela, and Carlos Monsiváis. "Un diálogo (¿o dos monólogos?) sobre la censura." *debate feminista* 5.9 (Mar. 1994): 25–50.

Elu de Leñero, María del Carmen. *¿Hacia dónde va la mujer mexicana?* Mexico City: Instituto Mexicano de Estudios Sociales, 1969.

———, ed. *La mujer en América Latina*. 2 vols. Mexico City: SepSetentas, 1975.

Espinosa Rugarcía, Amparo et al. *Palabras de mujer*. Mexico City: Editorial Diana, 1989.

Esquivel, Laura. *Como agua para chocolate. Novela de entregas mensuales con recetas, amores, y remedios caseros*. Mexico City: Planeta, 1988.

———. *Like Water for Chocolate. A Novel in Monthly Installments, with Recipes, Romances, and Home Remedies*. Trans. Carol Christensen and Thomas Christensen. New York: Doubleday, 1992.

Ezquerro, Milagros. *Juan Rulfo*. Paris: Editions L'Harmattan, 1986.

Faludi, Susan. *Backlash. The Undeclared War Against American Women*. New York: Doubleday, 1991.

Felski, Rita. *Beyond Feminist Aesthetics*. London: Hutchinson Radius, 1989.

fem. Publicación feminista. Mexico City, 1976–.

Female Studies. 10 vols. Pittsburgh, Pa.: Know, Inc., 1970–1975.

Fernández MacGregor, Genaro. *La santificación de Sor Juana Inés de la Cruz*. Mexico City: Cultura, 1932.

Fernández Olmos, Margarita. "Latin American Testimonial Narrative, or Women and the Art of Listening." *Revista Canadiense de Estudios Hispánicos* 13.2 (Winter 1989): 183–195.

Filgueira, Carlos. "Proyecto sobre estratificación y movilidad social en América Latina" *Mujeres en América Latina*. Ed. Marshall Wolfe. Mexico City: CEPAL; Fondo de Cultura Económica, 1975. 52–56.

Flores, Ana María. *La magnitud del hambre en México*. Mexico City: Ed. Impresos Modernos, 1973.

Flynn, Gerard. *Sor Juana Inés de la Cruz*. New York: Twayne, 1971.

Foster, David William. "Latin American Documentary Narrative." *PMLA* 99.1 (Jan. 1984): 41–55.

Franco, Jean. *Plotting Women. Gender and Representation in Mexico*. New York: Columbia University Press, 1989.

Frontiers: A Journal of Women's Studies (1975–).

FS, Feminist Studies. College Park, Md.: Feminist Studies, Inc. (1972–).

Fuentes, Carlos. "El día de las madres." *Agua quemada*. Mexico City: Fondo de Cultura Económica, 1981. 11–42.

———. "Mother's Day." *Burnt Water*. Trans. Margaret Seyers Peden. New York: Farrar Straus Giroux, 1980. 24–57.

————. *Gringo viejo.* Mexico City: Fondo de Cultura Económica, 1985.

————. *The Old Gringo.* Trans. Margaret Sayers Peden and Carlos Fuentes. New York: Farrar Straus Giroux, 1985.

Galindo, Hermila. *Estudio con motivos de los temas que han de absolverse en el segundo congreso feminista de Yucatán.* Merida, Mexico: Imprenta del Gobierno Constitucionalista, 1916.

Galván, Mariano. *Calendario para las señoritas mexicanas.* Mexico City: Imprenta de Mariano Murguía, 1838.

Gaos, José. "El sueño de un sueño." *Historia mexicana* 10.1 (1960): 54–71.

Garcés, Jesús Juan. *Vida y poesía de Sor Juana Inés de la Cruz.* Madrid: Ediciones Cultura Hispánica, 1953.

García Calderón, Carola. *Revistas femeninas. La mujer como objeto de consumo.* 3d ed., rev. Mexico City: Ediciones El Caballito. 1988.

García y Garma, Irma O. "Algunos factores asociados con la mortalidad infantil en México." *Demografía y economía* 17.3 (1983): 289–320.

Gilbert, Sandra M., and Susan Gubar. *The Madwoman in the Attic.* New Haven, Conn.: Yale University Press, 1979.

Gissi Bustos, Jorge. "Mythology About Women with Special Reference to Chile." *Sex Roles and Class in Latin America.* Ed. June Nash and Helen Safa. New York: Bergin, 1980. 30–45.

Glantz, Margo. *Sor Juana Inés de la Cruz: ¿Hagiografía or autobiografía?* Mexico City: Grijalbo, 1995.

Gómez, Jewelle. "Dream Merchants." *Hurricane Alice* (Spring/Summer 1984): 7.

Gómez, Roy. "The Bitter Fruit of Mango Street." *VíAztlan* (Mar. 1985): 21.

González, Natalicio. *Sor Juana Inés de la Cruz. Primero Sueño.* Mexico City: Editorial Guaranía, 1951.

González Berry, Erlinda, and Tey Diana Rebolledo. "Growing up Chicano: Tomás Rivera and Sandra Cisneros." *International Studies in Honor of Tomás Rivera.* Ed. Julián Olivares. Houston: Arte Público, 1986. 109–119.

González Boixó, J.C. "Bibliografía de Juan Rulfo." *Cuadernos hispanoamericanos* 421–423 (1985): 469–490.

————. *Claves narrativas de Juan Rulfo.* León: Universidad de León, 1983.

González Casanova, Pablo. *Democracy in Mexico.* Trans. Danielle Salti. London: Oxford University Press, 1970.

González Montes, Soledad, ed. *Mujeres y relaciones de género en la antropología latinoamericana.* Mexico City: El Colegio de México, 1993.

Graciarena, Jorge. "Notas sobre el problema de la desigualdad sexual en sociedades de clase." *Mujeres en América Latina.* Ed. Marshall Wolfe. Mexico City: CEPAL; Fondo de Cultura Económica, 1972. 26–45.

Greer, Germaine. "The Tulsa Center for the Study of Women's Literature: What We Are Doing and Why We Are Doing It." *Tulsa Studies in Women's Literature* 1.1 (1982): 5–26.

Guillermo, Juan. "Política. ¿Libertad diferencial?" *fem.* 13.79 (July 1989): 26–31.

Guimarães Rosa, João. *Grande Sertão: Veredas*. 1956. Rio de Janeiro: J. Olympio, 1968.

Gutiérrez Marrone, Nila. *El estilo de Juan Rulfo: Estudio lingüístico*. New York: Bilingual Press, 1978.

Gutiérrez Revuelta, Pedro. "Género e ideología en el libro de Sandra Cisneros: *The House on Mango Street*." *Crítica* 1.3 (1986): 48–54.

Gutiérrez y Gutiérrez, Raúl. "La desnutrición en México."*Reunión Nacional sobre Problemas de Salud, Alimentación, Asistencia y Seguro Social*. México, 1970.

Habermas, Jürgen. *The Theory of Communicative Action*. Boston: Beacon, 1987. 2: 374–403.

Heilbrun, Carolyn G. *Toward a Recognition of Androgyny*. New York: Alfred A. Knopf, 1973.

Hernández, Luisa Josefina. "La fiesta del mulato." *Tramoya* 17 (Oct.–Dec. 1979): 4–29.

———. "The Mulatto's Orgy." *Voices of Change in the Spanish American Theatre*. Ed. and trans. William I. Oliver. Austin: University of Texas Press, 1971. 219–255.

Hernández Tellez, Josefina. "La Lucha. Segunda jornada por la infancia. UNMM." *fem*. 13.81 (Sept. 1989): 42–43.

Herrera-Sobek, María. "The Politics of Rape: Sexual Transgression in Chicana Fiction." *Chicana Creativity and Criticism: New Frontiers in American Literature*. Ed. María Herrera-Sobek and Helena María Viramontes. Albuquerque: University of New Mexico Press, 1996. 245–256.

Herrera Zapién, Tarsicio. *Buena fe y humanismo en Sor Juana*. Mexico City: Porrúa, 1984.

Higonnet, Margaret, ed. *Borderwork. Feminist Engagements with Comparative Literature*. Ithaca, N.Y.: Cornell University Press, 1994.

Horan, Elizabeth Rosa. "Matrilineage, Matrilanguage: Mistral's Intimate Audience of Women." *Revista Canadiense de Estudios Hispánicos* 14.3 (Spring 1990): 447–457.

Humm, Maggie. *An Annotated Critical Bibliography of Feminist Criticism*. Boston: G. K. Hall, 1987.

Irigaray, Luce. *This Sex Which Is Not One*. Trans. Catherine Porter and Carolyn Burke. Ithaca, N.Y.: Cornell University Press, 1985.

Iser, Wolfgang. *The Act of Reading*. Baltimore: Johns Hopkins University Press, 1978.

———. *The Implied Reader*. Baltimore: Johns Hopkins University Press, 1974.

Jagger, Alison M. "Prostitution." *The Philosophy of Sex*. Ed. Alan Soble. Totowa, N.J.: Rowman and Allanheld, 1980. 348–368.

Jara, René, and Hernán Vidal, eds. *Testimonio y literatura*. Minneapolis: Institute for the Study of Ideologies and Literature, 1986.

Jiménez de Báez, Yvette. *Juan Rulfo, del páramo a la esperanza. Una lectura crítica de su obra*. Mexico City: El Colegio de México y Fondo de Cultura Económica, 1990.

Jiménez Rueda, Julio. *Sor Juana Inés de la Cruz en su época*. Mexico City: Porrúa, 1951.

Johnson, Irmgard W. "Dress and Adornment." *The Ephemeral and the Eternal of Mexican Folk Art*. Ed. Leopoldo Méndez and Marianne Yampolsky. Mexico City: Fondo Editorial de la Plástica Mexicana, 1971. 161–268.

Jorgensen, Beth E. *The Writing of Elena Poniatowska. Engaging Dialogue.* Austin: University of Texas Press, 1994.

Junco, Alfonso. *Gente de México.* Mexico City: Ediciones Botas, 1937.

Kaminsky, Amy K. "Gender as Category and Feminism as Strategy in Latin American Literature Analysis." *Reading the Body Politic: Feminist Criticism and Latin American Women Writers.* Minneapolis: University of Minnesota Press, 1993. 14–26.

Kirkwood, Julieta. "El feminismo como negación del autoritarismo." *Y hasta cuándo esperaremos mandan-dirun-dirun-dán: Mujer y poder en América Latina.* Caracas: Editorial Nueva Sociedad, 1989. 53–62.

Knight, Alan. *The Mexican Revolution.* Vol. 2. Lincoln:, University of Nebraska Press, 1990.

Kristeva, Julia. *Desire in Language. A Semiotic Approach to Literature and Art.* Ed. Leon S. Roudiez. Trans. Thomas Gora, Alice Jardine, and Leon S. Roudiez. New York: Columbia University Press, 1980.

———. *La Révolution du langage poétique.* Paris: Seuil, 1974.

———. "The System and the Speaking Subject." *The Tell-Tale Signs: A Survey of Semiotics.* Ed. Thomas A. Sebeok. Lisse, Netherlands: Ridder, 1975. 45–55.

Lacan, Jacques. *The Four Fundamental Concepts of Psycho-Analysis.* Ed. Jacques Alain Miller. Trans. Alan Sheridan. New York: Norton, 1978.

Lamas, Marta. "Editorial." *debate feminista* 1.1 (1990): 1–5.

Latin American and Caribbean Women's Collective. *Slaves of Slaves: The Challenge of Latin American Women.* London: Methuen, 1980.

Lavrín, Asunción. "Unlike Sor Juana? The Model Nun in the Religious Literature of Colonial Mexico." *Feminist Perspectives on Sor Juana Inés de la Cruz.* Ed. Stephanie Merrim. Detroit: Wayne State University Press, 1991. 61–85.

Leal, Luis. "Growing up on Mango Street." Paper read at the National Association for Chicano Students. San Diego (Feb. 1987).

———. *Juan Rulfo.* Boston: Twayne, 1983.

León Portilla, Miguel. *Aztec Thought and Culture: A Study of the Ancient Nahuatl Mind.* Trans. Jack Emoy Davis. Norman: University of Oklahoma Press, 1970.

Leonard, Irving A. *Baroque Times in Old Mexico.* Ann Arbor: University of Michigan Press, 1959.

Lewis, Oscar. *The Children of Sánchez: Autobiography of a Mexican Family.* New York: Random House, 1961.

———. *Five Families: Mexican Case Studies in the Culture of Poverty.* New York: New American Library, 1959.

"Ley Revolucionaria sobre las mujeres." *EZLN. Documentos y comunicados (1 de enero / 8 de agosto de 1994).* Mexico City: Ediciones Era, 1994. 1: 45–46.

Like Water for Chocolate. Dir. Alfonso Arau. Mexico, 1991.

Lillo, Gastón. "El reciclaje del melodrama y sus repercusiones en la estratificación de la cultura." *Archivos de la filmoteca* 16 (1994): 65–73.

Lima, María de la Luz. "La historia infantil en México." *fem.* 83 (1989): 10–21.

Lindstrom, Naomi. *Twentieth-Century Spanish American Fiction*. Austin: University of Texas Press, 1994.

Lippard, Lucy. "Up, Down, and Across: A New Frame for New Quilts." *The Artist and the Quilt*. Ed. Charlotte Robinson. New York: Knopf, 1983. 32–43.

Loeb, Catherine R., Susan E. Searing, and Esther F. Stineman. *Women's Studies: A Recommended Core Bibliography. 1980–1985*. Littleton, Colo.: Libraries Unlimited, 1987.

Lombardi, Susan. "Recipes for Reading: Summer Pasta, Lobster à la Riseholme and Key Lime Pie." *PMLA* 104.3 (1989): 340–347.

López González, Aralia, Amelia Malagamba, and Elena Urrutia, eds. *Culturas en contacto*. 2 vols. Mexico City: El Colegio de México and El Colegio de la Frontera Norte, 1988–1990.

Ludmer, Josefina. "Tricks of the Weak." *Feminist Perspectives on Sor Juana Inés de la Cruz*. Ed. Stephanie Merrim. Detroit: Wayne State University Press, 1991. 86–93.

Lugo, Carmen. "El matrimonio y el derecho en México." *fem.* 28(1983): 4–8.

Lustig, Nora. "La desigualdad económica." *Nexos* 11.128 (Apr. 1988): 8–11.

———. "Distribución del ingreso y consumo de alimentos en México." *Demografía y Economía* 14.2.42 (1980): 214–245.

———. "Distribución del ingreso y consumo de alimentos: estructura, tendencias y requerimientos redistributivos a nivel regional." *Demografía y Economía* 16.2.50 (1982): 107–145.

Marcos, Subcomandante Insurgente. "Dicen algunos miembros del EZLN, 30 de enero [1994]." *EZLN. Documentos y comunicados (1 de enero / 8 de agosto de 1994)*. Mexico City: Ediciones Era, 1994. 1: 106–110.

Marting, Diane, ed. *Women Writers of Spanish America. An Annotated Bio-Bibliographical Guide*. Westport, Conn.: Greenwood Press, 1987.

Massolo, Alejandra. *Por amor y coraje. Mujeres en movimientos urbanos de la ciudad de México*. Mexico City: El Colegio de México, 1992.

———, ed. *Mujeres y ciudades. Participación social, vivienda y vida cotidiana*. Mexico City: El Colegio de México, 1992.

———. and Martha Schteingart, eds. *Documentos de trabajo. I. Participación social, reconstrucción y mujer. El sismo de 1985*. Mexico City: El Colegio de México, 1987.

McCracken, Ellen. "Sandra Cisneros' *The House on Mango Street*: Community-Oriented Introspection and the Demystification of Patriarchal Violence." *Breaking Boundaries: Latina Writing and Critical Readings*. Ed. Asunción Horno-Delgado et al. Amherst: University of Massachusetts Press, 1989. 62–71.

Meacham, Cherie. "The Process of Dialogue in *Gringo viejo*." *Hispanic Journal* 10.2 (1989): 127–137.

Medina, David. "The Softly Insistent Voice of a Poet." *Austin American Statesman*, Mar. 11, 1986: 14–15.

Menchú, Rigoberta, with Elizabeth Burgos-Debray. *I, Rigoberta Menchú: An Indian Woman in Guatemala*. Trans. Ann Wright. London: Verso Editions, 1984.

Méndez Plancarte, Alfonso. *Obras completas de Sor Juana Inés de la Cruz*. 4 vols. Mexico City: Fondo de Cultura Económica, 1951–1957.

Menéndez y Pelayo, Marcelino. *Historia de la poesía hispanoamericana.* 2 vols. Santander, Spain: Aldus, 1948. 1: 67–77.

Merrim, Stephanie, ed. *Feminist Perspectives on Sor Juana Inés de la Cruz.* Detroit: Wayne State University Press, 1991.

Meyer, Doris. *Against the Wind and the Tide: Victoria Ocampo.* Austin: University of Texas Press, 1990.

Miller, Barbara. "Women and Revolution: The *Brigadas femeninas* and the Mexican Cristero Rebellion, 1926–1929." *Women and Politics in Twentieth-Century Latin America.* Ed. Sandra F. McGee. Williamsburg, Va.: Studies in Third World Societies, 1981. 57–66.

Miller, Francesca. *Latin American Women and the Search for Social Justice.* Hanover, N.H.: University Press of New England, 1991.

Miller, Nancy K. "Arachnologies: The Woman, the Text, and the Critic." *The Poetics of Gender.* Ed. Nancy K. Miller. New York: Columbia University Press, 1986. 270–295.

Millet, Kate. *Sexual Politics.* Garden City, N.J.: Doubleday, 1970.

Milligan, Bryce. "*The House on Mango Street*: Gritty, Street-wise." *Express-News* (San Antonio), October 14, 1984.

Mina V., Alejandro. "Estimaciones de los niveles, tendencias y diferenciales de la mortalidad infantil y en los primeros años de vida en México, 1940–1970." *Demografía y Economía* 15.1 (1981): 85–142.

Mink, Louis O. *Historical Understanding.* Ed. Brian Fay, Eugene O. Golob, and Richard T. Vann. Ithaca, N.Y.: Cornell University Press, 1987.

Moi, Toril. *Sexual/Textual Politics: Feminist Literary Theory.* London: Methuen, 1981.

Monsiváis, Carlos. *Entrada libre. Crónicas de la sociedad que se organiza.* Mexico City: Ediciones Era, 1987.

———. "Mexicanerías: ¿Pero hubo alguna vez once mil machos?" *Escenas de pudor y livianadad.* Mexico City: Grijalbo, 1981. 103–117.

———. "Sexismo en la literatura mexicana." *Imagen y realidad de la mujer.* Ed. Elena Urrutia. Mexico City: SepSetentas, 1975. 102–125.

Monteil, Noelle. "Las mujeres, instrumento de la iglesia institucional para mantener las estructuras de dominación." *Religión y política en México.* Ed. Martín de la Rosa and Charles A. Reilly. Mexico City: Siglo XXI, 1985. 159–176.

Montross, Constance M. *Virtue or Vice? Sor Juana's Use of Thomistic Thought.* Washington, D.C.: University Press of America, 1981.

Muncy, Michele. "Entrevista con Luisa Josefina Hernández." *Latin American Theater Review* 9.2 (1976): 69–77.

Muñoz Valle, Yazmin. "Salvar a los niños callejeros, un desafío para el gobierno mexicano." *Excélsior* (May 6, 1992): 1, 10.

The Name of the Rose. Dir. Jean-Jacques Annaud. Italy-Germany-France, 1986.

Nash, June, and Helen Safa, eds. *Sex and Class in Latin America.* New York: Bergin, 1980.

———, eds. *Women and Change in Latin America.* South Hadley, Mass.: Bergin and Garvey, 1986.

Nervo, Amado. *Juana de Asbaje. Obras completas de Amado Nervo.* Vol. 8. Madrid: Biblioteca Nueva, 1910.

Nigro, Kirsten. "Entrevista con Luisa Josefina Hernández." *Latin American Theater Review* 18.2 (1985): 101–105.

———. "'La fiesta del mulato' de Luisa Josefina Hernández." *Latin American Theater Review* 13.2 (1980): 81–86.

The Old Gringo. Dir. Luis Puenzo. Columbia Pictures, United States, 1988.

Olivares, Julián. "Sandra Cisneros' *The House on Mango Street,* and the Poetics of Space." *Chicana Creativity and Criticism: New Frontiers in American Literature.* Ed. María Herrera-Sobek and Helena María Viramontes. Albuquerque: University of New Mexico Press, 1996. 233–244.

Oliveira, Orlandina, ed. *Trabajo, poder y sexualidad.* Mexico City: El Colegio de México, 1989.

Oppenheimer, Andres. *Bordering on Chaos: Guerrillas, Stockbrokers, Politicians, and Mexico's Road to Prosperity.* Boston: Little, Brown, 1996.

Ortega, Julio. "*Pedro Páramo.*" *La narrativa de Juan Rulfo.* Ed. Joseph Sommers. Mexico City: SepSetentas, 1974. 76–87.

Ortega Galindo, Luis. *Expresión y sentido de Juan Rulfo.* Madrid: Porrúa Turanzas, 1984.

Pacheco, Cristina. *Amores y desamores.* Mexico City: Gobierno del Estado de Tabasco, Instituto de Cultura de Tabasco, 1989.

———. *El corazón de la noche.* Mexico City: Ediciones El Caballito, 1989.

———. *Cuarto de azotea.* Mexico City: SEP/Ediciones Gernika, 1985.

———. *Para mirar a lo lejos.* Villahermosa, Mexico: Selector, 1996.

———. *Para vivir aquí.* Mexico City: Editorial Grijalbo, 1982.

———. *Sopita de fideo.* Mexico City: Ediciones Océano, 1984.

———. *La última noche del "Tigre".* Mexico City: Ediciones Océano, 1987.

———. *Zona de desastre.* Mexico City: Ediciones Océano, 1986.

Paz, Octavio. *The Labyrinth of Solitude.* Trans. Lysander Kemp, Yara Milos, and Raphael Phillips Belash. New York: Grove, 1961.

———. "Sor Juana Inés de la Cruz." *Las peras del olmo.* Mexico City: UNAM, 1957. 34–48.

———. *Sor Juana Inés de la Cruz o Las Trampas de la Fe.* Mexico City: Fondo de Cultura Económica, 1982.

———. *Sor Juana or, The Traps of Faith.* Trans. Margaret Sayers Peden. Cambridge, Mass.: Harvard University Press, 1988.

———. "Sunstone." *The Collected Poems of Octavio Paz. 1957–1987.* Ed. and trans. Eliot Weinberger. New York: New Directions Books, 1987. 2–35.

Peden, Margaret Sayers. "Introduction." *A Woman of Genius. The Intellectual Bibliography of Sor Juana Inés de la Cruz.* Salisbury, Conn.: Lime Rock Press, 1987. 1–13.

Peralta, Violeta, and Liliana Befumo Boschi. *Rulfo. La soledad creadora.* Buenos Aires: Fernando García Cambeiro, 1975.

Pfandl, Ludwig. *Sor Juana Inés de la Cruz. La décima musa de México. Su vida, su poesía, su psique.* Ed. F. de la Maza. Trans. J.A. Ortega y Medina. Mexico City: UNAM, 1963.

Pimentel, Luz Aurora. "'Los caminos de la eternidad': El valor simbólico del espacio en *Pedro Páramo.*" *Revista Canadiense de Estudios Hispánicos* 16.2 (1992): 267–291.

Poniatowska, Elena. *Hasta no verte, Jesús mío.* Mexico City: Ediciones Era, 1969.

———. *La "Flor de lis".* Mexico City: Ediciones Era, 1988.

———. *Luz y luna, las lunitas.* Mexico City: Ediciones Era, 1994.

———. "El hombre del pito dulce." *Juchitán de las mujeres.* Ed. Pablo Ortiz Monasterio. Fotografía de Graciela Iturbide. Mexico City: Ediciones Toledo, 1989. 11–26.

———. *Nada, nadie. Las voces del temblor.* Mexico City: Ediciones Era, 1988.

———. Prologue to *Se necesita muchacha,* by Ana Gutiérrez. Mexico City: Fondo de Cultura Económica, 1983. 7–86.

Portal, Marta. *Análisis semiológico de Pedro Páramo.* Madrid: Narcea, 1981.

Portugal, Ana María. "Introducción." *Mujeres e iglesia. Sexualidad y aborto en América Latina.* Ed. Ana María Portugal. Washington, D.C.: Catholics for a Free Choice, 1989. 1–7.

Pozas, Ricardo. *Juan Pérez Jolote.* Mexico City: Fondo de Cultura Económica, 1952.

Prado Garduño, Gloria. "Cuando la injusticia encuentra su voz." *Palabras de mujer.* Ed. Amparo Espinosa Rugarcía et al. Mexico City: Editorial Diana, 1989. 65–73.

Puga, María Luisa. "Inmóvil sol secreto." *Jaula de palabras.* Ed. Gustavo Sainz. Mexico City: Editorial Grijalbo, 1980. 365–377.

Pupo-Walker, C. Enrique. "Personajes y ambiente en *Pedro Páramo.*" *Cuadernos Americanos* 167.6 (1969): 194–204.

Ramos Escandón, Carmen. "Receta y feminidad en *Como agua para chocolate.*" *fem.* 15.102 (1991): 45–48.

——— et al. *Presencia y transparencia: La mujer en la historia de México.* Mexico City: El Colegio de México, 1987.

Register, Cheri. "American Feminist Literary Criticism: A Bibliographical Introduction." *Feminist Literary Criticism. Explorations in Theory.* Ed. Josephine Donovan. 2d ed. Lexington: University Press of Kentucky, 1989. 1–28.

Revista Canadiense de Estudios Hispánicos. Special issue, "Presencia y ausencia de la mujer en las letras hispánicas." Ed. M. E. de Valdés. 14.3 (Spring 1990).

Ricoeur, Paul. *Le discours de l'action.* Paris: Centre National de Recherche Scientifique, 1977.

———. "Ethics and Culture. Habermas and Gadamer in Dialogue." *Political and Social Essays.* Ed. David Stewart and Joseph Bien. Trans. David Pellauer. Athens: Ohio University Press, 1974. 243–270.

———. "The Hermeneutical Function of Distanciation." *Hermeneutics and the Social Sciences. Essays on Language, Action and Interpretation.* Ed. and trans. John B. Thompson. Cambridge, England: Cambridge University Press, 1981. 131–149.

———. "The Human Experience of Time and Narrative." *A Ricoeur Reader: Reflection and Imagination.* Ed. M. J. Valdés. Toronto: University of Toronto Press, 1991. 99–116.

———. "The Model of the Text: Meaningful Action Considered as a Text." *Hermeneutics and the Social Sciences. Essays on Language, Action and Interpretation.* Ed. and trans. John B. Thompson. Cambridge, England: Cambridge University Press, 1981. 197–221.

———. *Oneself as Another*. Trans. Kathleen Blamey. Chicago: University of Chicago Press, 1992.

———. *The Rule of Metaphor*. Trans. Robert Czerny. Toronto: University of Toronto Press, 1977.

———. *Time and Narrative*. Trans. Kathleen McLaughlin and David Pellauer. Vol. 1. Chicago: University of Chicago Press, 1984.

———. "Violence and Language." *Political and Social Essays*. Ed. D. Stewart and J. Bien. Athens: Ohio University Press, 1974. 88–101.

———. "What is a Text? Explanation and Understanding." *A Ricoeur Reader. Reflection and Imagination*. Ed. M. J. Valdés. University of Toronto Press, 1991. 43–64.

———. "Word, Polysemy, Metaphor: Creativity in Language." *A Ricoeur Reader: Reflection and Imagination*. Ed. M. J. Valdés. University of Toronto Press, 1991. 65–67.

Rivers, Elias L. *Antología de Sor Juana Inés de la Cruz*. Salamanca: Anaya, 1965.

Rocard, Marcienne. "The House Theme in Chicana Literature: A New Sense of Place." *Hispanorama. Chicanoliteratur* (Feb. 1990): 106–107, 146–147.

Rodríguez, Juan. "*The House on Mango Street*, by Sandra Cisneros." *Austin Chronicle*, Aug. 10, 1984.

Rodríguez-Luis, Julio. "Algunas observaciones sobre el simbolismo de la relación entre Susana San Juan y Pedro Páramo." *Cuadernos hispanoamericanos*, 270 (1972): 584–594.

Rof Carballo, J. *Entre el silencio y la palabra*. Madrid: Aguilar, 1960.

Rogers, Katharine M. *The Troublesome Helpmate. A History of Misogyny in Literature*. Seattle: University of Washington Press, 1986.

Rombauer, Irma S. *The Joy of Cooking*. New York: Bobbs, 1931.

Rorty, Richard. *Contingency, Irony, and Solidarity*. Cambridge, England: Cambridge University Press, 1989.

Rosaldo, Renato. *Culture and Truth: The Remaking of Social Analysis*. Boston: Beacon, 1989. 160–167.

Ruffinelli, Jorge. "El lugar de Rulfo." *El lugar de Rulfo y otros ensayos*. Xalapa: Universidad Veracruzana, 1980. 9–40.

Ruiz de Velasco, Marcela. "Para no pensar en ti. . . ." *Palabras de mujer*. Ed. Amparo Espinosa Rugarcía et al. Mexico City: Editorial Diana, 1989. 105–113.

Ruiz Harrel, Rafael. "La violación en México." *fem.* 4 (1977): 18–21.

Rulfo, Juan. "Paso del Norte." *El llano en llamas*. México: Fondo de Cultura Económica, 1953.

———. *Pedro Páramo*. Trans. Lysander Kemp. New York: Grove Press, 1959.

———. *Pedro Páramo*. Ed. José Carlos González Boixo. Madrid: Ediciones Cátedra, 1983.

Sabat de Rivers, Georgina. "Octavio Paz ante Sor Juana Inés de la Cruz." *Modern Language Notes* 100.2 (Mar. 1985): 417–423.

———."Sobre la versión inglesa de *Las trampas de la fe* de Octavio Paz." *Sor Juana Inés de la Cruz y otros poetas bárrocos de la colonia.* Barcelona: Promociones y Publicaciones Universitarias, 1992. 341–355.

———."Sor Juana Inés de la Cruz." *Historia de la literatura hispanoamericana. Tomo I: Epoca colonial.* Ed. Luis Iñigo Madrigal. Madrid: Cátedra, 1982. 275–293.

———. *El "Sueño" de Sor Juana Inés de la Cruz: Tradiciones literarias y originalidad.* London: Tamesis Books, 1976.

Sacoto Salamea, Antonio. "Pedro Páramo." *Cinco novelas claves de la literatura hispanoamericana.* New York: Eliseo Torres, 1979. 55–128.

Saldierna, Georgina, and Victor Zendejas. "En seis años, 500 mil denuncias de violencia familiar en México." *La Jornada* (Nov. 26, 1996).

Saldívar, Jose David. "*The House on Mango Street.*" *Melus* (1984).

Saldívar, Ramón. *Chicano Narrative.* Madison: University of Wisconsin Press, 1990. 181–186.

Salles, Vania, and Elsie McPhail, eds. *Textos y pre-textos. Once estudios sobre la mujer.* Mexico City: El Colegio de México, 1991.

Samanes Cadillo, Rut. "Entrevista. Cristina Pacheco." *fem.* 13.82 (Oct. 1989): 26–28.

Sánchez Robayna, Andrés. *Para leer "Primero sueño" de Sor Juana Inés de la Cruz.* Mexico City: Fondo de Cultura Económica, 1990.

Sartre, Jean Paul. *Being and Nothingness.* Trans. Hazel Barnes. New York: Philosophical Library, 1956. 396–405.

Schaefer-Rodríguez, Claudia. "Embedded Agendas: The Literary Journalism of Cristina Pacheco and Guadalupe Loaeza." *Latin American Literary Review* 19.38 (1991): 62–76.

———. *Textured Lives. Women, Art and Representation in Modern Mexico.* Tucson: University of Arizona Press, 1992.

Schons, Dorothy. "Some Obscure Points in the Life of Sor Juana Inés de la Cruz." *Feminist Perspectives on Sor Juana Inés de la Cruz.* Ed. Stephanie Merrim. Detroit: Wayne State University Press, 1991. 38–60.

Sedgewick, Henry Dwight. *Italy in the Thirteenth Century.* Boston: Houghton, 1912.

Séjourné, Laurette. *Burning Water: Thought and Religion in Ancient Mexico.* Trans. Irene Nicholson. New York: Vanguard, 1957.

Showalter, Elaine. *A Literature of Their Own.* Rev. ed. London: Virago Press, 1982.

———. "Piecing and Writing." *The Poetics of Gender.* Ed. Nancy K. Miller. New York: Columbia University Press, 1986. 222–247.

Signs: Journal of Women in Culture and Society (1975–).

Sklodowska, Elzbieta. *Testimonio hispanoamericano.* New York: Peter Lang, 1992.

Smith, Sidonie. *A Poetics of Women's Autobiography.* Bloomington: Indiana University Press, 1987.

Snow, Kimberly. "A Voice of Hope on Mango Street." *News-Press* (Santa Barbara) Oct. 19, 1986: 23, 27.

Sommer, Doris. "'Not Just a Personal Story': Women's *Testimonios* and the Plural Self." *Life/Lines. Theorizing Women's Autobiography.* Ed. Bella Brodzki and Celeste Schenck. Ithaca, N.Y.: Cornell University Press, 1988. 107–130.

Soustelle, Jacques. *La vida cotidiana de los aztecas*. Trans. Carlos Villegas. Mexico City: Fondo de Cultura Económica, 1970.

Spivak, Gayatri Chakravorty. "The Political Economy of Women as Seen by a Literary Critic." *Coming to Terms*. Ed. Elizabeth Weed. New York: Routledge, 1989. 218–229.

Steele, Cynthia. *Politics, Gender, and the Mexican Novel, 1968–1988. Beyond the Pyramid*. Austin: University of Texas Press, 1992.

Steiner, George, and Elizabeth Hall. "Interview with George Steiner." *Psychology Today* 6.9 (Feb. 1973): 57–69.

Steinsleger, José. "Los costos de la modernización." *Mujeres en acción* 4 (1994): 17–20.

Stevens, Evelyn. "*Marianismo*: The Other Face of *machismo* in Latin America." *Female and Male in Latin America. Essays*. Ed. Ann Pescatello. Pittsburgh, Pa.: University of Pittsburgh Press, 1973. 90–101.

Stimpson, Catharine R. *Where the Meanings Are*. New York: Methuen, 1988.

———, with Nina Kressner Cobb. *Women's Studies in the United States*. New York: Ford Foundation, 1986.

Suárez del Real, Enrique. "El problema alimenticio en México." *Revista Mexicana de Sociología* 24 (1962): 367–379.

Suleiman, Susan Rubin. "Pornography, Transgression and the Avant-Garde: Bataille's *Story of the Eye*." *The Poetics of Gender*. Ed. Nancy K. Miller. New York: Columbia University Press, 1986. 117–136.

Tarrés, María Luisa. "Introducción." *La voluntad de ser. Mujeres en los noventa*. Ed. María Luisa Tarrés. Mexico City: El Colegio de México, 1992. 21–46.

Tavard, George H. *Juana Inés de la Cruz and the Theology of Beauty: The First Mexican Theology*. Notre Dame, IN: University of Notre Dame Press, 1991.

Taylor, Charles. *Sources of the Self. The Making of Modern Identity*. Cambridge, Mass.: Harvard University Press, 1989.

Thomas Aquinas, Saint. *Introduction to St. Thomas Aquinas*. Ed. Anton C. Pegis. New York: Random House, 1948. 429–442.

Tittler, Jonathan. "*Gringo viejo/The Old Gringo*: 'The Rest is Fiction.'" *The Review of Contemporary Fiction* 8.2 (1988): 241–248.

Trueba, Marta. "Hipótesis sobre una escritura diferente." *fem.* 6.21 (Feb.–Mar. 1982): 9–12.

Trueblood, Alan S., trans. *A Sor Juana Anthology*. Foreword by Octavio Paz. Cambridge, Mass.: Harvard University Press, 1988.

Tuñon, Enriqueta. "La lucha política de la mujer mexicana por el derecho al sufragio y sus repercusiones." *Presencia y transparencia: La mujer en la historia de México*. Ed. Carmen Ramos Escandón. Mexico City: El Colegio de México, 1987. 81–89.

Urrutia, Elena. "La casa y la propia identidad." *fem.* 10.48 (1986): 32–33.

———. "La mujer y la cultura." *fem. 10 años de periodismo feminista*. Mexico City: Planeta, 1988. 283–289.

———, ed. *Directorio de investigadoras sociales, y programas de estudio e investigación sobre la mujer en América Latina y el Caribé*. 3d ed., rev. Mexico City: El Colegio de México, 1993.

————, ed. *Documentos de trabajo. 2. Organizaciones no gubernamentales que trabajan en beneficio de la mujer.* Mexico City: El Colegio de México, 1990.

Valdemoro, Ana. "Crimen contra las mujeres." *fem.* 4 (1977): 22–23.

Valdés, María Elena de. "Paraliterature as a Sociocultural Index of Mexico." *NorthSouth NordSud NorteSur NorteSul* 3–4 (1977): 197–206.

————, and Margaret Higonnet, eds. *New Visions of Creation. Feminist Innovations in Literary Theory.* Tokyo: International Comparative Literature Association, 1993.

Valdés, Mario J. *World-making: The Literary Truth-Claim and the Interpretation of Texts.* Toronto: University of Toronto Press, 1992.

Valente, Luiz Fernando. "Mediação e Afetividade: O Leitor em Sertão: Veredas." *Travessia* 7.15 (Florianópolis, Brazil, 1987): 107–124.

Vigil, José María. *Poetisas mexicanas. Siglos XVI, XVII, XVIII y XIX.* Mexico City: Instituto de Investigaciones Filológicas de la UNAM, 1977.

Wallace, Elizabeth. *Sor Juana Inés de la Cruz. Poetisa de corte y convento.* Mexico City: Xochitl, 1944.

Watson, G. Llewellyn. *Feminism and Women's Issues: An Annotated Bibliography and Research Guide.* 2 vols. New York: Garland, 1990.

Weed, Elizabeth. "Introduction: Terms of Reference." *Coming to Terms. Feminism, Theory, Politics.* New York: Routledge, 1989. ix–xxxi.

Westheim, Paul. *Arte antiguo de México.* Trans. Mariana Frenk. Mexico City: Ediciones Era, 1970.

Wittgenstein, Ludwig. *Philosophical Investigations.* Trans. G. E. M. Anscombe. New York: Macmillan, 1968.

Wolff, Cynthia Griffin. "A Mirror for Men: Stereotypes of Women in Literature." *Women: An Issue.* Boston: Little, Brown, 1972. 205–218.

Women's Studies Abstracts (1980–).

Women's Studies Quarterly (1972–).

Woolf, Virginia. *Jacob's Room.* London: Hogarth, 1976.

————. *A Room of One's Own.* London: Harcourt Brace Jovanovich, 1929.

Yarbro-Bejarano, Yvonne. "Chicana Literature From a Chicana Feminist Perspective." *Chicana Creativity and Criticism: New Frontiers in American Literature.* Ed. María Herrera Sobek and Helena María Viramontes. Albuquerque: University of New Mexico Press, 1996. 213–219.

Zola, Emile. *Germinal.* Ed. L. W. Tancock. Harmondsworth: Penguin Books, 1954.

Index